The Limits of American Isolation:
The United States and the Crimean War

# The Limits of American Isolation: The United States and the Crimean War

by

## Alan Dowty

**Foreword by Hans Morgenthau**

1971

NEW YORK: New York University Press

327.73
D752ℓ
1971

© 1971 by New York University
Library of Congress Catalog Card Number: 73-124522
ISBN 8147-1752-7
Manufactured in the United States of America

# Acknowledgments and Dedication

I count myself among the many who have been deeply influenced by the scholarly logic and personal humanity of Hans Morgenthau, who not only wrote the foreword for this book, but has helped in every imaginable way since it was conceived.

Other past and present University of Chicago faculty members who must be cited—but not implicated in the book's shortcomings—are Walter Johnson, William T. Hutchinson, and Bernard Weisberger. Yehoshua Arieli and Martin Seliger of the Hebrew University read and commented upon the manuscript.

Other acknowledgments are relatively few, this being an old-fashioned kind of book *not* made possible by grants-in-aid, extended leaves of absence, conferences or consultations, access to data banks, or lavish secretarial assistance. The University of Chicago and the Hebrew University are both large and prestigious institutions in which research is considered an honorable pursuit. The personnel of the National Archives were unusually efficient and helpful, a fact singular enough to deserve mention. I am indebted to Gerard F. McCauley, of Gerard McCauley, Inc., for advice and assistance in publishing the book; I have also enjoyed a very good relationship with the editors of New York University Press, an establishment I can recommend without hesitation to other scholars. My father-in-law, J. Richard Gordon, financed the necessary photocopying documents, and my wife, Nancy Gordon Dowty, furnished what clerical assistance I had.

This book is dedicated to the Shimer College "dissidents" of 1966-1967.

# Foreword

It is an open question whether America has been harmed more by the actual policy of isolation it pursued in the inter-war period or by the misconceptions about its isolationism that are current in historiography, folklore, and polemics. The United States has actually embarked twice upon isolationist policies: during the first decade of its history and in the inter-war period. These two policies are radically different both in philosophic conception and political purpose. The isolationism of the Federalist period, as formulated in Washington's Farewell Address, saw in America's isolation from the conflicts of European powers, whose colonies surrounded the United States on three sides, a precondition for its survival as an independent nation. It sought to achieve this end by an active foreign policy, keeping the European powers away from the United States. In other words, American isolation was conceived not as a condition to be preserved by abstention, but as a goal to be attained by action. On the other hand, the isolationism of the '20s and '30s assumed the isolation of the United States as a fact of nature, which could best be maintained by political inactivity abroad.

In the historic recollection of America, these two periods and types of isolationism have merged, and the isolationism that dominated the inter-war period transformed in retrospect the Federalist type in its own image. Thus, the isolationism of the 20th century was able to justify itself as a contempo-

rary application of the great example of statecraft which the
Founding Fathers had set in the initial period of American
foreign policy. A deviation from the isolationism of the inter-
war period could thus be proven wrong not only on pragmatic
grounds but also as a departure from the standards established
for American foreign policy by the founders of the republic.

The myth that American foreign policy was conceived by
the founders in the image of 20th-century isolationism cast its
shadow over the whole intervening century. Thus American
diplomatic history from the beginning through the inter-war
period was conceived as a continuum dominated by isolationism and but temporarily interrupted by the Spanish-American
War and the First World War. In consequence, 20th-century
isolationism appeared as the organic continuation of a tradition established by the founders and adhered to throughout
American history. More particularly, the rejection of Wilsonian internationalism in 1919 could then appear as the resto-
ration of the American tradition in foreign policy, from which
Wilson had proposed to deviate.

This conception of American foreign policy is as mytho-
logical as is the interpretation of the foreign policy of the
Federalist period as a model for 20th-century isolationism. It
is the great merit of Professor Dowty's book to have redis-
covered the reality behind the myth and thereby to have taken
an important step toward a radical revision of American
diplomatic history in the 19th century.

The tradition of American foreign policy throughout the
19th century followed indeed the pattern established by the
founders, but that pattern consisted of an active diplomacy
serving a dual purpose: the protection of the United States
from involvement in the conflicts of European nations and
the promotion of the interests of the United States in the
Western Hemisphere. American diplomacy during the Crimean War provides the classic example of that pattern. The
quantity and quality of that diplomacy are impressive. To call
it isolationist is untenable in view of the evidence adduced in
this book. The United States made its diplomacy serve its
perennial interest of maintaining and, if need be, restoring

the balance of power in Europe. To that end, American diplomacy played one side out against the other and supported the one which appeared to be the weaker of the two, all the while trying to use its diplomatic assets vis-à-vis the European powers for the benefit of America's hegemonial position in the Western Hemisphere. The American diplomats played the game according to its long established rules, and they did so successfully and at times brilliantly. To call their foreign policy isolationist tells more about the state of mind and the political purposes of those who use such an inappropriate term than about the actual nature of that foreign policy.

Hans J. Morgenthau

# Contents

# Introduction

This study is basically an account of United States foreign policy from 1853 to 1857, during the Presidential administration of Franklin Pierce. But if its only aim were to recount Pierce's foreign policy, there would be little justification for undertaking such a project. Works on foreign policy have already covered this period in some depth. Monographs, many of them excellent, have been written on nearly every phase and aspect of the diplomacy of our fourteenth President, and competent biographies of Pierce, Marcy, Buchanan, and most of the other important figures of the age have been published. Most of the material in this work has appeared in one form or another elsewhere.

The uniqueness of and justification for this study is twofold. First, the events of this period are viewed as a case study, as part of an attempt to investigate a larger interpretative question. Secondly, and partly as a result, the diplomatic events of 1853-1857, which have usually been studied as a series of separate and unrelated episodes, are considered as parts of a whole. Results of research on one strand of foreign policy, however excellent, may have an entirely different significance when related to the foreign and domestic background and to other contemporary diplomatic affairs.

The original aim of the study was to investigate the nature of the isolation of the United States in the nineteenth century.[1] As there appeared to be little empirical research on the actual content of this much-discussed principle of United States foreign policy, a study in depth of its relationship to European events, over a short period of time, seemed suitable. I chose the period between 1853 and 1857 because it was a time of turbulence in European affairs. The high level of diplomatic activity in Europe during the Crimean War, coinciding with a surge of expansionism in the foreign policy of the United States, seemed likely to amplify and illuminate the connections, if any, between the international politics of the two hemispheres.

The problems of such research are great. The connection between the diplomacies of the New and Old Worlds may be limited to the influence which events in one hemisphere exert on decisions taken in the other. These influences may never be recorded in print, or if they are, they may be obscured by ideological disguises. They are, nevertheless, still political relationships that are relevant to a study of isolationism. We must distinguish between actual policy and declaratory policy, which are by no means always synonymous.

It is also important to sort out the interpretative theories that have grown up about the foreign policy of the United States in the nineteenth century, from the thoughts and ideas of contemporaries. This study seeks to reappraise the former and to set the latter, so far as possible, in their proper historical setting. The study begins, therefore, with an outline of the historical theories about nineteenth-century isolationism that have developed, distinguishing them from the actual or declaratory policies they seek to explain.

# NOTES

1. A clear distinction should be made between eighteenth, nineteenth, and twentieth century isolationism. The foreign policy of the United States before 1815, especially under Washington and Hamilton, is seldom referred to as "isolationist." The neutrality of the United States during these years was viewed in traditional terms, as a policy of realistic advantage. The isolationism of the twentieth century is usually described as a policy of withdrawal and subordination of political considerations to ideological traditions, which may differentiate it considerably from earlier U.S. foreign policy. We are concerned here only with nineteenth century isolationism, at least as it appeared at mid-century.

# The Theory of Nineteenth-century Isolationism

## CHAPTER ONE

It is true that Washington thought a time might come when, our institutions being firmly consolidated and working with complete success, we might safely and beneficially take part in the consultations held by foreign states for the common advantage of nations. Since that period occasions have frequently happened which presented seductions to a departure from *what, superficially viewed, seemed a course of isolation and indifference.*

William H. Seward, 1863 [1]

The refusal to take sides or become involved in any way in the internal political quarrels of Europe is known as the isolation policy. It is the oldest doctrine of American foreign policy, and it was defined by example during the first decade of our national life and by precept in Washington's farewell address. Since the foundation of the republic, in every crisis that has arisen in the relations of America with Europe, the isolation doctrine has been reaffirmed and has met with the approval of the American people.

Herbert Adams Gibbons, 1924 [2]

*Isolation,* as the word is usually used, implies more than neutrality. It suggests, to most modern diplomatic historians, an attitude and policy of passivity that goes beyond the simple requirement of remaining unaligned in international politics. To be neutral is to pursue an active policy of avoiding open conflicts in order to enjoy the advantages of peace and maximum freedom of action; to be isolated is to withdraw from active diplomacy and to seek complete noninvolvement in political relationships between other states. The distinction is made clearly, for example, by Richard W. Leopold. Isolationism is defined as a set of ideas, "largely negative—a limitation upon the action of the United States government. It required the avoidance of permanent alliances and of involvement in the diplomatic affairs of other continents." Neutrality, in contrast, is "a policy of a nation in remaining aloof from a war between other states, while expecting from them certain rights and observing for them certain duties." In addition, neutrality "can be adhered to, modified, or abandoned as the national interest dictates." [3]

Following this distinction, it is claimed that the United States, during a period of its history corresponding roughly to the nineteenth century and sometimes extended to World War II, pronounced and practiced a self-limiting policy of isolation. The United States, in short, was not only neutral but also isolated in international politics during the nineteenth century. Leopold, again, gives clear expression to this idea:

The cardinal principle undergirding the foreign policy of the young republic was isolationism. . . . Second only to isolationism as a pole star of American diplomacy in the formative years was the principle of neutrality.[4]

The first obstacle that Leopold's claim must meet is the absence of references to isolationism in nineteenth-century writings and speeches. Contemporary policy was described then as "neutral" or "nonaligned" but not as isolated. In fact, "isolationist" was an epithet throughout most of the nineteenth century. The only apparent use of the word in political discourse was to discredit an opponent: the "Young Americans" of the 1850s and the expansionists of the late 1890s both described nonsympathizers in such terms.[5] It was not until the second of these disputes, during the late 1890s, that isolation was used as an objective description of the foreign policy of the United States as well as an invective term.

This paradox can be partially explained by the relatively recent entry of the word into the English language. The French *isolé* was first used during the eighteenth century; the *British Critic* of October, 1800, confirmed the change of spelling: "The affected, frenchified, and unnecessary word *isolated* is not English, and we trust never will be." [6] Noah Webster's first dictionary of 1807 documented the word's transatlantic passage, defining "isolated" as "detached, standing alone." Similar definitions, with added explanations of the word's scientific connotations, prevailed throughout Webster's various nineteenth-century editions. The first specifically political definition in Webster did not appear until 1912, when the first edition of the *New International Dictionary* explained that an isolationist was "one who favors what is considered to be a policy of isolation in national affairs."

The expansionists of the 1890s, though not the first to describe their opponents as isolationists, were the first to extend both the word and the concept to describe the actual content of previous United States foreign policy. As advocates of change, the spokesmen of manifest destiny were willing to condemn all past diplomacy as well as the contemporary policies that they opposed. Earlier accusations of "isolation" were directed at those presumed to be out of touch with the main stream of events; now the charge was directed at a whole era in foreign policy. Alfred Thayer Mahan was one of the first to express these feelings when he declared that international law was an insufficient guarantee for the protection of American interests and called for increased political activity to offset "our self-imposed isolation in the matter of markets, the decline of our shipping interest in the last thirty years." [7] Broad use of the term did not come, however, until after the popularization of the "splendid isolation" idea in British political debates. This term was first used by Sir Wilfred Laurier of Canada in 1896, and in the British context did not, of course, have the same negative connotations it acquired in American usage.[8]

Richard Olney's statement in May, 1898, shows the way in which the idea of isolationism came into use during this period:

> I . . . invite you to consider for a few moments a feature of our foreign policy which may be described as the "international isolation of the United States."
>
> What is meant by the phrase "international isolation" as thus used is this. The United States is certainly now entitled to rank among the great powers of the world. Yet, while its place among the nations is assured, it purposely takes its stand outside the European family circle to which it belongs, and neither accepts the responsibilities of its place nor secures its advantages. It avowedly restricts its activities to the American continent and intentionally assumes an attitude of absolute aloofness to everything outside those continents.[9]

This view was adopted by a number of "manifest destiny" revivalists. One typical herald of the new age began by asking "whether this country is to continue in its policy of political isolation, or is to take its rightful place among the great World-Powers." He advocated in particular an "Anglo-American system" and colonial acquisition: "From the blood of our heroes, shed at Santiago and Manila, there shall arise a New Imperialism, replacing the waning Imperialism of Old Rome; an Imperialism destined to carry world-wide the principles of Anglo-Saxon peace and justice, liberty and law." [10]

The use of the isolationist idea to describe nineteenth-century foreign policy was by no means universally accepted at first. Those who resisted the "internationalism" of this age would not willingly accept the designation of isolationists, even if they were allowed to claim that American tradition was on their side. *The Nation,* for example, asserted that "in equally important respects we have not isolated ourselves," pointing in particular to immigration. Furthermore, the magazine continued, "what of the isolation that the party in power has practised and boasted of?" Their protectionist trade policy, it was argued, constituted a veritable policy of "isolation." [11] John Bassett Moore, writing in 1918, accepted most of the tenets of what was to become the "isolationist" view of United States foreign policy, but avoided the term itself.[12] Detachment and separation were accepted as distinguishing features of American neutrality, but the supporters of "tradition" were not yet prepared to accept the belittling label of "isolationists."

The theory of nineteenth-century isolationism came into full bloom only after World War I. In the dispute over United States foreign policy brought on by the war and by the fight over the League of Nations, those who advocated a return to what they believed to be "traditional non-entanglement" were often willing to describe their policy as isolationist. Since "isolation" in the twentieth-century United States required the strongest conscious effort of withdrawal in view of the country's size and importance, the task of isolationists was to emphasize as much as possible the historic extent of nineteenth-century isolationism which was to serve as the model. They assumed that "until recently the peoples of America have not had to worry over what was happening to the people of Europe." In the absence of real interests, the principal danger was self-enforced passivity: "an honest intention to remain aloof from foreign conflict, a refusal to be stampeded by unneutral propaganda, a knowledge of the law and a capacity to stand upon it. . . ." [13]

The internationalists of the 1920s and 1930s could logically meet the isolationist argument in two ways. They could, on the one hand, deny the historic validity of isolationism and emphasize the elements of involvement in the past that would forge a continuous link with the policies they advocated for the present. Or they might accept the view that the United States had practiced a policy of isolation for either moral or political reasons, but emphasize the way in which "changed world conditions" made a different policy necessary. The second argument was, of course, much more similar to the "internationalist" arguments made in the 1890s. In any event, many nonisolationists accepted the general historical truth of isolation and, as a consequence, helped to confirm the theory in the public mind.

Edward Meade Earle, for example, arguing in *Against This Torrent,* admitted that Washington's Farewell Address stated "the theory of isolation . . . with so much dignity and eloquence." Isolation itself was "a worthy foundation for American policy," and only a change of circumstances altered its application: "It is possible for situations to arise in which the isolation appropriate to the young American republic is inadequate to safeguard the peace and security of the great nation we have become." [14] "To keep out of Europe's quarrels," added another internationalist, "and at the same time to profit by them on every occasion, expanding and fortifying ourselves at Europe's expense—such has been our sagacious policy." Only new interests, brought about by a "closer structure" in the world, enabled the author to ask rhetorically "whether these new interests can best be furthered by cooperative means, or by means of isolation." [15]

This "consensus" on the historic validity of nineteenth-century isolationism coincided, significantly, with the first rash of general histories of American diplomacy, published in the interwar period. In these works the canons of nineteenth-century isolationism were generally accepted, given a common terminology, and codified into a set of assumptions that have often served as a substitute for fresh thought and research in subsequent periods. This was generally the case whether the author favored internationalist or isolationist policies for the period in which he was writing.[16]

It was assumed that the isolationist period of United States history, beginning in 1776, 1793, 1815, or 1823, and ending in 1898 or 1917 (or not yet ended), could be treated as a unit so far as foreign policy was concerned: "In all the more than a century of foreign relationships which remains for us to consider, we shall find scarcely a new principle, but merely a further working out of the principles of Washington's administration." [17] During this period the United States had avoided European politics by a conscious policy of insulating and separating itself from "European broils": "Indifference to the affairs of Europe was the true policy of the country." [18] Such a policy was not a temporary expedient, but was based on lasting principles. "By 1829 we had not only shaken ourselves loose from the entanglements of European international politics, but we had formulated rules of conduct designed to make that separation permanent." [19] As a result of this "separation from the diplomacy of Europe," the country was directly and indirectly unaffected by European developments, and "the American diplomatic contribution to world history so far as Europe was concerned was negligible." [20] European relations with the United States were therefore simple and needed no elaboration; apart from a few minor episodes involving limited conflicts, the United States succeeded in keeping the record of its involvement in European diplomacy totally blank. On the whole,

> American annals were 'short and simple.' The United States was politically isolated and apart from European interests; it cared nothing for Europe's balance of power, its intrigues, and its wars.[21]

This view of nineteenth-century isolationism was also dominant in the writings of the generation of diplomatic historians that came to prominence during the 1930s, and whose work has influenced all succeeding studies. Samuel Flagg Bemis, though usually avoiding the term "isolation," accepted "abstention from the entanglements of European politics" as a foundation of American policy and described the separation of Old and New World interests as basic to American success:

> The continental position has always been the strength of the United States in the world. American successes in diplomacy have been based on a continental policy. . . . A continental policy was instinctive with the Fathers.

American activity with European powers, in his account, revolved around a small number of specific disputes, and United States diplomats committed only a "few minor errors" as a result. The entry of the United States into world politics "began the great mistakes of American diplomacy." [22] Over twenty years later Bemis' view of nineteenth-century isolation was basically unchanged:

> One is impressed by the routine character of American diplomatic contacts with European countries during the years of the twentieth century before 1914. As long as the question of neutral rights remained asleep the United States could keep profitably aloof from all European politics and generally did so.[23]

Thomas A. Bailey and Dexter Perkins, also among the most influential modern diplomatic historians who wrote during this period, have accepted the same general view of nineteenth-century foreign policy. Bailey explained that a policy of isolation, pursued "notably in the nineteenth century," meant that "the American people have wished to work out their own destiny in the Western hemisphere without becoming embroiled in the conflicts of the outside world." [24] Perkins has declared that the distinctive feature of the first hundred years of United States foreign policy, in addition to expansion, was "the crystallization of the tradition of what has come to be called isolation," in pursuit of which the United States "could and did . . . increasingly neglect the European scene." The "notion of the two spheres," he added, "cut deep into the American mind. . . . In the nineteenth century there was little disposition to interfere in Europe or in Asia, in the political sense." [25]

This view of nineteenth-century isolationism is still the "orthodox" interpretation of the issue, even among later writers.[26]

# NINETEENTH-CENTURY DECLARATORY POLICY

While contemporary writings do not describe the foreign policy of the United States as isolated, policy pronouncements made in the nineteenth century often seem to recognize the practice of isolation in so many words. Spokesmen in the nineteenth century, in other words, actually enunciated many elements of what was to become known later as the theory of isolation. As one critic of isolationism's historicity has written, "it can not be denied that the literary evidence in support of the tradition of isolation during the period 1825-1900 and even since that time is very strong." [27] *Declaratory* policy, at least, seems to have been partially or largely "isolationist." In particular, at least three basic assumptions of the isolationist theory, as stated in the twentieth century (above and beyond simple neutrality), can be traced to the thinking of the nineteenth century.

The first assumption might be called the belief in moral differentiation, or the uniqueness of American institutions. This attitude began with the view that as "an experiment in democracy" the United States faced a hostile world and only the policy of withdrawal enabled it "to follow unhindered the bent of [its] political genius." [28] From this followed a

whole range of contentions supporting the higher and finer
idealism of the United States in international politics, expressed in a policy so purely moral that it could be preserved
only by avoiding contacts with the less enlightened European
states. There is, of course, no problem in documenting this
attitude of moral differentiation in nineteenth-century America (or any other period), and the Monroe Doctrine expresses
it clearly enough:

> The political system of the allied powers is essen-
> tially different in this respect from that of America. . . .
> To the defense of our own, which has been achieved
> by the loss of so much blood and treasure . . . this
> whole nation is devoted.

Writers during the twentieth century have expressed
this attitude even more extremely: One, for example, referred
to American diplomacy as "the policies of the golden rule—
honest diplomacy, arbitration rather than war, and peace
among the nations." [29] Another said of American neutrality
that "seldom had any country resisted so strong temptations,
urgings, threats, and what not, to array itself on the side
of an alien belligerent. The world stood astonished at the
measure of our resistance and forbearance." [30] The protection
of virtue, in modern eyes, demanded not only active defense
but also the avoidance of seductive situations.

A second attitude that tied twentieth-century isolationist
historiography policy pronouncements made in the nineteenth
century involves the nature of international politics. Some
historians believe that a nation can make a choice between
pursuing a policy based on power considerations or a policy
based on freely-chosen ideals. The United States, with its
superior political institutions and ideals, has usually chosen
the latter, and by an act of will, ignored all considerations
of the balance of power. James K. Polk, in his first annual
message, laid down such a rule:

The American system of government is entirely different from that of Europe. Jealousy among the different
sovereigns of Europe, lest any one of them might become too powerful for the rest, has caused them an-
xiously to desire the establishment of what they term
the "balance of power." It can not be permitted to have
any application to the North American continent, and
especially to the United States.[31]

Because it was not based on international political relationships United States foreign policy was, according to most
nineteenth-century writings, based on international law
or international morality (although some twentieth-century
historians claimed it lacked even these bases).[32] Most, however, agreed with the nineteenth-century historians, that the
U.S. "made itself the conspicuous protagonist of principles
of international law so advanced and exalted as to command
the wonder and the not always ungrudging admiration of
the world." [33] In any event the United States avoided "drifting
into the position . . . of holding the balance of power" since
it was obvious that "by taking sides interests and ideals are
both inevitably compromised." [34]

Nineteenth-century historians of United States diplomacy
provide adequate evidence of the legalistic bent to American
thinking about foreign relations during this period. The first
"diplomatic history," written by Theodore Lyman in 1826,
deals almost exclusively with treaty negotiations, primarily
on issues of neutral rights; and it concludes with the warning that "not one of the neutral doctrines, for which America
has always contended, and from the violation of which she
has suffered so much, has yet been secured by treaty stipula-
tion." [35] William Henry Trescot's history of the diplomacy
of Washington and Adams, published in 1857, showed a similar appreciation of "the progress of international law." The
task of the Washington administration, according to Trescot,
was "in negotiating such treaties as were absolutely necessary
for the interests of the country, to avoid all political engage-

ments." [36] Yet it was one of the leading nineteenth-century
American diplomats who sang the classic paean of praise to
the United States for basing its foreign policy not on politics
but on international law. Speaking of the principle of neutrality, Charles Francis Adams said:

> I think the world owes the practical adoption of
> this principle mainly to the long and painful struggles
> of the Government of the United States. . . .
>     Yes, it shall "sway the rest," not by its power, but
> by its example; not by dictation, but by adhering, in
> the day of its strength, to the same pure and honorable
> policy which it proclaimed and defended when relatively
> weak. Yea, and still more, by developing the system
> which has been inaugurated, as far as it may be car-
> ried, to secure peace to non-combatants everywhere. [37]

Nineteenth-century historians of United States diplomacy
also furnish a clear example of the third attitude underlying
isolationism. In the absence of any apparent continuity in
United States foreign relations, it is possible to view each
issue or episode in our diplomatic history independently of
any larger considerations. The study of American diplomacy
can thus be broken down by country or event, and each frag-
ment treated separately. The resultant picture reveals a complete absence of any political ties or considerations save in
the few "disputes" or "crises" involving, ordinarily, a single
country, which are discusssed primarily in legal terms. Lyman,
for example, concentrates upon treaty negotiations by country, with the issues in one case carefully insulated from the
issues in another. The legalistic accounts of Trescot, Foster,
and others follows the same pattern. Modern historians dis-
cussing nineteenth-century foreign policy have similarly frag-
mented the subject, on the assumption that

> The political dealing of the United States with
> Europe from the time of the Monroe Doctrine to the

year 1914 were confined almost entirely to warning
European powers against territorial extension in the
Americas. . . . Aside from such matters controversial
dealings with Europe related almost entirely to the
settlement of disputed claims, to boundary and fishing
disputes, and to attempts to harmonize conflicting
theories of expatriation, naturalization, immigration,
and the rights of neutrals in time of war.[38]

Bemis gives full expression to this trend in historical
thinking. In his work the arguments behind each dispute involving the United States and other powers are given comprehensive, knowledgeable, and generally judicious treatment.
But beyond these particular affairs "the diplomacy of the
United States in Europe was limited to the maintenance of
friendly commercial and cultural contacts, the technical problems of citizenship and immigration, and participation in
multilateral international conferences of a humanitarian
rather than a political nature." [39] The question is whether
this fragmentation in studies of United States diplomacy ob-
scures underlying political relationships that are expressed
not so much in signal events as in the general atmosphere
within which policy is conducted. The theory of isolationism
is involved, for the differences between "isolation" and a
simple policy of neutrality lie, to a great extent, in the presence or absence of political relationships not likely to appear
in the superficial anatomy of particular disputes.
    These assumptions used to differentiate isolation from
neutrality—moral-political uniqueness, freedom from power
politics, and fragmentation of diplomatic issues—establish
a continuity between much nineteenth-century declaratory
policy and twentieth-century diplomatic historiography. The
most that could be said to separate the two is that later historians have placed an added emphasis on passivity or conscious insulation that seems uncharacteristic of nineteenth-
century diplomats, who regarded their "moral superiority"
as a virtue to be flaunted rather than a motive for isolation.
    One reason for the acceptance of historical isolationism

by twentieth century internationalists is the fact that they often accepted these same assumptions on the nature of American institutions and behavior. Their plea for internationalism thus rested on arguments that, given a different slant, could be used to support isolationism. Thus an internationalist of one period, such as Henry Cabot Lodge, promoted the isolationist position later with little or no inconsistency in his basic assumptions. The Wilsonian internationalists argued for their policy not on grounds of concrete interest but from arguments *against* the "selfishness" of the United States and *for* the promotion of international morality and law.[40] But if the United States were on a different moral and ideal plane from the rest of humanity, the argument for withdrawal was at least as logical as the plan to carry American ideals abroad.

Taking policy pronouncements of the nineteenth century at face value, then, the argument for the historical truth of isolationism is strong. If, as declaratory policy would have it, a belief in the uniqueness of American institutions motivated a conscious effort to withdraw from power politics that proved largely successful, diplomatic historians are justified in treating this period of American diplomacy in terms of such subjective considerations. But if, as it has been claimed, "America's foreign relations are no exception to the cardinal rule that objective conditions largely shape and govern a nation's external relations," [41] we might look for some differences between the pronouncements of United States foreign policy in the nineteenth century and the actual content of that policy. It is to the question of the actual policy that we now turn.

# AN ALTERNATE THEORY:
# THE TWO BALANCES OF POWER

Criticisms of the theory of nineteenth-century isolationism, based primarily on the content of actual policy, date back almost as far as the theory itself. In general they originally consisted of limited qualifications and as time progressed, developed into attacks on the basic assumptions of the theory. At least four different lines of attack (by no means mutually exclusive) were used in these criticisms: (1) specific exceptions to the rule of total separation, (2) general exceptions to the practice of isolation, (3) description of nineteenth-century policy in terms of concrete advantage rather than ideology, and (4) denial of the contention that any nation could pursue a policy totally unrelated to the world balance of power.

Albert Bushnell Hart, writing in 1901, said that "historically there has never been such an isolation" as was then being claimed because "the power of the Unitd States has usually been in reserve, . . . and whenever the interests of the nation seemed sufficiently affected, our place has been made manifest." [42] The idea that the general policy of isolation had not been followed when national interests directed otherwise was accepted by a number of historians who, unlike Hart, believed that the rule stood despite the exceptions. Some expressed the view that "American isolation always breaks down in war . . . because it is based on a physical misconception—the idea that the Atlantic is an impossible barrier." [43] It was felt that Washington's expressed desire of avoiding European quarrels was a "pious hope," for American interests were involved during the worst conflicts. The rule of isolation remained the general principle, but "it might be temporarily departed from on particular occasions whenever the interests of the United States could be subserved thereby." [44]

These criticisms of the theory of isolationism were enlarged upon by Richard W. Van Alstyne, who argued that "it is natural to assume that the Father of His Country was expressing himself somewhat in terms of the doctrine of the two spheres, but he was too practical a statesman to carry the reliance upon geographical separation to an extreme." It followed, therefore, that United States policy in the Washington tradition was "isolationist only to the extent that it regards with indifference issues which are purely local to Europe," and that the United States reserved to itself the right to determine when a question ceased to be local. Van Alstyne put great emphasis on the Washingtonian distinction between the *ordinary* and the *extraordinary* vicissitudes of European politics, with the understanding that the latter issues were likely to cross the Atlantic. This objection provides exceptions in special cases to the general practic of isolation, but accepts the unhindered operation of the policy during normal, peaceful periods of European history.[45]

Other writers enlarged the list of specific exceptions to the practice of isolationism. Pitman Potter, one of the few internationalists of the 1920s, who chose to challenge the historical truth of isolationism, thought that the exceptions were sufficient to disprove the rule: "The legend of national isolation as a description of American policy is sheer myth." Potter accepted the argument that in special cases the defense of national interests had always taken precedence ("when we have had definite interests to defend or objects to promote, we have taken action without regard for any a priori theory of abstention"), and added the fight against commercial restrictions and "crusading demarches" for liberty and democracy to the list of non-isolationist practices." [46] Others also argued that American interest in promoting liberal political movements abroad was a departure from general isolationist policy, leading to an "anomalous position" for the average citizen, since the supposition of popular abstention from such matters "was in flagrant contravention of the facts." [47] In the same category were American interests in the pursuit of peace in world politics and American intervention in pursuit of important principles or doctrines, activities that have not been infrequent in the diplomacy of the United States.[48]

Historians have also noted more general exceptions to American isolation, although both the general and specific exceptions still left the doctrine of isolation intact, if reduced in dimension. The distinction between specific and general exceptions is a matter of degree, of course, but in general the latter excluded whole areas of political activity from the sway of the abstentionist doctrine. John Bigelow, writing in

1914, limited the proscription to "entangling alliances," which in his view had not affected alliances prior to 1796 (the Farewell Address), temporary alliances, impartial alliances, Western hemisphere alliances, or most forms of political contact or intervention.[49]

A more thorough examination of the content of "isolationism" as the United States practiced it was made by Albert K. Weinberg, who arrived at the conclusion that "the concept of isolation is useful only in so far as it indicates the misunderstanding of an ideology, serves as a point of departure for investigation, and contains in its connotation certain suggestive half-truths." Weinberg found that isolation was better described as a "policy of reserve" based on the principle of maintaining the greatest possible measure of independence and national sovereignty. This policy prohibited eight types of action: (1) entangling alliances, (2) intervention in domestic affairs of other states, (3) interference in purely European matters, (4) joint as opposed to coincident action, (5) commitments limiting future freedom of action, (6) limitation of any sovereign rights, (7) acceptance of any political "super-authority," and (8) any action or lack of action creating entanglements. But the general exception to isolation left "at least as much outside as within": "Permissible because lacking in commitment or meddlesomeness is all single-handed action, from interposition to war, in behalf of national rights, and, when in accord with comity, in behalf of world interest." [50]

Enumeration of exceptions led some to attack the idea of isolationism itself. Rippy was one of the first to promote the view that isolationism, even during its normal "quiet" periods of operation, was a policy of advantage based upon the maintenance of neutrality during the times of discord in Europe. "The conviction of the superiority of our political system and moral standards" and "the belief that European and American interests were not parallel" provided motives for the belief in the idea of isolationism. Actual policy, however, was based not on a moralistic desire to avoid entanglement with European politics but on a practical understanding of the benefits of an active exploitation of a neutral position. Far from being an evil from which this country should insulate itself, European conflicts were an important foundation of our entire foreign policy: "The significant fact—a fact too much ignored by provincial historians of the foreign relations of the United States—is that Europe's strife has been America's shield." [51] This view, though accepting the existence of a policy of isolation in the nineteenth century, in fact calls into question the moralistic basis that underlay much of the distinction between isolation and neutrality. The United States could keep itself out of balance-of-power politics, but did so out of advantage and not because of political or moral differences.

Finally, there were those who denied the United States could in fact avoid balance-of-power politics. These writers contended that no nation had a choice between involving itself in power politics or withdrawing into a position free of such considerations, whether for reasons of morality or advantage. The United States, it was said, not only benefited from the upheavals in European politics, but was inevitably involved in pursuing policies designed to preserve the European balance of power and maintain the advantages of neutrality. The United States could be said, in this view, to be neutral but not isolated, except in the sense of being temporarily freed of any need to act in European politics when European nations maintained the advance of power themselves. Most writers continued, however, to use the word "isolation" even while limiting its content to what in this study has only the meaning of "neutrality."

This strand of attack on the theory of isolationism was begun at least as early as 1928 by the writer who called isolation a "misnomer" because "from the beginning of our national independence, our foreign policy has been influenced by the affairs of Europe. Without the balance of power in Europe, our history would undoubtedly have been quite different." [52] Rippy hinted at this when he outlined the ways in which the United States had benefited from a balanced Europe in which "Russia wished to keep on friendly terms with the

United States as a counterpoise to England." [53] But the most complete statement of this view of American involvement in the world balance of power came from Nicholas John Spykman, who wrote that

> the New World, notwithstanding its insular character, has not been an isolated sphere on which political forces were permitted to find their natural balance without interference from outside. On the contrary, the power structure has been dependent not only on the power potentials inherent in the geography of the continent, but also on the amount of power that states in Europe were able to make available in this area.[54]

Spykman further argued that "the position of the United States in regard to Europe as a whole is, therefore, identical to the position of Great Britain in regard to the European continent." The two countries had, as a consequence, followed similar policies and had "become involved in the same cycles of isolation, alliance, and war." At the outbreak of the first World War, for example, "the United States indulged in a good deal of selfrighteousness," but growing concern with the threat to the European balance of power served to draw it into the conflict.[55] Further studies along these lines in the last fifteen years have strengthened the arguments against the traditional theory of nineteenth-century isolation.

An additional line of attack has been the emphasis placed on the differences between "isolation" as a realistic aim of nineteenth-century policy and "isolationism" as an unrealistic policy of withdrawal, the "very negation of foreign policy," practiced in the 1920s and 1930s.[56] These criticisms have had, at best, a limited effect on the general direction of diplomatic historiography.[57] There is still, for example, no general history of United States diplomacy based squarely upon those assumptions that most fundamentally challenged the traditional concept of isolation, treating the everyday foreign policy of the United States in terms of its continual relationship to the European balance of power and the advantages gained from active exploitations of neutrality.

If American foreign policy were to be considered in these terms, what sort of an international system might be envisioned? What would a theory constructed of the various criticisms of isolationism resemble? And what kind of historical research would be required to validate it? Certainly any theory must recognize the fact that during the nineteenth century the major issues of world politics were settled in Europe, and the European balance of power, to a great extent, was the world balance of power. The Western hemisphere could be described as a local system or balance of power subordinated to the dominant world balance of power.[58] Located on the periphery of the main conflicts in world politics, the United States could hope to wield a decisive influence in the Western hemisphere as long as outside powers did not intervene in great force. Thus Alexander Hamilton could proclaim: "Let the thirteen States . . . concur in erecting one great American system, superior to the control of all transatlantic force or influence, and able to dictate the terms of the connection between the old and the new world!" [59]

The geographical distance of the United States from the main centers of world conflict would increase its autonomy in the Western hemisphere to the point of making neutrality a feasible and profitable policy for the United States. American neutrality in European politics and her insistence on European restraint in the New World could be seen as elements of an instinctive policy to "dictate the terms of connection" most favorable to the young country. These terms would clearly require the United States not to interfere in the Old World as far as possible, for the influence of the United States would in any event count for little there, while it could act with a free hand in the Western hemisphere, where there was no significant opposition. Such might be its aim. But the terms for the connection between the New World and the Old could not be entirely of American choosing. The material interests of European countries and the threatened dominance of the New World by the aggressive young "Colossus of the

North" would make this impossible. In addition, the New
World might play a role as makeweight in European politics;
it was, significantly, an English statesman who boasted that
"I called the New World into existence, to redress the balance
of the Old." [60]

If the United States was never completely involved and
never completely uninvolved in European politics, the terms
of its "connection" would be a matter of constant dispute and
adjustment. Here the importance of Britain's role as the link
between the two systems emerges. In the first place, British
interests were in many respects similar to American interests.
Both countries sought to prevent the domination of the European continent by any one power, and the British fulfillment
of this aim would relieve the United States of concern with
European politics, under ordinary circumstances.[61] Britain
also sought to keep other Old World powers from interfering
in the New World and thus acquiring the strength to challenge
British interests and upset the world balance of power. The
resulting situation has been described as a world "policed by
the British fleet, a world in which Englishmen grew rich and
Americans prospered peacefully." [62]

Yet the British position was anomalous. As main protector of the autonomy of the New World, she could also be the
main threat. To the American position, American historians
have pointed out that British aims were not as expansive as
they might have been: "It has been little less fortunate that
the strongest of these European powers has been opposed
to the intervention of the Old World states in America while
displaying small disposition to control Hispanic-American territory for itself." [63] Yet others have recognized that additional
factors might have been involved. As it was in the British
interest to see the European continent balanced, it could be
said that the American interest was to see it balanced in a
manner which would keep Britain occupied. The United States
could be best assured of a free hand in the New World only if
the European continent were not too well balanced: "Only
complete success or complete failure of British foreign policy
would mean replacement of equilibrium by the domination of

a single power, a situation sufficiently serious to warrant American intervention." [64]

It has been pointed out that conflicts between the United States and Britain were most frequent when Britain's attention could be relaxed in Europe. During such interludes Britain could look out after its own interests and try, at least in a feeble manner, to thwart the further expansion of the power of the United States, which threatened to turn the New World balance permanently in its own favor. The British, sometimes with French assistance, were said to practice what might be loosely labelled a policy of "containment" against the lusty young giant. This, of course, could bring about closer ties between the United States and Britain's European foes (e.g., Russia), thus mixing the major elements of the two balance of power systems.[65]

The Monroe Doctrine, guiding star of United States policy, during this period can be seen as a symbol of the kind of separation between the two balances of power which the United States desired. Although never accepted explicitly by the British, its rough similarity to British aims could be described as a major factor in its success. In any event, the simple logic of its idealistic appeal could serve as a good weapon in the hands of American diplomats and, as time went on, as a powerful rallying cry for public opinion.[66] Another guiding aim of American foreign policy, expansionism, can also be related to the desire of American diplomats to restrict European activity in the New World. From this, one would expect to find that the greatest exponents of expansion were also the greatest opponents of the British or any other nation seeking to maintain the New World balance.[67]

The fact that such a theory has not been reflected in empirical historical studies does not prove it barren. Historical research often overlooks important factors that raise difficult methodological questions. The theory outlined above assumes the existence of underlying, concealed, and undramatic forces in politics that are often acted upon instinctively but may receive little or no recognition in the written sources with which historians deal. Ideological concealments, meaningless policy pronouncements, legalistic thinking, moralistic assumptions, partisan issues, and the fragmentation of politics into specific disputes all tend to obscure the underlying calculations, often only half-conscious to begin with. The historian must try to probe beneath all the disguises and self-deceptions of politics and, at the same time, avoid reading his own assumptions into the evidence.

Two alternative interpretations, therefore, can be made by the historian of United States foreign policy. The first considers policy to be actually as well as theoretically based on moral preference rather than power, free of connections to European affairs and legitimately expressed in legal and moral terms. The second interpretation sees it as based on considerations of national interest and unavoidably connected to the world balance of power. One interpretation assumes the freedom of the United States from European power politics and its insulation from European conflicts; the other assumes at least a peripheral involvement in European power politics and the exploitation of advantages derived from European conflicts. The question might be phrased: Was the United States isolated, or merely neutral?

# NOTES

1. Seward to William L. Dayton (Minister to France), May 11, 1863, quoted in John Bassett Moore, *A Digest of International Law*, VI (Washington: Government Printing Office, 1906), 23. Italics mine.

2. Herbert Adams Gibbons, *America's Place in the World* (New York and London: The Century Co., 1924), p. 31.

3. Richard W. Leopold, *The Growth of American Foreign Policy* (New York: Alfred A. Knopf, 1962), pp. 17, 29.

4. *Ibid.*

5. Merle E. Curti, "Young America," *American Historical Review*, XXXII (October, 1962), 34-55; Albert K. Weinberg, "The Historical Meaning of the American Doctrine of Isolation," *American Political Science Review*, XXXIV (June, 1940), 539.

6. James A. H. Murray, ed., *A New English Dictionary on Historical Principles*, V (Oxford: Clarendon Press, 1901), 508.

7. Alfred Thayer Mahan, "The United States Looking Outward," *Living Age*, CLXXIV (December, 1890), 818, 821.

8. Murray, *op. cit.*, V, 508.

9. Richard Olney, "International Isolation of the United States," *Atlantic Monthly*, LXXXI (May, 1898), 578.

10. John W. Proctor, "Isolationism or Imperialism?" *Forum*, XXVI (September, 1898), 14, 15, 26.

11. "The Isolation of Our Country," *The Nation*, LXVII (August 4, 1898), 86-87.

12. "The situation of the United States was essentially different. Physically remote from the Old World, its political interests also were detached from those of Europe. . . . The political arrangements of Europe . . . were treated as belonging to what was called the European system, while those of the independent nations of America were jealously guarded as belonging to the 'American system' . . . No other principle has so distinguished the foreign policy of the United States; . . . it is probable that the ramifications of that principle will not be wholly overlooked in the consideration of any future plan of concert." John Bassett Moore, *The Principles of American Diplomacy* (New York and London: Harper & Brothers, 1918), pp. 35, 444-45.

13. Gibbons, *op. cit.*, p. viii; Edwin Borchard and William Potter Lage, *Neutrality for the United States* (New Haven: Yale University Press, 1937), p. 350.

14. Edward Meade Earle, *Against This Torrent* (Princeton: Princeton University Press, 1941), pp. 35, 37, 39.

15. Paul Scott Mower, *Our Foreign Affairs* (New York: E.P. Dutton & Company, 1924), pp. 37, 86.

16. "The separation of the European and American Systems, is on the contrary as vital and essential today as it was when it was first enunciated." (Willis Fletcher Johnson, *America's Foreign Relations*, I [New York: The Century Co., 1916], 349-50). "People began to realize that the isolation proclaimed in 1823 as desirable was only a means adapted to the conditions of that time." Carl Russell Fish, *American Diplomacy* (New York: H. Holt and Company, 1923), p. 2.

17. Johnson, *op. cit.*, I, 201.

18. Robert L. Jones, *History of the Foreign Policy of the United States* (New York: G.P. Putnam's Sons, 1933), p. 108.

19. Fish, *op. cit.*, p. 2.

20. Theodore Clarke Smith, *The United States as a Factor in World History* (New York: Henry Holt and Company, 1941), pp. 46, 57.

21. James Quayle Dealey, *Foreign Policies of the United States* (Boston: Ginn and Company, 1926), pp. 303-04. See also John Holloday Latané, *A History of American Foreign Policy* (Garden City, N. Y.: Doubleday, Page & Company, 1927), especially pp. 579-81; John Mabry Mathews, *American Foreign Relations* (New York: The Century Co., 1928), especially pp. 26, 30-31; Benjamin H. Williams, *American Diplomacy* (New York and London: McGraw-Hill Book Company, 1936), especially pp. 18-19, 25, 29-30; and Louis Martin Sears, *A History of American Foreign Relations* (New York: Thomas Y. Crowell Company, 1936), especially p. 182.

22. Samuel Flagg Bemis, *A Diplomatic History of the United States* (1st ed.; New York: Holt, Rinehart, and Winston, Inc., 1936), pp. 209, 802, 809.

23. Bemis, *A Short History of American Foreign Policy and Diplomacy* (New York: Henry Holt and Company, Inc., 1959), p. 364. This does not mean Bemis' view of *twentieth-century* (interwar) isolation has not changed. In the second edition of his general history (New York: Holt, Rinehart and Winston, Inc., 1942), Bemis dropped his affirmation of the "continental policy" for contemporary foreign relations and adds (p. 878) that "the policy of abstention . . . was admirably calculated to suit American interests as long as Europe was balanced in power." The United States, he said (p. 865), entered World War II "because it was scared for its own safety," and the neutrality legislation (p. 879) was "better designed to keep the nation out of the last war than out of the next war." See also the fourth edition of the same work (New York: Holt, Rinehart and Winston, Inc., 1955), pp. 963-64, 968.

24. Thimas A. Bailey, *A Diplomatic History of the American People* (1st ed.; New York: F. S. Crofts & Co., 1940), pp. 755, 757. Subsequent editions have not changed the sense of this view.

25. Dexter Perkins, *The Evolution of American Foreign Policy* (New York: Oxford University Press, 1948), pp. 40, 53, 54.

26. "Isolation is a theory about a theory of American foreign policy" (Weinberg, 539).

27. Pitman B. Potter, *The Myth of American Isolation* ("A League of Nations," Vol. IV, No. 6; Boston: World Peace Foundation, 1921), p. 478.

28. Latané, *op. cit.*, p. 98.

29. Dealey, *op. cit.*, p. 135.

30. Johnson, *op. cit.*, I, 202.

31. James D. Richardson, ed., *A Compilation of the Messages and Papers of the Presidents*, IV (Washington: Bureau of National Literature and Art, 1908), 398.

32. See, for example, Borchard and Lage, *op. cit.*, pp. 32, 349-350.

33. Johnson, *op. cit.*, I, 200.

34. Latané, *op. cit.*, p. 686; Gibbons, *op. cit.*, p. 216.

35. Theodore Lyman, *The Diplomacy of the United States* (Boston: Welles and Lilly, 1826), pp. 373-74.

36. William Henry Trescot, *The Diplomatic History of the Administrations of Washington and Adams* (Boston: Little, Brown and Company, 1857), p. 3.

37. Charles Francis Adams, *The Struggle for Neutrality in America* (New York: Charles Scribner and Co., 1871), pp. 2, 46. See also John W. Foster, *A Century of American Diplomacy* (Boston: Houghton, Mifflin and Company, 1900), pp. 3, 439.

38. Dealey, *op. cit.*, p. 141.

39. Bemis, *op. cit.*, *A Short History of American Foreign Policy and Diplomacy*, p. 364.

40. "The escape from the responsibilities of organized society into hermitlike isolation [will bring about] an easier triumph on this planet of lawlessness, brute force, and war" (Cordell Hull, "Spirit of International Law," *United States Foreign Policy*, ed. Julia Johnsen [New York: The H.W. Wilson Company, 1938], pp. 90, 91). "In the mandate also there is the beginning of a new era for the peoples of lower civiliza-

30 THE LIMITS OF AMERICAN ISOLATION

tion. . . . In such matters of international morality the United States
must have a voice" (Dealey, *op. cit.*, p. 368).

41. Kenneth W. Thompson, "Isolation and Collective Security,"
*Isolation and Security*, ed. Alexander De Conde (Durham, N.C.: Duke
University Press, 1957), p. 159.

42. Albert Bushnell Hart, *The Foundations of American Foreign
Policy* (New York: The Macmillan Company, 1901), pp. 2-3, 49.

43. J. Fred Rippy and Angie Debo, *The Historical Background of
the American Policy of Isolation* (Northampton, Mass.: Smith College,
1924), p. 72.

44. Randolph Greenfield Adams, *A History of the Foreign Policy
of the United States* (New York: The Macmillan Company, 1924), p. 21;
James Witford Garner, *American Foreign Policies* (New York: New
York University Press, 1928), pp. 55, 57.

45. Richard W. Van Alstyne, *American Diplomacy in Action*, 1st
ed. (Stanford, Calif.: Stanford University Press, 1944), pp. 6, 47, 619.

46. Potter, *op. cit.*, pp. 433, 451, 436-37, 463, 472-73. Potter also disputes the validity of isolation as a declaratory policy, capitalizing upon
the qualifications in official statements (see especially p. 478).

47. Malbone W. Graham, *American Diplomacy in the International
Community* (Baltimore: The John Hopkins Press, 1948), pp. 82-84.

48. J. Fred Rippy, *America and the Strife of Europe* (Chicago: The
University of Chicago Press, 1938), pp. 46-47; Doris Appel Graber,
*Crisis Diplomacy: A History of U.S. Intervention Policies and Practices*
(Washington, D.C.: Public Affairs Press, 1959), pp. 28-29.

49. John Bigelow, *American Policy: The Western Hemisphere in
its Relation to the Eastern* (New York: Charles Scribner's Sons, 1914),
pp. 33, 39-41.

50. Weinberg, *op. cit.*, 539, 543-45.

51. Rippy, *op. cit.*, pp. 15-17, 103, 131.

52. John Mabry Mathews, *American Foreign Relations* (New York:
The Century Co., 1928), p. 18.

53. Rippy, *op. cit.*, pp. 132-33.

54. Nicholas John Spykman, *America's Strategy in World Politics*
(New York: Harcourt, Brace and Company, 1942), p. 89.

55. *Ibid.*, pp. 123-24.

56. See Hans J. Morgenthau, *In Defense of the National Interest*
(New York: Alfred A. Knopf, 1952), pp. 9-10, 28-29; Alexander De
Conde, "On Twentieth Century Isolationism," in De Conde, *op. cit.*

57. For recent views reflecting caution, see Julius Pratt, *A History
of the United States Foreign Policy* (Englewood Cliffs, N.J.: Prentice-
Hall, Inc., 1955), pp. 4, 69, 777, and De Conde, *A History of American
Foreign Policy* (New York: Charles Scribner's Sons, 1963), pp. 2, 54,
140, 441.

58. Hans J. Morgenthau, *Politics Among Nations*, 3rd ed. (New
York: Alfred A. Knopf, 1961), pp. 198-203.

59. Alexander Hamilton, "Federalist No. 11," in Hamilton, John
Jay, and James Madison, *The Federalist on the New Constitution* (New
York: Williams & Whiting, 1810), I, 79.

60. *Speeches of the Right Honourable George Canning*, VI (London, 1836), 111.

61. "Because Great Britain is interested in balanced power and actively engaged in the pursuit of that objective, the United States felt that she could disinterest herself in European political questions most of the time" (Spykman, p. 123). See also Forrest Davis, *The Atlantic System* (New York: Reynal and Hitchcock, 1941), especially pp. xi-xvi.

62. De Conde, *A History of American Foreign Policy*, p. 7.

63. Rippy, *op. cit.*, p. 132.

64. Spykman, *op. cit.*, p. 123.

65. *Ibid.*, p. 85; Rippy, *op. cit.*, pp. 108-110.

66. Leonard Lawson, *The Relation of British Policy to the Declaration of the Monroe Doctrine* (Published Ph.D. Dissertation, Columbia University, 1922), p. 125; Rippy, *op. cit.*, pp. 29-30, 126.

67. Rippy, *op. cit.*, pp. 64-65.

# Expansion and Containment, 1853-1854

## CHAPTER TWO

E'en so, when Young America demands
Her rightful share of Nicaraguan lands,
Poor John Bull Bumble stands aghast, and cries:
"Why, Brother Jonathan! you'll want the skies
If you check not these bad propensities;
We are your mother, and sure know what's best." [1]

## NEW WORLD AND OLD WORLD

On March 4, 1853, Franklin Pierce of New Hampshire was inaugurated as the fourteenth president of the United States. During the same month, Tsar Nicholas I of Russia dispatched Prince Alexander Menshikov, a hard-bitten soldier, on his ill-fated diplomatic mission to Constantinople.

No obvious or direct connection between these events is apparent. Menshikov's mission, to wrest certain concessions from the Turkish government in order to enlarge Russia's powers as protector of Orthodox Christians within the Ottoman Empire, was the first important episode in the series of events that led to the outbreak of the Crimean War. It was also related to an old set of issues, known as the Eastern Question: What was to happen to the strategically important Ottoman-Turkish territories which the Turks could no longer effectively control or defend against the Great Powers? The United States had never openly interfered with the Eastern Question, central though it might be to European diplomacy. Any effects on American diplomacy, then, would be indirect.

This does not mean that there were not, in early 1853, outstanding diplomatic issues between the United States and the powers directly affected by Menshikov's mission. There were, in fact, a large number. Viewed separately, these issues were mostly disputes of a legal nature concerning the relationship of the United States to neighboring American states or colonies in which European powers had an interest. Viewed together, these issues indicated a pattern of American expansion into neighboring areas, with Europe almost unvaryingly opposed.

In 1853, the United States was involved in two particularly important disputes with Great Britain, her major opponent. The first of these involved competition between the two parties in Central America; the second, the relationship of the United States to British North America. In both cases the conflict was framed in circumscribed legal terms; the Central American dispute revolved around the interpretation of the Clayton-Bulwer Treaty of 1850, and the Canadian dispute grew out of conflicting claims regarding the rights of American fishermen in Canadian waters, along with the ever-present problem of trade restrictions.

The Clayton-Bulwer Treaty of April 19, 1850, bound the United States and Great Britain to cooperate in the construction of any Isthmian canal in Central America and further provided that neither party would "occupy, or fortify, or colonize, or assume or exercise any dominion over Nicaragua, Costa Rica, the Mosquito Coast, or any part of Central America." The competition of the two powers in Central America was to be allayed by mutual abstention. From the

British point of view, expressed by Sir Henry Bulwer himself, the treaty was of great value because it bound the United States against further annexations in Central America, "Honduras and Nicaragua being at that time desirous to annex themselves." The treaty also facilitated the construction of a canal over which Britain was assured partial control; and finally it "tacitly set aside the Munro [sic] doctrine, viz., that the States of Europe have nothing to do with the States of America." [2] From the American point of view, the treaty recognized the United States for the first time as "an American power, equal in every respect to the only other first-class American power, Great Britain." [3]

But whatever the mutual advantages, the treaty merely changed the form of the Central American dispute; it did not resolve it. Territorial conflicts in Central America had been allayed only by the use of general terms; as one historian concluded, "both negotiators deliberately consented to the use of ambiguous language in order to conceal their official differences." [4] When the treaty was applied, these differences soon reappeared as sharply as before. The United States maintained that under the terms of the treaty the British must relinquish their "protectorate" over the Mosquito Indians on the east coast of Nicaragua, cease their occupation of the Bay Islands off the coast of Honduras, and reduce their settlement in Belize (later British Honduras) to its original limits.[5] One particular source of irritation was the continued occupation of Greytown (formerly San Juan), Nicaragua's only port and a probable terminal point on any Nicaraguan canal, by the Mosquito Indians, whom the British had sponsored; another was the organization of the Bay Islands Colony in 1852. In response to these demands the British insisted that the treaty was not retroactive, and thus did not affect settlements or occupations established before 1850. The battle over Central America was to be a staple of Anglo-American diplomacy during the 1850s.

The Canadian situation was no less dangerous. British officials in Canada were frightened by an annexationist movement there, caused, to a large extent, by the economic dislocation following the repeal of the Corn Laws in Great Britain. They sought to reduce the strength of the movement by securing American markets to replace the lost British markets. One method of pressuring trade concessions from the United States was to enforce the Convention of 1818 against American fishermen in Canadian waters, the restrictions of which they had long ignored with impunity. The British fleet in the area was enlarged, and in the storm that followed open naval warfare seemed likely to break out. The situation had, however, led President Millard Fillmore to open negotiations on the related questions of the fisheries and trade restrictions. The situation was sensitive from both points of view. The British sought sufficient economic ties between the two countries to reduce Canadian economic discontent without increasing American influence past a tolerable point, while Americans viewed the annexationist movement with scarcely concealed approval and saw in the fisheries dispute, in Daniel Webster's words, "questions of a very serious nature, threatening the peace of the two countries." [6]

Distrust of American expansionism ran deep, and was often linked to other issues of no apparent relevance to foreign policy. Harriet Martineau, for example, linked the expansionism of the United States to the evils of Southern slavery, claiming that "the spirit of the Southern slave-power was ruling at Washington" and adding that

> the war with Mexico astonished that part of the world which did not understand that slavery brings after it both the lust and the need of fresh territory. . . . No adequate cause for the Mexican war appeared to anybody outside of the United States; and nothing had happened yet which so lowered the Republic in the eyes of older nations.[7]

Slavery, of course, might well be marginal to the deeper issues of the conflict, insofar as the American expansionist impulse cannot be attributed solely to this one factor. A more inclusive point of view, comprehending the serious diplomatic aspects of the problem, was clearly expressed by John Crampton, British Ambassador to the United States, one month before Pierce's inauguration:

> The point of time seems to me to have come when it behoves us to come to a determination as to whether these aggressive [U.S.] plans are of such vital importance to our Interests as to oblige us to resist them. . . .
>
> It seems to me quite clear that if carried out to their full effect, we should be forced to resist them somewhere, and the question remains as to the point at which it would be advisable to make a stand.
>
> All these considerations would give an impression of a very dangerous state of things: but I think nevertheless that there are two checks upon which we may generally concede as preventing the aggressive spirit of this People from being carried to extremes. The one is the inextinguishable struggle between the North and South, Free States and Slave States. . . . The other is the real injury to the material and commercial interests of a practical and moneymaking people which they are perfectly aware would result from a serious quarrel with England. . . .[8]

French policy toward the United States was based on the same attitude. French diplomats and statesmen also sounded constant warnings about the expansionism of the United States and disturbance of the balance of power; Francois Guizot, Louis Philippe's Premier, remarked in 1846 that while Britain checked the Russian threat to the balance of power in Europe, no one checked the threat of the United States in the Western hemisphere.[9] The theme of European cooperation, especially with England, to contain the Yankee threat, was repeatedly expressed; Eugene de Sartiges, French Ambassador to the United States through most of the 1850's, claimed that one interest united these two countries with the rest of Europe and Latin America: "to resist the endless invasions of the North Americans." [10] The French, as did the British, feared the expansionism of the United States into a number of locations: Central America, Cuba, Hawaii, the Amazon (where American filibustering was feared), and even the Galapagos Islands near Ecuador (where Americans sought guano deposits). By its own report France regarded the checking of the United States in the Western hemisphere [11] as a cornerstone of its foreign policy.

Under Louis Napoleon, however, the goals of French policy were not merely negative ones. Though full fruition of his plans could not be achieved until the United States was occupied with the Civil War, Napoleon's pledge, made in 1853, to "support Mexico against American inroads" was not empty.[12] Following the publication of a pamphlet urging the creation of French colonies in Northern Mexico to check United States expansion,[13] one French adventurer, Count Raousset de Boulbon, actually attempted to capture the state of Sonora in late 1852. The responsibility of the French government for this undertaking is uncertain: Though formally disapproving, the French consul in San Francisco privately favored the scheme, and asked for the dispatch of a French warship to the Gulf of California. In any event, the suspicions of many American newspapers and political figures, especially pro-expansionists such as Senator Lewis Cass of Michigan, were thoroughly aroused by this episode.[14] The American chargé d'affaires in Paris was especially concerned about some of Raousset's efforts to gain support from influential Frenchmen, and in mid-1853 relayed to Secretary of State William Marcy a letter claiming that the French aims did not stop at the border between Mexico and the United States.[15]

The extent of British and French opposition to United States expansion was shown clearly by their concern over American intentions in one particular area where they themselves had no formal interest. This was the question of Cuba, technically only an issue between Spain and the United States. In 1848 President James K. Polk had offered to buy Cuba from Spain for one hundred million dollars. Spain had, of course, refused.[16] Three more American "filibusters," attempting to wrest Cuba from Spain by planned invasions and revolution, were carried out within the next three years. These not only strengthened Spanish determination to hold Cuba, but led to British and French support of the weak Spanish authority. This began with the dispatch of French naval forces in 1850 to help stop further American expeditions, a move which led to full-fledged naval intervention in 1851, and finally, in late 1852, to a proposal to the United States government for a tripartite treaty guaranteeing Cuba. Such an admission by a European power of interest in an "American affair" was, of course, anathema to any American politician, and Whig Secretary of State Edward Everett made a widely publicized response on December 1, 1852, rejecting the scheme in no uncertain terms and condemning British and French interference. In response the British and French fleets in the West Indies were strengthened.[17]

To this explosive situation was added a series of incidents such as the Crescent City affair of 1852, involving the treatment of American ships by Cuban authorities, which served as irritants to Washington and might have become a *casus belli* at any time. Such incidents were aggravated by the fact that redress to American shipowners and sailors could only be obtained through appeal to the Spanish government in Madrid, an uncertain and tedious procedure at best. The Cuban problem, with Great Britain and France taking Spain under their protection against the threatened onslaught of American expansionism, was perhaps the most delicate problem in the relationship of these powers. As Crampton expressed the British viewpoint to his home government,

This matter of Cuba is one which involves very serious considerations for us, and one which I think is now come to such a point that we can no longer avoid looking it in the face and making up our minds as to what we are to do or not to do about it. The question, as you truly observe, involves Peace or War, or, at all

events a risk of war. . . . We must either take a step
further in the same direction by making, in conjunction
with France, a declaration to the United States similar
to that which the United States has made to us . . . or
. . . we must take a step backwards . . . and make up
our minds to see Cuba annexed to this Country. . . .
Now, if we adopt the first of these two courses, we
must not blink the fact that it would engage us to go
to War under certain future contingencies, and also
that the brunt of that War would fall on our
Shoulders. . . .[18]

Austria shared some of the Anglo-French apprehensions
of United States expansion; but, since it did not have any
direct interest in the Western hemisphere and did have serious domestic problems, it was more concerned with the possible extension of American power *in Europe*. Baron Hülsemann, Austrian chargé d'affaires in the United States from
1841 to 1855, constantly warned his government of this danger
and, while sympathizing with English and French policy,
urged restraint. He was especially disturbed by American
negotiations for a naval base in Lisbon in 1851 and by the
welcome extended to the Hungarian refugee Louis Kossuth
that same year. In the latter case he entered an official protest
which earned a well-publicized rebuke from Secretary of
State Daniel Webster.[19] Austria also gave "moral support"
to Spain on the Cuban problem, although in 1850 Hülsemann advised selling the island before it was too late. Hülsemann also predicted later (December, 1853) that a European
war at that time would give the United States the opportunity
to seize Canada and Hawaii as well.[20] But, on the whole,
Austrian involvement in the Western hemisphere was, for
realistic reasons, minimal.

# CRIMEAN PRELUDE AND UNITED STATES POLICY

"The policy of my Administration," declared Franklin Pierce in his inaugural address, "will not be controlled by any timid forebodings of evil from expansion. Indeed, it is not to be disguised that our attitude as a nation and our position on the globe render the acquisition of certain possessions not within our jurisdiction eminently important for our protection. . . ." [21]

Many forces impelled Pierce in the direction of an expansionist foreign policy. As his biographer has remarked, "his scruples would not permit a very broad domestic program, but the Constitution wrote no 'laissez-faire' across the pages of state department instructions." [22] The traditional anti-British and expansionist policies of the Democratic party, due partly to its cultivation of such voting blocs as the Irish-Americans, also encouraged Pierce to choose two of his principal diplomatic agents (Secretary of State William Marcy and Minister to Great Britain James Buchanan) from the cabinet of his good friend James K. Polk. Pierce's entire political career, from his beginning as a disciple of Andrew Jackson through his service as a General in the Mexican War, led him to take a strong stand in questions of foreign policy. His close ties with the rabid Southern expansionists in his own party (Harriet Martineau's "Southern slave power") increased these tendencies, and, finally, the delicate situation regarding slavery in the period following the Compromise of 1850, which Pierce regarded as having permanently settled the issue, led to a concentration on "unifying" foreign issues, particularly expansion, rather than "divisive" domestic conflicts.

No one doubted the popular appeal of expansion, and the most far-fetched projects received open discussion during this period; a popular newspaper could say baldly that

we suppose we must concede, though we do it with
reluctance, that Great Britain has a title to the possession of Canada at present . . . but we cannot imagine
the reason why she and France want little Greytowns
and Honduras Islands. . . . We can never consent to
it, for we want them all ourselves.[23]

Even a considerable number of Whigs, particularly those
led by Senator William H. Seward of New York, could denounce meekness toward expansion: "Has the imperial usurpation of Louis Napoleon struck a damp into the heart of
American as well as European republicans?"[24]

In his inaugural address Pierce not only set the expansionist tone for his administration, but also subscribed
to the popular belief that European affairs had no effect on
American policy:

Of the complicated European systems of national
polity we have heretofore been independent. From their
wars, their tumults, and anxieties we have been, happily, almost entirely exempt. Whilst these are confined
to the nations which gave them existence . . . they
can not affect us except as they appeal to our sympathies
in the cause of human freedom and universal advancement.[25]

What is interesting is not Pierce's acceptance of popular
ideology, but his affirmation of a complete separation of the
New and Old Worlds in almost the same breath as his declaration of a vigorous foreign policy which was certain to create
problems with at least some of the European powers. Could
an active, expansionist American foreign policy (or any American foreign policy, for that matter) possibly be pursued
effectively without any involvement with the complications
of European politics?

Pierce's choice for Secretary of State was William L.
Marcy, former Governor of New York, who is best known

for his declaration that in politics "to the victors belong the spoils," the origin of the "spoils politician" designation. Marcy had no experience to speak of in foreign affairs.[26] Though not always in agreement with some of the more aggressive circles within the Pierce administration, Marcy was in favor of expansion and adopted the tone set in Pierce's inaugural address.[27] Marcy was also an ardent advocate of the outspoken expression of "Americanism" which was common at that time, especially in the ranks of his own party, and was particularly characteristic of the Pierce administration. Indicative of Marcy's attitude was his directive that only "the American language" should be employed in the diplomatic correspondence of the United States and even more so his famous "dress circular," which encouraged the diplomatic representatives of the United States abroad to appear in court "as far as practicable . . . in the simple dress of an American citizen." [28] The contrast between American republicanism and Old World despotism was intentionally underlined, and assertions of moral superiority, combined with boastful arrogance on the future growth of American power, set European nerves on edge during much of this period.

But Marcy was not the most outspoken advocate of this position. Nor was James Buchanan, a man of much diplomatic experience who was persuaded by Pierce to serve as Minister to Great Britain (although Buchanan did declare that he looked forward "to the day when the English language . . . will be the language of the larger portion of the habitable globe").[29] Two other sturdy Democrats, Judge James Y. Mason of Virginia and Governor Thomas H. Seymour of Connecticut, appointed respectively as Ministers to France and Russia, also supported an active and assertive foreign policy, but they, too, maintained a certain restraint in their public expressions. All of these men were "old fogies" in the view of the "Young America" Democrats, who advocated a program of aid to European republicans, wide expansion of American influence, support of filibustering expeditions in Latin America, and other expressions of nationalistic fervor characteristic of America's "coming of age." [30] The leading hero of the "Young America" movement was Stephen A. Douglas, although the movement's chief strength was in the South among the ardent expansionists who sought additional slave territory as a guarantee of Southern power within the Union.

The Pierce administration, despite the presence of such "old fogies" as Marcy, was perhaps more receptive to this strange mixture of pro-republican, pro-slavery, pro-expansion beliefs than any other presidency. In spite of Marcy's opposition, a number of "Young Americans" received important diplomatic posts. Pierre Soulé, noted for his advocacy of the seizure of Cuba, became, suitably, head of the mission in Spain. John L. O'Sullivan, originator of the "Manifest Destiny" slogan, was appointed head of the mission in Portugal. George N. Sanders, *Democratic Review* editor often cited as the leader of "Young America," was made Consul in London, and in the same city the dashing Daniel E. Sickles was chosen as secretary of the American legation under Buchanan. Through Sanders' influence, August Belmont, like Soulé a European republican refugee, returned to Europe as Minister to the Netherlands. Another friend of Sanders, Edwin de Leon, was sent as the representative of democracy to the despots of Egypt. Solon Borland, representing the United States in Central America, pursued many of the same aims.[31] The chances of preserving a clean separation of the Old World and the New, whatever they might have been objectively, were certainly diminished by the character which the Pierce administration revealed to the rest of the world. Pierce's declared intent of avoiding complication in European affairs did not receive even lip service from some "Young American" diplomats; August Belmont, for example, declared to Sanders that the Crimean War aided American aims and brought closer the day "when self-preservation will dictate to the United States the necessity of throwing her moral and physical force into the scale of European republicanism." [32]

The threat of increased pressure for expansion under the new administration made most of the European governments somewhat apprehensive. The French and British press spoke disparagingly of the election of Pierce and the probable influence of Young America Democrats in the new administration, greatly fearing a tendency to seek forceful solutions to outstanding issues. The Austrian and Prussian ministers in Washington both informed their governments that the new administration was likely to expand its influence in Europe as well as in the New World. Austria, because of this fear, had already decided to adopt a more conciliatory tone toward the United States. *Siècle,* a European republican newspaper, published a report that the Pierce administration favored intervention in Europe, causing no small amount of consternation. This feeling of apprehension was not dispelled in the following years; in 1855, for example, a French writer devoted a book to the theme that European governments should occupy themselves chiefly with checking the further expansion of the United States.[34]

The Pierce administration pushed forward vigorously during its first few months. One of the most pressing needs, from the American point of view, was protection for American fishermen subjected to the new indignities of law enforcement in Canadian waters. In July, 1853, Secretary of the Navy James C. Dobbin ordered the movement of a naval force to Portsmouth, New Hampshire, in order to assure "protection to such of our citizens as are there engaged in the fisheries." The commander of the force was told that "worthy citizens . . . have become apprehensive that there is a settled purpose to disturb them in the enjoyment of their fishing rights," and was ordered to "take such steps as in your judgment will be best calculated to check and prevent such interference," particularly from the sizable British Fleet which had been moved to the area.[35] The dangers of an open clash between the opposing forces were obviously not slight.

Another problem existed at the same time on the country's other international border. Many expansionists had not been completely satisfied with the results of the Mexican War only a few years earlier, and in addition railroad interests were pressing for the acquisition of a piece of territory needed for a good southern route to the Pacific. Although Santa Anna, head of the Mexican government, was extremely hostile to the United States, he was also badly in need of money. James Gadsden, U.S. Minister to Mexico, was thus instructed to arrange a purchase of territory in northern Mexico, which he succeeded in doing. Although the Pierce administration was disappointed with the small size of the purchase, the treaty was swiftly ratified.[36]

Santa Anna, in the estimate of many, negotiated the treaty partly in order to avoid war; in any event his fears of American aggression were frequently reflected in the Mexican press, which he controlled.[37] This inevitably brought the European powers into the picture; Santa Anna himself sought aid and support against the United States from England, France and Spain. With the last of these powers he concluded a claims convention in 1853 and proposed an offensive and defensive alliance to protect Cuba and Mexico from American attack.[38] As far as French support was concerned Louis Napoleon's remarks gave intermittent comfort to the Mexican government, and Santa Anna's relationship to the British was demonstrated by his relaying all Gadsden's notes to the British Minister in Mexico, Percy William Doyle, who sent them on to the British Foreign Office. Santa Anna even offered to step down in favor of any European prince who would be given definite support by the European powers, but the British avoided any outright commitments and advised the Mexican ruler to avoid conflict with the United States.[39]

Mexican relations remained strained throughout Pierce's term; Gadsden was a boisterous diplomat with little respect for the autocratic Mexican regime, which eventually asked for his recall.[40] America's desire for more Mexican land continued, and the involvement of the European powers in the Russo-Turkish imbroglio presented her with a fresh opportunity. As James Gordon Bennett's expansionist *New York Herald* put it in mid-1853, shortly before Russia occupied the Danubian provinces in retaliation for the Turkish defiance of Menshikov:

Look at the glory and the power which he [Pierce] and half his cabinet have reaped from the last war, and look at the gathering distractions in the democratic party, and answer us then, dispassionate reader, if there is not a prospect for another brush with Mexico distinctly visible to the naked eye? Peace or war, however, we must abide the issues for Providence, the action of the administration, and the upshot of the *ultimatissimum* between Russia and Turkey. Is that thunder? [41]

It was in late 1853, while war clouds were gathering on the Bosporus, that the Pierce administration had its first real chance to assert American principles to another great power through a show of force. The occasion arose in 1853, when Austrian authorities in Smyrna, Turkey, seized Martin Koszta, a Hungarian refugee who had participated in the uprising of 1848 and 1849, and put him on board an Austrian ship. Turkish authorities took no action, but because Koszta had declared his intention of becoming an American citizen, the American Chargé d'Affaires in Constantinople ordered Captain Ingraham, commander of the United States corvette "St. Louis," to demand that Koszta be surrendered to him. After Ingraham had threatened to clear his deck for action, the Austrians transferred the prisoner to the French consulate in Smyrna pending settlement of the dispute. George Perkins Marsh, hold-over Whig Minister in Constantinople who had been temporarily out of the city, returned soon after and upheld the actions of his subordinates over the protests of the Austrian internuncio.[42] On August 29, 1853, Baron Hülsemann submitted to the United States government a strongly worded protest against "this act of hostility." The Austrian Minister demanded that Koszta be returned to Austrian custody, and that the United States disavow its agents and give "a satisfaction proportionate to the magnitude of the outrage."

In response to the Austrian note, on September 26 Marcy

submitted a lengthy note which, after a point by point, devastating attack on the Austrian position according to international law, refused every single one of the Austrian demands, concluding with the "confident expectation that the Emperor of Austria will take the proper measures to cause Martin Koszta to be restored to the same condition he was in before he was seized in the streets of Smyrna on the 21st of June last." [43] Marcy's note was greeted with almost universal approbation in the United States and even won grudging admiration abroad from such a noted anti-American as Lord Palmerston.[44] No situation could have been better designed for an assertion of America's position and a test of patriotic feeling. By a fortunate coincidence, the decision of the Austrian government to allow Koszta to return to the United States was announced three days after publication of the note, further increasing the impact of Marcy's diplomatic "triumph." [45] The incident was one in the series of episodes that helped to make clear America's determination to pursue its aims in the face of European opposition.

British relations with the United States during these months remained calm. The British government managed to avoid open conflict over the fisheries question, and Joseph R. Ingersoll, Buchanan's predecessor as Minister to the Court of St. James, wrote Marcy that "there is undoubtedly an existing sentiment of respect founded upon a belief of the increasing power of the people and government of the United States." [46] Perhaps this attitude was not unrelated to "the state of things at Constantinople" which, Ingersoll reported a little later, were a "curious matter of speculation" and of constant interest in Britain, to an extent impossible in the United States, which was "happily aloof from the immediate contingencies of the balance of power in the European world. . . ." [47] It was the Central American question that worried the British most, and their concern over the steps that might be taken by the Pierce administration in this area were also reflected by Ingersoll: "I can discover symptoms of uneasiness, lest in the manner in which the whole affair may be treated by the United States, there may be incidental cause of irritation." [48] It would hardly be convenient for Britain to deal forcefully with the Central American issue at a time when the Eastern Question was again coming to a boil.

The Pierce administration, in fact, was moving in the direction of a forthright challenge to the British presence in Central America. Marcy, for one, saw the issue as more than a legalistic quarrel, and was fully prepared to press the case for American influence on the isthmus. In instructing Borland on American policy in that area, he declared that

> The detriment which some of these states have received from the intermeddling of England in their affairs on the pretense of a protectorate over a miserable and degraded tribe of savages—the Mosquitos—and by unwarrantably extending her restricted grants is an instructive lesson to them on this subject. So far as advantages are to be obtained from the friendship of the other nations, they can look to the United States with better hopes and more confidence than to any other power.[49]

This confidence in the benevolence of America as the potentially dominant power in Central America was translated into vigorous and renewed insistence on British withdrawal. By prior agreement with Buchanan, negotiations on this subject were to be carried on in London under the latter's direction, while the trade and fisheries questions were to be handled in Washington.[50] Buchanan's instructions were finally approved by the Cabinet and sent to him in early July, 1853. Based explicitly on the Monroe Doctrine, which at the time was being challenged not only by the British but by many American politicians as well,[51] these instructions were "a reversion to the old Monroe-Doctrine principles of the Polk administration, which, according to Buchanan, aimed to sweep geographic Central America clear of all British influence which had developed since 1786. . . ." [52]

Buchanan was to insist on British evacuation of all but Belize, in which it was to restrict its settlement to the original limits of the Spanish grant of 1786 and to abide by the terms of this grant, which covered only the right of cutting logwood. The government of the United States thus chose the moment of increasing British involvement in the Eastern Question to enlarge its demands in Central America and to press them with renewed determination.[53]

British influence was not to be exorcised in Central America alone. Marcy also declared that "the course of England and France in sending their ships of war on to our coast during the late disturbances respecting that Island," meaning the attempted Cuban filibusters, "was (to use the mildest expression) not respectful to this Republic." This spurred the Secretary to a rousing defense of American expansion against the "unworthy suspicions" of the European powers:

> It is true we have in the last half century greatly enlarged our territories; and so have Great Britain and France enlarged theirs, but we have done it in a manner that may proudly challenge the most rigid scrutiny of mankind. . . . England and France should reluctantly be our accusers.

Marcy was obviously concerned about British and French efforts to preserve the rule of Spain in Cuba. Buchanan was to ascertain British intentions in this regard and warn that country that the United States would regret to see any outside aid given to Spain. If he should discover that Britain had entered into any commitment to maintain Spanish rule in Cuba, he was to "have recourse to such arguments and persuasions as in your judgment will induce her to abandon them." It was clear that American policy-makers would be relieved if they could be certain that the British considered it prudent to limit their actions to moral support of Spain.[54]

Marcy had already received some information on this

question from another source. Daniel M. Barringer, serving his last months as Minister to Spain, had informed the Secretary that in his opinion "both these great powers would go as far as they possibly could short of an actual collision with the United States to protect and maintain the continued dominion of Spain over the Island," adding that France might even "be willing to risk the consequences of such a collision." There was, however, one encouraging factor from the American point of view. "In the present combustible state of the Continent . . . France would have enough to do to take care of the enemies of the Empire within and without her own borders." Barringer also spoke of French and British rivalry for ascendancy in Spain as a possible limitation on their actual support of Spanish rule in Cuba.[55]

The same questions were very much in Marcy's mind when he wrote Soulé's instructions three weeks after relaying Buchanan's. In addition to the expected statement that the United States "would be willing to contribute something more substantial than their good will" toward a "voluntary separation of Cuba from Spain," Marcy told Soulé that this country would "resist at every hazard the transference of Cuba to any European nation" and "would exceedingly regret to see Spain resorting to any power for assistance to uphold her rule over it." Accepting the assumption that Spanish rule could not continue long unaided, Marcy expressed the "deep and direct interest" of the United States in the future destiny of the island, a question with which some of the principal European powers had unfortunately also "seen fit to concern themselves." Marcy also talked of the dangers of a European protectorate for Cuba, citing Central America as an example of how such a status might be used to "annoy" the United States.[56]

It can be assumed that none of this was unwelcome to Soulé. The appointment of this French republican emigré and avid expansionist to the court at Madrid had been taken as an indication that the United States would adopt a forceful policy toward Cuba. On November 3, 1852, Edward Everett had recorded in his diary a prophecy by Caleb Cushing,

who became Pierce's Attorney General and was thought by
many to be the real power in the administration, that Soulé
would go to Madrid with an offer to purchase Cuba, and that,
in case of failure, "a quarrel is to be picked and the island
invaded." [57] If a quarrel were to be picked, the choice of
Soulé as Minister was masterful, for controversy dogged his
footsteps. Even his presentation to the Spanish court created
a stir, for the Spanish government insisted that sections of
the bombastic message he had prepared for the occasion
be deleted. This Soulé did after much argument, complaining
to Marcy that what remained was "emasculated and insipid." [58]
Within a very short period of time, Soulé had also managed to
involve himself in a duel with the French Ambassador to
Spain, the Marquis de Turgot, following a duel between his
son and the Duke of Alba, brother-in-law of Louis Napoleon.
Turgot was crippled for life, and the Spanish court viewed
the episode as another example of "American aggression." [59]

A diplomat as ambitious as Soulé was quick to emphasize
the connection between French and British opposition in
Cuba and the events in Europe that were gathering momentum during this period. While en route to his post in Madrid,
Soulé had had an interview with Drouyn de Lhuys, the
French Foreign Minister, in which he had sought leverage
against the French by asserting that Russia had asked the
United States to mediate on the Eastern Question. Whatever
his private thoughts might have been, the French statesman
had minimized the importance of such a request to Soulé,
intimating that the Tsar would be insincere in any such
proposals. The British Minister in Paris, Lord Henry R. G.
Cowley, reported the incident to his government,[60] which
was worried enough to initiate an inquiry through its
Minister in Washington, John Crampton. Crampton managed
to obtain from Marcy a confirmation that "no such application has been made by Russia to the United States." [61]

Soulé continued to use this weapon to disconcert the
Allies, however. In one of his initial interviews with the
Spanish Foreign Minister Don Frances Inglis Calderon de
la Barca, shortly after the outbreak of hostilities between

Russia and Turkey, Soulé expressed the view that Russia and the United States were the only great powers of the future and that all other nations were decadent and must "seek an alliance with one or other of these leviathans." "It is not, in my humble opinion, improbable," observed Lord Cowley in reporting the incident, "that Monsieur Soulé's bombastic tone at Madrid may have its source in the knowledge that the Eastern Question has produced an intimacy, inimical to Great Britain, between his own Government and Russia." [62]

Whatever the extent of the intimacy between the United States and Russia, and of Soulé's exploitation of British and French fears concerning that intimacy, it was apparent that the United States Minister in Madrid appreciated the fact that the Eastern Question made support of Spain by the Western Allies, Great Britain and France, more unlikely. In a long despatch to Marcy in December, Soulé discussed the extent of French and British influence in Spain, warning of the hostile implications of this for the United States, and pointing out that the French in particular had "the idea of sounding how far the United States were vulnerable physically and politically." He added that "Spain never moves in any question without consulting either France or England." But, while discounting Spanish insistence that there was no arrangement between England and Spain regarding Cuba, Soulé believed that in a future collision with Spain, which he considered "hardly to be avoidable," Spain would be forced to fight the United States "alone, as the state of public affairs in Europe would allow neither France nor England to divert their attention and strength from the great struggle in which they must soon be involved." The outcome of this fortunate state of affairs was obvious: "Cuba, therefore, may well be considered as lost to Spain in a proximate future. . . ." [63]

Henry Sanford, charge d'affaires in France during the long interval before Mason's arrival took a consistently conservative view of the likelihood of war between Russia and the Western powers. "The opinion in the Diplomatic circles," he informed Marcy in June, "is decidedly that there will be a pacific solution of existing difficulties." [64] The only possibility of war, he felt, came from "the warlike and fanatical spirit manifested by the Turkish population," and he made no effort to suggest that the Eastern Question would hinder the Allies in their opposition to the United States. Even after the outbreak of war between Russia and Turkey in October, he advised his government that "confidence is still entertained . . . that, by the coming spring . . . the efforts of friendly Powers will avert the threatened calamities of war." [65] Sanford derived no explicit consequences for the policy of the United States from this analysis.

Ingersoll, in London, likewise discounted the likelihood of war in his correspondence.[66] Buchanan, in one of his first despatches from London, also felt that France and England were "indisposed to go to war with Russia," and would avoid it if they could, adding that "the greatest danger came from the attitude of the Turks." [67] Certainly in late 1853 there was no reason for an American statesman to make any projections based upon the predicted outcome of the Russo-Turkish affair, with the possible exception of "the perfect understanding and union between France and England," which Buchanan declared had been demonstrated by the crisis and which had clear and negative implications for American policy.[68]

Central American negotiations proceeded slowly during this period as the British claimed that the Eastern Question left them little time for other problems. In one of their interviews, however, Clarendon hinted to Buchanan that the British might be willing to execute a graceful retreat from the Mosquito Coast if the United States could "assist in constructing a bridge to enable them to pass honorably" from it, as Clarendon claimed the Allies were doing for Russia in the Danubian principalities. During the same interview Buchanan chided the British government for opposing the expansion of the United States while continually enlarging her own dominions, adding that he could not imagine "why England should object to our annexation; we extended the English language, Christianity, liberty, and law wherever we went upon our own continent. . . ." [69] But these discussions did not pass beyond generalities, leaving the major issues unsettled and American resentment of British and French interference as strong as ever during the months of tension that preceded the entry of the two countries into the Russo-Turkish conflict.[70]

# CRIMEAN OUTBREAK AND UNITED STATES POLICY

On November 30, 1853, the Russian Black Sea fleet destroyed a Turkish naval squadron at Sinope, an act which brought the Allied fleets into the Black Sea and which may have been the decisive factor in bringing on the Crimean War. Six days later, Franklin Pierce transmitted his first State of the Union message to Congress, in which he continued to emphasize a vigorous policy of national expansion: "The United States have continued gradually and steadily to expand through acquisitions of territory, which, how much soever some of them may have been questioned, are now universally seen and admitted to have been wise in policy [and] just in character. . . ." [71]

These two events, if not directly related, were at least intertwined. Only two weeks before Sinope, one of Clarendon's colleagues had remarked to him that "the shoals of Neutral Rights and Right of Search are quite enough for Great Britain to weather in her relations with her transatlantic children, in the event of an European War, without having any tangible territorial grievance to settle with them into the bargain." [72] That this kind of thinking was responsible for Clarendon's overtures to Buchanan on the Central American question a few days earlier is uncertain. But it does seem evident that British restraint on one issue was logical, given the inflammation of the other, and that the British government might be expected to try to put the Central American question on ice for the time being. One writer has concluded, as a matter of fact, that "without making any important

concessions, the British diplomats managed to continue negotiations on Central America for several months. . . ." [73]

The pressure of the impending conflict was also felt
from another quarter. From Madrid, Soulé reported that
Spain, unable under ordinary circumstances to make large
reinforcements in Cuba, was now faced with demands from
England and France for a contribution of 30,000 men for the
Russo-Turkish theatre. Whether or not this information was
accurate, Soulé then proceeded to make his strongest stand
to that date on Cuba, telling the Spanish Foreign Minister
that the United States would "sternly and unbendingly oppose and combat any and every arrangement by which Spain
with France or Spain with England or with them both and
with the world in arms should attempt in the slightest degree
to render the Island an injury or a danger to us." [74] Spanish
abstention from the Crimean War, despite British and French
pressure, might well have been influenced by considerations
of the threat to Spanish interests in the Western hemisphere
—a threat of which Soulé himself was a constant reminder.

By January Buchanan was beginning to get impatient
about the British delays on the Central American negotiation.
Reporting to Marcy that he had been unable to press the
issue since November, Buchanan attributed British slowness
to the unsettled condition of the British Cabinet and to "the
state of the Russo-Turkish question to which the ministry
have been devoting themselves, fruitlessly as it is now believed
to the task of preventing a war between Great Britain and
Russia." Buchanan did believe, however, that "my omission
to press the Central American questions at the present most
important crisis between Great Britain and Russia has been
properly appreciated by Lord Clarendon." [75] But Clarendon's
continued reluctance to reach a bargain on the terms offered
by the United States led Buchanan, in their next interview,
to declare to the former that "the British Statesman, particularly at the present momentous crisis in the affairs of
the world, who shall be instrumental in settling all the questions pending between the two Governments . . . will do more
for his country . . . than any Statesman who has arisen in

England since the days of Lord Chatham." Clarendon responded by complaining of the "prejudice" entertained by the American people against the British, which he declared was not reciprocated by the latter.[76]

Shortly after this, American statesmen were confronted with the possibility that the Anglo-French involvement in the Eastern Question held certain dangers for the United States as well as advantages. If the United States insisted on choosing this period to press its declared aims, the Crimean alliance, the British and French could reason, might also be applied to the Western hemisphere. The strongest statement of this warning came from Lord Clarendon himself in a speech to the House of Lords on January 31, 1854:

> The happy and good understanding between France and England have been extended beyond Eastern policy affecting all parts of the World, and I am heartily rejoiced to say that there is no portion of the two hemispheres with regard to which the policy of the two countries, however heretofore antagonistic, is not now in entire harmony.[77]

The transatlantic storm raised by this statement was considerable. Marcy immediately called in the British and French Ambassadors for an explanation, which failed to satisfy him. Following this, he asked Buchanan to make inquiries in London, commenting in instructions which his biographer called "the angriest of his career" that "this assumed guardianship by these nations over the political affairs of this part of the world will not be acquiesced in by the United States." [78] Senator Lewis Cass, one of the most outspoken anti-British expansionist Democrats in Congress, in vigorous language called the attention of the Senate to the threat contained in Clarendon's speech:

> Now, there is no misunderstanding that statement. It is intended to be a notice to us that France and England

have come to an agreement with respect to the schemes
of aggrandizement of the United States, and mean to
stop it. It means Cuba. It means any place where we
wish to procure the acquisition of territory . . . France
and England have said what they would do. Have we
ever said that we were dissatisfied? What ground have
we taken? I would let them know exactly what we would
do; that is to say, I would let them know what our
rights are.[79]

Cass also read into the record some resolutions introduced
in the House which promised physical resistance to the intervention of foreign powers in American affairs "upon this
continent." [80]

The spirited American response to Clarendon's speech
thus revealed a great sensitivity to the nuances of Great
Power relations. Nor was the response limited to unofficial
circles; the principal diplomatic agents of the government
of the United States moved quickly to assess and discourage
the threatened "universal alliance." In a despatch written
before Marcy's instructions of March 11 had reached him,
Buchanan recounted a conversation with Clarendon in which
"I playfully observed that as Great Britain and France did
not seem to be content to confine themselves to the regulations
of the balance of power in Europe, but were willing to extend
their care to our hemisphere, it might be necessary for us
to ally ourselves with Russia for the purpose of counteracting
their designs." Buchanan also called the Foreign Secretary's
attention to Cass's remarks in the Senate. Clarendon's response was to minimize the impact of his speech, claiming
that, as far as the Western hemisphere was concerned, the
alliance was intended to apply only to joint action on the
River Plata in South America. Clarendon also assured Buchanan that Britain and France had no formal commitment
with Spain respecting Cuba.

Minister Mason in Paris likewise sent a word of warning
to his government shortly after Clarendon's speech: "How
far, if successful in Europe, the disposition to regulate dis-

putes between other nations by the intervention of allied powers, may be manifested in other parts of the world, remains to be seen." [82] A month later Mason's fears were even more fully expressed, for on February 27 the Anglo-French alliance was confirmed by the ultimatum delivered to Russia to evacuate the provinces:

> And if we consider the circumstances which have brought the league into existence, and the avowed object of taking up the settlement of disputed questions between other nations, it is not improbable that these two powerful nations, now abjuring all conquests and undertaking to protect the weak against the strong, will be disposed, after this war is over, to carry their supervisory powers into another hemisphere. [83]

Thomas Seymour, Pierce's representative to the Tsar, was by this time beginning to discover numerous arguments for the Russian point of view in the Eastern Question. His viewpoint, as he made clear, was not unrelated to apprehensions of joint British and French action in the Western hemisphere: "If the people of the United States look upon the Anglo-French coalition in the light in which I confess it now appears to me, they will . . . be careful how they give their countenance to an alliance whose purposes are not confined merely to affairs on this side of the Atlantic." [84] Carroll Spence, who had been sent as envoy to Constantinople, shared the same feelings, informing Marcy that "your remarks in reference to the course of policy which France and England intend to adopt towards our country I have every reason to believe are correct." He added, however, the assurance that "the good understanding now existing between those two nations is not destined to be of long continuance," since he daily witnessed "evidence of their animosity towards each other." [85]

The imminence of war in the Near East also raised some immediate practical questions for American foreign

policy. As Buchanan warned Marcy in early February, due
to the likelihood of war "the rights and the duties of the
United States, as a neutral nation, will become a subject for
serious consideration." [86] In his next despatch Buchanan
urged Marcy to send instructions on the course to be taken
in the protection of United States commerce. He hinted that
this was the time to strike for the "free ships make free
goods" doctrine, as several other European countries were
presumably ready to join the United States in advocating this
definition of neutral rights, which had never been accepted
by Great Britain.[87] In truth, the United States was in a position to press their advantage here, and British statesmen
recognized that relations between the two countries might
become strained on this issue alone. Again, the situation was
not equivalent regarding the two sets of belligerents. The
allies posed the only threat to neutral commerce, while Russia,
as the inferior naval power, would certainly support the
broadest definition of neutral rights.

American diplomats were quick to seize this opportunity.
Mason, after reminding Marcy that American commerce
would be subject again, as in past European wars, to violation
by naval powers, asked: "Will not the opportunity be favorable, to an effort, by general consent of nations, [to obtain]
a prohibition of private war?" [88] Of great advantage to the
American bargaining position was the fear felt by the French
and British, as the Minister to France put it, "on the subject of the employment of privateers in the impending war,
and of citizens of the United States, engaging in that service."

In view of the size of both the Allied and American
merchant fleet, such fears were very real. Russia herself
could pose very little threat to British and French shipping,
but an armada of enterprising Yankee ships under Russian
auspices turned loose, to prey on their far-flung commerce,
would be a different matter. Mason reported having told the
French government that the extent of privateering by Americans might depend on the British and French policy on
neutral rights. If the Allies did not allow neutral commerce
the greatest freedom, he stated, the cooperation of Ameri-

can shipowners would be hard to obtain, and, in the absence of such voluntary cooperation, privateering would be impossible to control. "The combination of circumstances is most auspicious," he advised Marcy,

> to the establishment of our cherished principles of neutral rights. . . . There is, in my opinion, an anxious desire to avoid any collision with us. . . . I feel an anxiety, which I have difficulty in adequately expressing, that the opportunity should not be lost.[89]

In London the situation was much the same. Buchanan reported in late February that he had again pressed Clarendon on the Central American issues, reminding him of their "urgency and importance," and warning the British Foreign Secretary that, before the rapidly approaching adjournment of Congress, the President "would certainly expect to be able to communicate to them the result of the negotiation in regard to the Central American Questions." He reported that in the same interview Clarendon was "evidently apprehensive that Russian privateers may be fitted out in the ports of the United States, to cruise against [British] commerce. . . ."[90] Three weeks later the British "apprehension" resulted in the proposal of a tripartite treaty, between Great Britain, France, and the United States, providing that citizens of these countries serving on privateers against each other would be treated as pirates. The scheme, as Buchanan said, "undoubtedly was to prevent Americans from taking service in Russian privateers during the present war." Such a convention was clearly designed for the advantage of the two European powers with little compensation for the American position, and Buchanan recorded that "I stated my objections pretty clearly to such a treaty."[91]

The victory for American neutral rights, however, came at about the same time, without any guarantees on the American policy toward privateering. Ten days before their declaration of war against Russia, Clarendon read to Buchanan the text of the planned British policy toward neutral commerce. (France, a traditional supporter of neutral rights, subsequently accepted the same policy with little difficulty.) The statement not only adopted the principle of "free ships make free goods," except for contraband of war, but also guaranteed neutral property on enemy ships and accepted the American position on blockades (that a blockade must be effective, before it be respected). Buchanan stated his "approbation of it in strong terms," and Clarendon pointed out the departure from traditional British policy by remarking that the British government "had encountered great difficulties in overcoming their practice for so long a period of years and their unvarying judicial decisions." He attributed the change to the belief that "war should be conducted with as little injury to neutrals as was compatible with the interest and safety of Belligents." [92] The British were obviously anxious not to provoke an incident with the United States during the upcoming war, nor to give the latter any justification for countenancing irregular naval aid to Russia.

The timely British retreat on the neutral rights issue did, as a matter of fact, prevent an eruption over this potentially dangerous issue. Diplomatic activity on neutral rights, following the actual declaration of hostilities by Britain and France on March 27 and 28, was largely formal. During this period the United States exchanged information with other neutrals in the war, particularly the Scandinavian countries, to clarify and coordinate neutral practices. [93] Resolutions were introduced in Congress to obtain information from the administration on what, if anything, had been done to secure the full neutral rights of American commerce, and it was further suggested by one Congressman that the United States take advantage of the situation to place its definition of neutral rights "upon the firm basis of precedence as well as of natural right and justice." [94] The Pierce administration did take the view, however, that certain basic elements of the problem had not been resolved, and that the danger to neutral rights was by no means entirely eliminated by the moderate British declaration. As Marcy said to his

envoy in St. Petersburg, "with Great Britain and France
we may have some difficulty upon the subject of neutral rights
in regard to the coasting and colonial trade but between
this country and Russia I do not apprehend that any such
difficulty can arise." [95]

With neutral rights at least temporarily secured, attention could be directed to the many other schemes that
might have a greater chance of success because of the conflict; as Pierce's biographer said of the war, "The opportunity was too good to miss; seldom did destiny present such
a chance." [96] In the first few days of April, Marcy authorized
Soulé to negotiate for the purchase of Cuba, instructed the
American representative in Honolulu to conclude a treaty of
annexation with the Hawaiian king, and inquired of the Russian Minister concerning rumors that the Tsar was ready to
sell Alaska. In the following weeks Santo Domingo was added
to the expansionist program.[97] Most of these questions had
involved British and French opposition to the United States;
regarding Hawaii, for example, Buchanan had written only
a few weeks earlier that he had used these islands as an
argument to Clarendon that "there was at least one particular
in which Great Britain and France appeared to be acting in
concert in such a manner as might possibly affect the interest of the United States," citing joint protests of the British and French Ambassadors in Washington against American annexation. In response Clarendon had called attention
to efforts by Americans in Hawaii to bring about annexation
by revolution.[98]

These projects were quite tame, however, compared to
some of the grandiose plans of "Young Americans" in the
diplomatic service of the country. George Sanders, Consul
in London, provided headquarters in that city for the exiled
republicans of Europe who were planning the "revolution
of 1854." Sanders advocated open support of revolutionary
movements in Europe, going so far as to speak favorably
of assassinating Louis Napoleon. He also attempted to per-
suade Turkey to use Louis Kossuth to lead an army against
Austria during the Crimean War.[99] There was clearly little

"isolationism" in Sanders' thoughts or actions. One of the most famous incidents associated with him occurred during a dinner party he held on February 21, 1854—practically at the same time that conflict between the major European powers in the Near East had become a certainty. At the dinner, in addition to Sanders and Minister Buchanan, were Louis Kossuth, Giuseppe Garibaldi, Alexander Herzen, and a number of other leading European revolutionary figures, who all drank to "a future alliance of America with a federation of the free peoples of Europe." Unfortunately for Sanders, many of the Europeans lost interest in the cause of Young America when they discovered that the expansion of slavery was part of the program.[100]

The most promising opportunity for American expansionists, however, was the one closest to home. And for a while, in early 1854, the conjunction of the European conflict with events in Central America seemed to promise the accomplishment of an object which many Americans placed second to none.

# NOTES

1. "Young Twist and Young America," *United States Review* XXXVI (October, 1855), 331.
2. Sir Henry Bulwer, "History of the Mosquito Question," in Granville Papers, Public Record Office, London, quoted in Richard W. Van Alstyne, "British Diplomacy and the Clayton-Bulwer Treaty, 1850-60," *Journal of Modern History*, XI (June, 1939), 156.
3. *Ibid.*, 168.
4. Bailey, *op. cit.*, p. 291. The most complete account of the treaty and the disputes arising from it is by Mary Wilhelmine Williams, *Anglo-American Isthmian Diplomacy* (Baltimore: The Lord Baltimore Press, 1916), pp. 67-269.
5. This in spite of the fact that Clayton himself had declared, regarding Belize and the Bay Islands, that "to this settlement and these islands the treaty we negotiated was not intended by us to apply." Secretary of State John M. Clayton to the British Minister, July 4, 1850, Notes to the British Legation, records of the Department of State, National Archives, Record Group 59. Hereafter records in the National Archives are indicated by the symbol NA, followed by the record group (RG) number.

6. Quoted in Alexander De Conde, *A History of American Foreign Policy* (New York: Charles Scribner's Sons, 1965), p. 215. The United States based its position in the fisheries dispute on a differing interpretation of the three-mile limit, inside which American fishing was not allowed under the 1818 agreement. While the British took the traditional view that three miles should be measured from headland to headland in bays, American statesmen insisted that the line should follow the coastal indentations precisely. Though acceptance of the American definition of the three-mile limit would hardly have satisfied American fishermen, the entire American case in the fisheries dispute rested, technically, upon this sole point.

7. Harriet Martineau, *History of the Peace* (Boston: Walker, Fuller, and Company, 1866), p. 598.

8. John Crampton to George Villiers, Earl of Clarendon, February 7, 1853, quoted in Van Alstyne, "Anglo-American Relations, 1853-1857," *American Historical Review*, XLII (April, 1937), 495.

9. Quoted in Henry Blumenthal, *A Reappraisal of Franco-American Relations, 1830-1871* (Chapel Hill: The University of North Carolina Press, 1959), p. 35.

10. *Ibid.*

11. *Ibid.*, p. 51.

12. Quoted in Paul N. Garber, *The Gadsden Treaty* (Philadelphia: Press of the University of Pennsylvania, 1923), p. 99.

13. H. Du Pasquier de Donmartin, *Les Etats Unis et le Mexique* (Paris, 1852), pp. 74-76, cited by Blumenthal, p. 45.

14. *Ibid.*, pp. 45-46.

15. Henry Sanford to Marcy, June 30, 1853, Despatches from France, NA, RG 59.

16. U.S., Congress, *House Executive Documents*, No. 121, 32nd Cong., 1st Sess., 1851. For the fullest account of United States policy on Cuba during these years see Basil Rauch, *American Interest in Cuba: 1848-1855* (New York: Columbia University Press, 1948).

17. Amos Aschbach Ettinger, *The Mission to Spain of Pierre Soulé, 1853-1855* (New York: Yale University Press, 1932), pp. 39, 46-48, 79; Rauch, p. 275; Daniel Barringer, United States Minister to Spain, to Everett, December 14, 1852, Despatches from Spain, NA, RG 59.

18. Crampton to Clarendon, February 7, 1853, Van Alstyne, *American Historical Review*, XLII, 493.

19. Merle Eugene Curti, *Austria and the United States, 1848-1852* ("Smith College Studies in History," Vol. XI, No. 3; Northampton, Mass.: Smith College, 1926), pp. 144, 203-04.

20. *Ibid.*, pp. 145, 148-49.

21. James D. Richardson, ed., *A Compilation of the Messages and Papers of the Presidents*, V (Washington: Bureau of National Literature and Art, 1908), 198-99.

22. Roy Franklin Nichols, *Franklin Pierce* (Philadelphia: University of Pennsylvania Press, 1931), p. 325.

23. *Newark Daily Advertiser*, January 7, 1853, quoted in Elizabeth Brett White, *American Opinion of France from Lafayette to Poincaré* (New York: Alfred A. Knopf, 1927), p. 140.

66 THE LIMITS OF AMERICAN ISOLATION

24. *American Whig Review*, December, 1852, quoted in *ibid.*, p. 139.
25. Richardson, *op. cit.*, V, 199.
26. "I had not given until recently much attention to our foreign relations, and really was not qualified for the position assigned me." Marcy to Wetmore, August 17, 1853, quoted in Henry Barrett Learned, "William Learned Marcy," in Samuel Flagg Bemis (ed.), *The American Secretaries of State and Their Diplomacy*, VI (New York: Alfred A. Knopf, 1928), 168.
27. For fullest statement of Marcy's position as Secretary of State see Ivor Debenham Spencer, *The Victor and the Spoils* (Providence: Brown University Press, 1959), especially pp. 222-23.
28. *Ibid.*, p. 234.
29. John Bassett Moore, ed., *The Works of James Buchanan*, IX (Philadelphia and London: J. B. Lippincott Company, 1909), 175.
30. *Ibid.*, p. 224; see also Curti, "Young America," *American Historical Review*, XXXII (October, 1926), 34-55.
31. Spencer, *op. cit.*, pp. 230-31; Curti, *American Historical Review*, XXXII, 53-54.
32. Belmont to Sanders, August, 1854, Sanders MSS., quoted in *ibid.*
33. *Journal des Debats* (November 11, 1852). *Revue des Deux Mondes* (November, 1852; January, 1853). J. Addison Thomas to Marcy, December 26, 1852, Marcy MSS. Baron von Gerolt to the King of Prussia, December 13, 1852, Geheimes Staats-Archiv, Berlin. Baron Hülsemann to Count Buol-Schauenstein, April 10, 1853. All quoted in *ibid.*, pp. 45-47.
34. A. de Noges, *Influence Prochaine des Etats-Unis sur la Politique de l'Europe* (Paris, 1885), cited in *ibid.*
35. U.S., Congress, *House Executive Documents*, No. 21, 33rd Cong., 1st Sess., 1854, pp. 2-7.
36. Nicholas, *op. cit.*, p. 325; Spencer, *op. cit.*, pp. 287-88. For the fullest account see Garber, cited above.
37. *New Orleans Daily Picayune* (July 16, 1853).
38. John S. Cripps, Chargé d'Affaires to Mexico, to Marcy, June 19, 1856, Despatches from Mexico, NA, RG 59; Garber, pp. 98-99.
39. Doyle to Clarendon, December 3, 18, 1853; Foreign Office to Doyle, January 16, 1854. All quoted in Garber, pp. 99-100.
40. *Ibid.*
41. *New York Herald* (July 19, 1853).
42. Caroline Crane March, ed., *Life and Letters of George Perkins Marsh* (New York: Charles Scribner's Sons, 1888), pp. 332-34; U.S., Congress, *Senate Executive Documents*, No. 1, 33rd Cong., 1st Sess., 1853, pp. 25-30.
43. *Ibid.*, 30-49.
44. Spencer, *op. cit.*, p. 269.
45. *Ibid.*; U.S., Congress, *House Executive Documents*, No. 91, *Senate Executive Documents*, Nos. 40, 53, 33rd Cong., 1st Sess., 1853-54.
46. Ingersoll to Marcy, April 8, 1853, Despatches from Great Britain, NA, RG 59.

47. Ingersoll to Marcy, June 3, 1853, *ibid.*
48. Ingersoll to Marcy, April 22, 1853, *ibid.*
49. Marcy to Borland, June 17, 1853, Instructions to Central America, NA, RG 59.
50. This division of negotiations was partly the result of political jealousies. Pierce and Marcy feared that Buchanan would use the fishery negotiations to advance his own presidential ambitions, an apprehension the British shared. Quiet influence was exerted by both the British and key figures in the Pierce administration therefore, to have this dispute handled in Washington. Buchanan, resenting this decision and sometimes seeking to circumvent it, accepted the British mission with reluctance as a result. Mary Poindexter Silverstein, "Diplomacy and Politics: A British View of the Reciprocity Fisheries Negotiations, 1853-1854" (unpublished M.A. dissertation, Department of History, University of Chicago, 1961), especially pp. 28-30.
51. See, for example, the testimony quoted by Dexter Perkins, *Hands Off: A History of the Monroe Doctrine*, p. 102.
52. M. Williams, p. 152.
53. Marcy to Buchanan, July 2, 1853, Instructions to Great Britain, NA, RG 59; Spencer, p. 247.
54. *Ibid.;* Spencer, *op. cit.,* pp. 258-59.
55. Barringer to Marcy, May 7, 1853, Despatches from Spain, NA, RG 59.
56. Marcy to Soulé, July 23, 1853, Instructions to Spain, NA, RG 59.
57. Everett Papers, quoted in Ettinger, p. 369.
58. Soulé to Marcy, October 25, 1853, Despatches from Spain, NA, RG 59.
59. But the *New York Herald*, on January, 1854, commented: "The younger Soulé has done very well; and the elder Soulé has done well. 'All's well that ends well.' . . . Having had the pistols and coffee, now let us have the island."
60. Cowley to Clarendon, September 15, 1853, quoted in Ettinger, *op. cit.,* 185.
61. Crampton to Clarendon, October 10, 1853, quoted in *ibid.,* p. 187.
62. Cowley to Clarendon, November 3, 1853, quoted in Ettinger, *op. cit.,* p. 216.
63. Soulé to Marcy, December 23, 1853, Despatches from Spain, NA, RG 59.
64. Sanford to Marcy, June 7, 1853, Despatches from France, NA, RG 59. See also despatches of June 9, 13, 16, 23, 30, and July 7.
65. Sanford to Marcy, September 22, October 3, 20, 1853. *ibid.*
66. Ingersoll to Marcy, August 12, 1853, Despatches from Great Britain, NA, RG 59.
67. Buchanan to Marcy, September 2, 1853, *ibid.* In his despatch of September 22, Buchanan adds that "for some time it had appeared to me the danger of war proceeded from the Sultan rather than the Czar. . . ."
68. Buchanan to Marcy, November 1, 1853, *ibid.*

69. Buchanan to Marcy, November 12, 1853, *ibid.*

70. For an account of anti-British sentiment at this time, particularly in administration circles, see Nichols, pp. 326-27. For progress on Central American question see Williams, *op. cit.*, pp. 152 ff.; U.S., Congress, *House Executive Documents*, No. 1, 34th Cong., 1st Sess., 1855, pp. 42 ff.

71. Richardson, *op. cit.*, V, 212.

72. H. W. Addington to Clarendon, November 16, 1853, quoted in Rippy, p. 116.

73. *Ibid.*

74. Soulé to Marcy, January 20, 1854, Despatches from Spain, NA, RG 59.

75. Buchanan to Marcy, January 5, 1854, Despatches from Great Britain, NA, RG 59.

76. Buchanan to Marcy, January 10, 1854, *ibid.*

77. Great Britain, 3 *Hansard's Parliamentary Debates*, CXXX (1854), 43.

78. Spencer, p. 290; Marcy to Buchanan, March 11, 1854, Instructions to Great Britain, NA, RG 59.

79. U.S., *Congressional Globe*, 33rd Cong., 1st Sess., 1854, XXVIII, Pt. 1, pp. 483-84.

80. *Ibid.*

81. Buchanan to Marcy, March 17, 1854, Despatches from Great Britain, NA, RG 59.

82. Mason to Marcy, February 9, 1854, Despatches from France, NA, RG 59.

83. Mason to Marcy, March 6, 1854, *ibid.*

84. Seymour to Marcy, May 8, 1853, Despatches from Russia, NA, RG 59.

85. Spence to Marcy, April 24, 1854, Despatches from Turkey, NA, RG 59. In the same despatch Spence defended himself at length and with vehemence against the charge, evidently made in the American press, that he had gone too far in wishing the Sultan success in the war. In fact, Spence, as most members of the Pierce administration, held little sympathy for the Allied side, including the Turks; in his despatch of February 5, 1854, he had written that the Turks lacked enthusiasm for the war, being without money, energy, or religious fervor to arouse their "sluggish character," and that "their sole hope of success is based upon the support of England and France." *Ibid.*

86. Buchanan to Marcy, February 7, 1854, Despatches from Great Britain, NA, RG 59.

87. Buchanan to Marcy, February 10, 1954, *ibid.*

88. Mason to Marcy, February 20, 1854, Despatches from France, NA, RG 59.

89. Mason to Marcy, March 14, 22, 1854, *ibid.* As a former federal judge whose jurisdiction included admiralty law, Mason took a deep interest in the issue of neutral rights.

90. Buchanan to Marcy, February 24, 1854, Despatches from Great Britain, NA, RG 59.

91. Buchanan, "Memorandum," March 16, 1854, Moore, *The Works of James Buchanan,* IX, pp. 162-63.
92. Buchanan to Marcy, March 17, 1854, Despatches from Great Britain, NA, RG 59.
93. U.S., Congress, *House Executive Documents,* No. 103, 33rd Cong., 1st Sess., 1854, pp. 16-21.
94. *Congressional Globe,* 33rd Cong., 1st Sess., 1854, XXVIII, Part 2, 883-84.
95. Marcy to Seymour, April 14, 1854, Instructions to Russia, NA, RG 59.
96. Nichols, p. 329.
97. *Ibid.,* 329-30; Frank A. Golder, "Purchase of Alaska," *American Historical Review,* XXV (April, 1920), 412.
98. Buchanan to Marcy, March 17, 1854, Despatches from Great Britain, NA, RG 59.
99. Merle E. Curti, "George N. Sanders—American Patriot of the Fifties," *South Atlantic Quarterly,* XXVII (January, 1928), 80, 83, 86.
100. *Ibid.,* 79. Rauch, *op. cit.,* p. 283. *The Political Correspondence of the Late Hon. George N. Sanders* (New York: The American Art Association, 1914), pp. 71, 112, 132.

# The Enemy of My Enemy . . .

## CHAPTER THREE

> Should Russia be defeated . . . and crippled . . . and the
> *entente cordiale* between Great Britain and France con-
> tinue, their abstinence from intermeddling in our affairs
> can hardly be expected—this view of the subject is
> Russianizing some of our people.[1]

## RUSSIANIZATION: UNITED STATES POLICY TOWARD THE CRIMEAN BELLIGERENTS FOLLOWING THE OUTBREAK OF WAR

In his first despatch after assuming the post of Minister
to Russia, Thomas Seymour expressed a degree of surprise
over one of the first discoveries he made in that country.
Writing three days after the entry of Britain and France into
the war against Russia, he reported that "the threatening
attitude of the allied powers of France and England had
. . . directed the thoughts of a very considerable number of
persons here towards the United States, whose government,
it was intimated, might possibly take sides with its old and

faithful ally, the Emperor." Seymour had in response entered the customary disclaimer, telling the Russians that "with European wars, we have nothing to do; that the United States government gives itself no concern about the 'balance of power' in Europe. . . ." [2]

Juridically and formally the United States was, of course, neutral in the Crimean War. Like most of the minor European states, she had declared her neutrality upon the outbreak of the conflict. Formal American diplomatic contact with the war centered around questions of trading rights with the belligerents, with the United States taking its customary stand for the broadest possible definition of neutral rights. Other formal responses to the war included such traditional and innocuous moves as dispatching a military commission to observe the military preparations, weaponry, and methods of warfare on both sides.[3]

But, in the same sense that neutrality and isolation were not synonymous, there were alternative styles and models of neutrality. A country remaining neutral in a conflict between other states may nevertheless pursue an active or a passive policy toward that conflict. An active neutral, such as Austria in the Crimean War, may, like the belligerents of the war, be deeply involved in the underlying political issues of the conflict. At the other extreme, an "isolated" nation, by the usual implication, presumably avoids the slightest degree of involvement or even of emotional partiality in its official stance (though public opinion within the country may sympathize with one side or the other).

The United States, therefore, was continuously faced with the  task of defining its "neutrality" in the Crimean War. In practice this neutrality was often far from being simple and absolute. Seymour, for one, later revealed an appreciation of the nuances of American neutrality that was much more sophisticated than his initial reaction might have indicated:

Though far removed from the scene of European conflicts, the United States cannot regard the present

contest with indifference. As long as our government
has a commerce to look after, a commerce which has
recently outstripped that of every other nation, it will
be well to keep a strict watch on the operations of the
belligerents. It would not be strange, if the continuance
of a war, which manifestly is to be carried on for the
purpose of destroying the trade of Russia by sea, and
the destruction of her sea-port towns, should seriously
affect us.[4]

Protection of trade and commerce was one, but not the
only, complication of American neutrality during the Crimean
War.

Political considerations, while often remote, did, nevertheless, affect relations between the United States and Russia. The considerations were, of course, of much greater im-
port to the Russians than to the Americans, and it was the
former who acted more openly upon them although the Americans were certainly aware of underlying political motives.

The attitude of the Russian government itself was important in this respect. Seymour, after noting Russian hopes
for the participation of the United States in his first despatch,
appended to a later account of his very friendly reception by
Tsar Nicholas the comment that "it is not to be disguised,
I am aware, that the peculiar circumstances in which His
Majesty's government is placed at the present time, may have
kindled in his breast a more ardent desire for the friendship
of the United States. . . ." [5] The Russians had long considered
the United States a potential counterweight to the British,
who sought to contain the expansion of both, and as early
as the 1830s Russian diplomats had concluded that the United
States would of necessity become Russia's ally if the Tsar
became involved in a war with Britain.[6] In 1837, for example,
the Russian Minister to the United States had been explicitly
instructed that Russia desired the United States to be a
strong power so it could aid Russia in case of war.[7]

In the absence of any concrete cause for dispute, and
with good reason to favor any involvements that would keep

Great Britain and France out of the Western hemisphere, the United States naturally reciprocated Russian overtures in a noncommital but significant way. The "traditional friendship" of the two countries during this period has been noted by all the historians of Russo-American relations. There is more than routine importance to the remark, made by one of the United States attachés in St. Petersburg, that the American Minister's "relations with the leading Russians, from the Emperor down, were all that could be desired. . . ." [8] Benjamin Perley Poore, in his classic reminiscences of Washington, also recalled that "the Russian diplomats have generally been on the most friendly terms with Congressmen and citizens generally, while the Prussians and the Frenchmen have been several little difficulties with the Department of State and with the residents of Washington." [9] Such "little difficulties," are often, as is well known, merely representative of more fundamental sources of tension.

Austrian Minister Hülsemann, among others, was shocked by the appearance of a blatantly pro-Russian article written early in the Pierce administration for the *Washington Union,* the unofficial organ of the administration. The article, by Roger A. Pryor, was a scathing review of an anti-Russian book, *The War of Ormuzd and Ahriman,* written by Representative Henry Winter Davis of Maryland, an antislavery Whig who was later to become a Republican and in 1864 a co-author of the Wade-Davis Manifesto. Pryor, a "Young American" of some repute, proclaimed that Russia was "great and prosperous beyond any other country in Europe," and that the United States and Russia should "consolidate and perpetuate their friendly relations by the same just and pacific policy which has regulated their intercourse in times past." [10] Hülsemann was certain that the article represented the efforts of the Pierce administration to win Russian support in its difficulties with the colonial powers in the Western hemisphere.[11] Poore remembered that "it was the general belief at Washington that Mr. Pryor had been inspired by someone connected with the Russian Legation." [12] In any event the article was apparently too controversial for even the Pierce administration, and despite support from some of the expansionists, such as Caleb Cushing, Pryor was forced to resign from the paper. The fact that Pierce did not strongly disapprove of what Pryor had said was demonstrated soon after by the latter's appointment on a special mission to Greece.[13]

Such generous sentiments toward the Tsarist regime were echoed by American diplomatic representatives in Russia. Neill Brown, Seymour's predecessor, reported that in his last interview with Nicholas, "this great sovereign," the Tsar had inquired sympathetically about the plans of the United States for acquiring Cuba and had expressed general support for its position in Latin America. "His Majesty has as kind feelings towards the United States as he can have towards a country whose institutions are free," concluded Brown.[14] Seymour himself was an unapologetic Russophile. He found Nicholas "perfectly irresistible," called his handshake "a good republican grasp," and took the view that "after all the Autocrat of Russia had been much misrepresented." Expressing his overall opinion shortly after the Allied landing in the Crimea, Seymour observed:

Some of the faults of Russia may seem too great to be overlooked or forgiven; there are others which are trifling compared to those which stain the escutcheon of the powers opposed to her in this struggle. Much as I dislike her past history and the despotic power of her government . . . I should never think of giving any encouragement to the cause of her adversaries in this contest.[15]

Even the American Minister to "victimized" Turkey, who might be expected to see the Porte's position in a more favorable light, had little sympathy for the Allied cause. Speaking of the regime to which he was accredited, Spence declared that "by what means and in what manner a government . . . can be perpetuated, without talent to direct it—without integrity to guard it,—without available physical force to protect it,—without money to sustain it . . . is to me a source of surprise." [16]

With its established antipathy to English and French designs in general, the Pierce administration found the claims of the Russian position fairly easy to comprehend. There seemed to be disturbing parallels between the Anglo-French intervention against Russia and their tendency to oppose the United States in the Western hemisphere. During March, 1854, when both the Eastern question and the "Black Warrior" affair had become heated, Marcy was advised by Richard Rush, the veteran American diplomat, that the triumph of the Western Powers would lead to their intervention in the Western hemisphere and to the scrapping of the Monroe Doctrine. These two powers, said Rush, "have always been ready to strike at us," but "Russia never." [17] Marcy probably needed no reminders of this melancholy possibility; at almost the same time he himself had expressed similar feelings on the relation of American policy to Russian success in the Eastern War. The American people were being "Russianized," he said, by the possibility that Britain and France would meddle in American affairs if they defeated Russia. Concerning the Allies, he added:

They have shown—G.B. particularly—too much of a disposition to be guardians of the whole world. As our policy and practice has been to let them alone in their proper sphere of action—we have a right to ask and expect that they should do the same to us—will they do so if they weaken and humble Russia.[18]

This natural coincidence of interests between the United States and the Tsarist regime became a frequent note in Marcy's subsequent correspondence. Writing to Spence in Constantinople later in that month, for example, he expressed the same idea in general terms:

In relation to the political organization of her government the people of the U. States never can have any
sympathy with Russia and will always regret to see her
political system extended; but in regard to our international relations no nation on the face of the earth
has used us more fairly. . . .[19]

The ties of affection between the regime whose very
name symbolized despotism and the self-consciously republican American government did not escape the notice of the
common enemy. The British in particular were very uneasy
about the sympathy of the United States for Russia that they
had detected, particularly after the onset of the war. Buchanan
even warned Marcy early in 1854 that the feelings of the
United States toward Russia were clearly injuring the country's image in British public opinion.[20] The unfriendly tone of
the American press frequently led to retaliation in British
papers.[21]

There were, in the meantime, some concrete issues upon
which American neutrality could hardly fail to be expressed
in its particular shading. The area of neutral rights is an
example. Following the British retreat to the "free ships
make free goods" doctrine, Buchanan had observed to Marcy
that

should Russia be prevailed upon to adopt the liberal
policy toward neutrals announced in the Queen's declaration, we may expect a harvest for our carrying trade
such as it has never before experienced. I could almost
wish myself to be in St. Petersburg for a fortnight.[22]

There was actually little doubt as to what the Russian policy
would be. As a minor naval power, she had always supported
the broadest definition of the rights of neutral commerce.
As one historian said of the British surrender, "it was also
a boon to Russia. Freedom of the seas for neutral shipping

meant that she could keep open her trade and commerce with the outside world." [23]

The United States Government thus conceived the idea of using Russian sympathy and support in a campaign to gain from the reluctant British yet further concessions for freedom of the seas. The plan was carried out when Marcy addressed the Russian Chargé de Affairs, Edouard de Stoeckl, on April 14, 1854, to secure Russian consent to the definition of neutral rights already adopted by the British. After calling attention to the fact that Russia was the chief defender of these rights in Europe, and indicating his assurance that the Tsar woud assent to the British program, Marcy further proposed that, as the first step toward putting these principles permanently into international law, the two countries should conclude a convention accepting them. He added:

We are going to ask France and England to sign this convention; if they refuse, as I have every reason to think, we will conclude it with you alone in the first instance. We will then put forward the same proposals to the maritime powers of the second rank.

Having less means of defending their rights, they are, because of that very fact, interested in seeing them determined by rules in a definitive manner; and we have no doubt that they will give their consent to them, provided that they succeed in escaping English influence.[24]

In later instructions to Seymour, Marcy expressed optimism that the signing of a convention with Russia would win the approval of enough nations, including the Allies, to raise the American definition of neutral rights to a permanent principle of international law.[25]

The American proposal was clearly designed to exploit British apprehensions over the cooperation between Russia and the United States even more, by creating the spectre of a common struggle for a common goal, should England prove recalcitrant. The British, as expected, opposed the plan;

while they had accepted a broad view of neutral rights in 1854 for reasons of expedience, they were not willing to go so far as to make the same principles a permanent extension of international law. And they succeeded in withstanding American pressure despite the danger of forcing the Russians and Americans closer together, by prevailing on nearly all other states not to follow the Russian lead in acquiescing to the proposed convention. In the end Marcy had little to show for his efforts beyond a bilateral convention with Russia, ratified on October 31, 1854, which hardly gave the principles the status of universally accepted international law.[26]

The Russian government was, if anything, more active than the American government in its efforts to gain a concrete advantage from the convergence of interests between the two countries. Russian diplomats in Washington continually attempted to capitalize upon antipathy for the Allies and sympathy for the Tsarist cause. The Russian Foreign Office wrote their Minister in Washington, Alexander Bodisco, shortly before Britain and France declared war, to ask what the general policy of the United States toward the war would be and, more particularly, whether there was any chance that American citizens would be permitted to fit out privateers.[27] Bodisco replied that the United States would undoubtedly remain neutral, but that if Americans were tempted to trade with Russia through special favors different arrangements might be made.

Shortly after offering this opinion, on January 23, 1854, Bodisco—long a popular figure in Washington—died. Russian affairs in the United States then fell first into the hands of Constantin Catacazy, secretary of the legation, and finally those of Stoeckl, designated as Chargé d'Affaires. Catacazy immediately proposed an ambitious scheme designed to bring the United States into the war on Russia's side. He suggested engaging an American ship to carry goods through the British blockade of one of the Russian ports. This, he was certain, would unfailingly produce an incident dragging the two Anglo-Saxon states into war with each other.[28] But nothing came of this devious maneuver.

Stoeckl likewise tried to turn the rivalry between the United States and Great Britain to Russian advantage. Convinced that the two nations were already on the verge of open conflict, and encouraged by statements made by Marcy and other members of the administration (he reported that Pierce had said, "We desire to remain neutral but God alone knows whether it is possible"), Stoeckl advised that a small incident alone might achieve the desired effect. To accomplish this, he believed that encouragement of trade with Russia would be enough; the conflicting English and American views of neutral rights would, as in 1812, produce the inevitable incident.[29] Russian Foreign Minister Nesselrode received these suggestions favorably, even reporting that Nicholas had been impressed by them, and told Stoeckl to proceed with his plans.[30] But in the meantime the British had accepted the American view of neutral rights and all these plans came to nothing, for there was no longer a cause for dispute over trade. The American government had always respected the right of a belligerent to close an enemy's port to trade with an effective naval blockade, and this was the principal means by which Britain choked off Russia's maritime commerce and accomplished her purpose without running the risk of collision with the United States over neutral rights.

The Russians then turned to privateering. The legation had received numerous requests from American citizens to arm privateers under the Russian flag, and despite the very dubious legality of such actions, Stoeckl tried to get a firm answer from the American government on the policy it would pursue in this matter.[31] Marcy could not, of course, openly countenance such proceedings; and the Russian finally concluded that arming privateers in the United States was too risky. It was more important, he decided, to keep American friendship and good will for future need, a conclusion that Nesselrode shared.[32] To another of Stoeckl's ideas, that American privateers be fitted out in Russian Alaska, Nesselrode himself delivered the crushing blow, saying that such proceedings would still violate American laws, and this at a time when it was more than ever essential to keep American friendship.[33] The decisive argument against such a program was not, however, the attitude of the Pierce administration. As a matter of fact, Marcy had clearly intimated to Stoeckl that the United States would not pay close attention to what its citizens chose to do in foreign ports. It was fear of what the Allies would do to Americans sailing under a Russian flag, and, more importantly, fear of what the British would do to Alaska, that discouraged the Russians.[34]

Alaska also figured in Russian-American relations during the years of the Crimean War. The Russian Far Eastern policy at this time was clearly committed to the principle of cooperation with the United States, on the assumption that together both might be able to withstand British opposition in that area. The Russians were already considering the sale of Alaska to the United States as a seal on the arrangement, particularly since Russian advances in the Amur Valley of China made Alaska less valuable as a possession and its defense more difficult. Nicholas Muriavev, Russian Governor-General of Eastern Siberia, had told the Tsar:

This state of affairs may still be improved by a close alliance between the United States and our country. England will, of course, exert all her powers to prevent this; her agents everywhere, and with all means at their command, are now attempting to estrange the United States from us. . . . But, if on the one hand there is prepared under the above mentioned conditions a firm and suitable basis of power for our Russian-American Company on our western shores of the Pacific, in the place of the North American shore, and on the other hand our power expands quickly and firmly on the western shores of the Pacific belonging to us, it will be necessary for us to decide to transfer the Russian-American Company to the island of Sakhalin, from which trade might be carried on directly with Japan and Korea.[35]

Russian desires for a common anti-British policy in the Pacific were shared by many Americans, particularly those, such as Senator William M. Gwin of California, who were active promoters of the plan to purchase Alaska. Gwin and Stoeckl became very close friends through their mutual advocacy of a Russo-American *entente* to withstand British encroachments in the Pacific.[36] The harmony of interests in Russo-American relations, particularly in this part of the world, was further demonstrated by Marcy's action in warning Stoeckl, in March or April of 1854, that the British were planning either to blockade or take possession of Alaska.[37] The stage was clearly set for further cooperation in the Pacific between the two friendly powers.

With the outbreak of the Crimean War, the Russians faced a difficult problem in the defense of Alaska, due to its distance and their naval inferiority. This led foreign diplomats in Washington to speculate openly on the possible sale of the indefensible territory to the United States. Baron Hülsemann informed his government that Sitka would probably be ceded to the United States, and he observed that "no one doubts that this Government would be glad to extend its territory in that direction." [38] But the Russians, typically, had evolved even larger plans than this.

After the defeat of a rather far-fetched plan to hire Americans to defend Alaska, Stoeckl and his Vice-Consul in San Francisco, P. S. Kostromitinov, settled on the idea of a fictitious sale of the Russian-American Company holdings to an "American" company.[39] Kostromitinov, who was also an agent of the company, organized the "American-Russian Commercial Company" in San Francisco, and a pre-dated bill of sale of the Russian-American Company holdings was sent to Washington for clearance on January 30, 1854. After some discussion, however, Stoeckl and Marcy agreed that the British would easily see through the ruse, and the proposal was dropped.[40] According to Gwin's "Memoirs," Pierce favored the arrangement and backed down only because Marcy threatened to resign if the fraudulent scheme were carried through.[41]

All of these maneuvers and rumors of maneuvers had repercussions on British policy. On March 31, 1854, the British government ratified an agreement that both the Russian-American Company and the Hudson's Bay Company would remain neutral during the war and that the holdings of neither would be touched. This eliminated the need for defensive arrangements in Alaska, and, as Stoeckl recognized, the agreement was very much in Russia's favor since the British had control of the seas. A later report by Stoeckl gives some indication as to why the British were willing to come to such seemingly unfavorable terms: "I received this information from Mr. Marcy . . . that during the entire time of the war in the East, the English legation in Washington was on the alert to know whether there were really any question of the sale of our colonies to America." [42]

The Russians could thus point to at least one concrete advantage they had been able to reap from their friendship with the United States and from British opposition to the expansion of both countries.

# PUBLIC REACTIONS TO THE OUTBREAK OF THE CRIMEAN WAR

Public reactions to the Crimean War, like official policy, tended to reflect the country's international position, and particularly the underlying tension between the United States, on one hand, and Britain and France on the other, regarding crucial questions of Western Hemisphere politics. Public opinion, in other words, did not respond to the conflict in the random fashion that might have been expected if there really had been no sense of involvement in it. Nor can the response be explained in terms of either subjective motives (e.g. the American love-hate relationship with Britain) or concrete but limited economic interests such as commercial privileges. However muted, the public response was clearly sensitive to the same considerations that shaped a large part of the Pierce administration's thinking.

In the first place, the direct involvement and personal interests of American citizens in the Crimean War were, of course, quite limited. Even the effect of the war upon American commerce was not great. Trade with the Allies was almost unchanged as a result of the conflict.[43] While trade with Russia was almost cut off by the blockade of Russian ports (exports from the United States to that country dropped from $2,313,175 in 1853 to $48,940 in 1855), the amount of commerce affected by this was only a fraction of the United States trade.[44] Although it appears that businessmen tended to favor mediation in order to protect their trade (see pages 000-000), their interest in the war and their influence on government policy toward it seem to have been slight.

In addition to the expected commercial, cultural, and personal contacts between Americans and the British and French, there were also a surprising number between Americans and Russians at this time. Colonel Samuel Colt of Hartford, the famous arms manufacturer, and his colleague, Mr. Dickerson, an expert mechanical engineer, supplied the Russians with technical skill and materials. The Tsarist government had also hired about fifteen American mechanics to help build Russian railroads, and was planning to use "American genius and enterprise" in the modernization and enlargement of the Russian fleet.[45] There were about thirty American physicians and surgeons serving in the Russian army in the Crimea, most of them medical students from Paris. The United States Consul in Odessa, a Russian citizen of Greek birth, was kept busy serving these and other Americans who came to this area during the war.[46]

But the actual participation of Americans in the Crimean War was limited, for the most part, to the expression of sympathy for one side or the other. American interest in the events of the war, however, was extensive. Countless articles appeared in the major American newspapers and magazines on the battles, military plans, and diplomatic maneuvers of the conflict; the romance and excitement of military campaigns in distant lands evidently had a strong attraction for readers. *Harper's* magazine, in its column, the "Editor's Easy Chair," remarked:

> When we hear the elaborate discussions that arise about our Chair concerning the great war in the East, we often find ourselves asking our young friends whether, after all the enthusiasm with which they enter into the politics of other nations, they have any left for those of their own. . . .
> Now all this intelligence is worth something. This amount of accurate information, applied to other affairs, would be equally valuable. But is the West less than the East? Shall a man be so wise in another's interests, and know nothing of his own? Have contemporary foreign affairs the same charm as foreign history, so that a youth shall pore over the papers as he pores over books? Why is a young American so interested in the allied and Russian movements in the Crimea, and does not concern himself with American movements of which he is a part?

Nor was this interest dispassionate. The American public was often hotly partisan, and clearly felt no need to be "impartial in thought as well as in action." Throughout the mid-nineteenth century, the sympathies of citizens and political leaders for various states or groups in European politics were declared unhesitatingly.[47] The Crimean War was no exception; as one of the leading students of American opinion during this period has remarked, "there were certainly some Americans who were completely neutral, but probably the great majority took sides either with Russia or with the Allies."[48]

It can also be claimed, of course, that much of this feeling was superficial. Sympathy for one side or the other did not necessarily indicate a feeling of involvement, or an inclination to give active support to the favored side. It has been said that "the American people favored Russia or the Allies in the same spirit as spectators who had little at stake might favor one or another contestant in a horse-race." [49]

This may be true in the sense that the spectator felt no more directly involved than he might at a horse race. And yet his choice of horses was far from whimsical. Sympathies for the contestants in the Crimean war were clearly related to one's overall political position and attitude on *American foreign policy*.

This relationship can be seen, for example, in the press. Among the strongly pro-Russian publications—from the outbreak of the war until its close—were the leading pro-Administration, Democratic, expansionist, and Southern newspapers and magazines: the *Washington Union,* the *New York Herald,* the *Richmond Enquirer,* the *New Orleans Picayune,* the *United States Review* (formerly the *Democratic Review*), and *Debow's Review.* The neutral camp included moderate and middle-of-the-road journals such as the *New York Tribune* and *Putnam's Magazine.* The main publications that were sympathetic to the Allies were Whig periodicals, including the *Cincinnati Gazette,* the *American Review, A Whig Journal,* the *Washington Intelligencer, Harper's,* and the *North American Review.*[50] The number of pro-Allied papers may be considered disproportionately large in relation to public opinion, as the press generally seems to have over-represented the conservative point of view.

The fact that most Americans sympathized with the Tsarist cause has been confirmed both by contemporary and modern analysts. Gazley's cautious conclusion is that "perhaps a majority of Americans favored Russia and were opposed to the Allies.[51] Oliva believes that the American public was basically pro-Russian even though the press, by comparison, was much more favorable to the Allies.[52] A third student of American opinion has written that "there was a decided feeling against the two Western European powers in certain American circles." [53] And finally, one of the leading historians of Russian-American relations has expressed the view that "the American people knew little of either the causes of this

conflict or of the issues at stake, but they sided almost instinctively with Russia." [54]

There are numerous contemporary references to the pro-
Russian response of the American public to the war. In late
1854 the Washington correspondent of the *New Orleans
Picayune* wrote:

> During the week I have conversed much on the
> subject with intelligent, well-informed, diplomatic
> politicians and military men. It is clear to my mind
> that the prevailing sentiment is becoming settled
> against the Allies and in favor of Russia.[55]

The *New York Herald*, a little later, declared that "public
opinion here is undoubtedly favorable to Russia. There is
no necessity for disguising the fact. . . . Not that we love
Russia more, but that we hate her less." [56] Neutral or pro-
Allied papers such as the *Portland Transcript* or *Brownson's
Quarterly Review*, while disapproving, accepted as a fact a
strong pro-Russian tendency in American public sentiment.[57]

This sympathy of Americans for Russia is interesting
in view of the amount of anti-Russian writing to which the
country was subjected. Oliva points out that much of the
news of the war was inevitably from British or French
sources, and that all of the five books on Russia published in
the United States in 1854 were written by British or French
authors.[58] Typical of these was the popular work by Laurence
Oliphant, an Englishman, who wrote that Russia had long
pursued a policy "calculated to fill all Europe with dismay,"
and that once Russia controlled the Dardanelles she would
be in a position to maintain "command of the Mediterranean,"
which would "invest her with the supreme control of the
destinies of Europe." [59] But, whatever bias was inherent in
these sources of information, there existed even stronger
motivation for pro-Russian sentiment.

First of all, Russia was an underdog in the war. Fear

of the Muscovite giant seemed more and more absurd as the Russian war effort crumbled before the Allied onslaught. As one of the American diplomats in St. Petersburg later remarked, Russia, "powerful as she seems from the outside, is anything but strong when viewed from the inside." [60] Or, as another historian put it, to the average American, "it seemed as though two great maritime powers . . . were trying to humiliate a badly overmatched third." [61] There was also an antipathy to non-Christian Turkey; many Americans felt strongly about the fact that "the Allies were fighting the cause of Mohammedan Turkey against Christian Russia." [62]

Some groups within the country had more specific reasons to sympathize with the Tsar. To slave-owners and supporters of slavery it appeared that Russia was the strongest protector of this "natural" ordering of human relationships. The *Portland Transcript*, an antislavery paper that took a pro-Allied position, sarcastically advised Russia at one point not to free its serfs if it wanted to retain its supporters in the United States.[63] The *Richmond Enquirer* provided more positive proof of this feeling in its declaration that "no people in Christendom are so happy and contented as the Russians, except the people of our Southern states." [64]

Another source of pro-Russian, or more accurately, anti-British, feeling in the United States was the large number of politically active Irish immigrants. The potato famine of the 1840's had caused many to leave the island, and their political influence had increased considerably by the early 1850s. Typical of the Irish response to Crimea was the large public rally held in New York in 1854 to welcome the prominent rebel, William Smith O'Brien, who had been imprisoned by the British. Anti-British speeches were the order of the day, and inevitably, "three rousing cheers were given for the Czar." [65]

Yet these factors, while helping to explain pro-Russian feeling in the United States, do not explain the relationship of such sympathy to support of a certain foreign policy. The most fundamental motive for the pro-Russian sympathy ex-

pressed in public opinion or the Crimean war appears to have
been the previously discussed fear of British and French
opposition to American aims in the Western hemisphere.
This feeling was unmistakable. One of the Russians writing
about the United States during these years, called attention
to the fact, which he regarded as perfectly apparent on the
basis of comments in the American press, that "hatred toward
Great Britain is the main reason for their sympathy for the
Russians," adding that "the sympathies . . . of Americans
for Russians are of a harmless nature. . . ." [66] The average
American seemed to understand perfectly well what the major
source of opposition to the fulfillment of the "Manifest Destiny" of his country was. "Far more important [than other
causes of pro-Russian sympathy] was the fairly common
conviction among Americans that France and England were
opposed to any further expansion of the United States in
North America. . . ." [67]

The potential extension of the Crimean alliance to the
Western hemisphere was the most frequent allusion made
by the American press to American interests in the Crimean
War. Clarendon's notorious speech of January, 1854, had
aroused the *New York Herald* as well as the officials of the
Pierce administration (see pg. 57 above). For the *Herald,*
a pro-Russian view of the war was the natural result of
a continuing apprehension of British and French designs
that antedated the war and that varied according to the
nature of the threat. After the war the *Herald* merely re-
directed its fire to the new seat of troubles:

The emperor of Russia has filed a protest against
the interference of France and England in the affairs
of Naples. The ground taken is simply that the maritime powers have no more right to mix in the politics
of Italy than Russia had to mix in the affairs of Turkey. . . . The argument of the Russian State department appears to be strictly logical; and a fair case
made out against the courts of England and France.[68]

The *Richmond Enquirer* and the *New Orleans Picayune* both stressed the dangers of the British and French alliance from a Southern viewpoint. The *Enquirer* took the view that the Allies had a deep plot to pick a war with the United States and seize control of the Western hemisphere, adding that the proofs of this scheme had outraged American opinion. The *Picayune* took much the same line, declaring that only a disavowal of any intention to interfere with American annexation of Cuba would enable this country to sympathize to any extent with the Allied position in Crimea. Both papers saw in the scattered instances of French and British opposition evidence of a broad pattern of determined hostility, and called on American citizens to recognize this hostility for what it was and resist it with all their might.[69]

Some Americans took the more moderate position that the Anglo-French alliance was indeed directed at the United States as well as Russia, but that it could not function well enough to be a great threat to either. The *New York Atlas* declared that the coalition "will prove a humbug and do no harm to the Czar."[70] But, as is mentioned above (page 87), even those publications that took a generally anti-Russian stand, recognized the fact that the Allies had alienated American opinion by creating an impression of hostility to goals that many Americans felt to be highly desirable and even essential.[71]

The most outspoken advocates of the Russian cause, as mentioned, were in general the most ardent American expansionists, the most uncompromising sympathizers with Southern slavery, and the groups that most staunchly supported the administration. These points of view were mutually congenial, of course, and were particularly held by the "Young Americans." The *United States Review* (long known as the *Democratic Review*) was this group's leading organ of expression, and was dominated by such figures as John L. O'Sullivan and George N. Sanders, both appointed to diplomatic positions by Pierce. The journal boldly proclaimed anti-British and pro-Russian sentiments that were only mildly touched upon elsewhere. The relationship between the expansionist aims of an active United States foreign policy and the European conflict was accepted without apology by those who were most deeply involved in promoting the extension of American influence.

Summing up its feelings on the Crimean alliance, the *Review* remarked in early 1855:

> Taking into view the mutual declarations of Great Britain and France, clearly intimating a scheme whose object is equally to arrest the progress of the United States and Russia, it must be obvious to all who reflect on the subject, that the former have a deep and direct interest in the result of the present European war. If it should terminate in the success of the Anglo-French alliance, and the attainment of all its objects without absolutely exhausting or crippling the victors, there can be no reasonable doubt that the attempts already made and now being made to overawe and intimidate the United States, and to counteract their policy everywhere in the New World, will be followed by more direct exhibitions of hostility that will place before them the unavoidable alternative of resistance or acquiescence.[72]

If, in the view of the expansionists, Allied victory would endanger American interests, the United States could, in the first place, act to redress the balance without endangering its traditional neutrality, which was not defined as the absence of interests or policies in European political configurations. Secondly, if pressed too hard, Americans could always remember that Washington's injunction was only against *permanent* alliances:

> Without some sufficient counterpoise to the Anglo-French alliance, which is gradually either bullying or subsidizing all the minor states of Europe into becoming accomplices in their own subjugation, there will be no safety to the rights of nations, and they must depend

altogether on the moderation and magnanimity of England and France for the establishment of the just
"equilibrium of power." This counterpoise can at any
time be established and maintained by a cordial good
understanding between the United States and Russia
without an alliance offensive and defensive, which will
only be required in the event of the Anglo-French alliance persisting in its war of diplomacy and intimidation, and in preventing any cooperation of the states
of the New World in establishing a continental system
which will enable them to maintain their commercial
and political rights.[73]

In order to encourage this "good understanding" it was
necessary to improve the image of the Tsarist autocracy in
American public opinion. The *United States Review* was eager
to explain the positive side of the Russian régime, particularly
since the Young Americans were presumably promoting the
United States as the world agent of republicanism. Abstract
ideals of government were not allowed to stand in the way
of an advantageous confluence of interests with the Muscovite
dynasty. As a first step in the justification of Tsarism, Allied
and Russian iniquities were equated:

It is true that the government of Russia is a despotism
—it is also true that ours, of the United States, is
republican; but the despotism of the present day is not
so bad and outrageous, even in Russia, as the reign of
Henry VIII., in England. It bears no comparison with
that of Charles I., and yet the Allies would call on us
to break our faith with Russia, and stultify ourselves
by hurrahing for them. We have no apologies to make
for Russia. . . . We can see little or no difference between Botany Bay, and St. Helena of England; and the
Kamtschatka and Siberia of Russia—between crushing
the body and soul in the factories of Manchester, or
the mines of Cornwall; and performing the same labor
of love in the serfdoms and saltmines of Russia and
Cracow.[74]

The *United States Review* attributed the view of Russian despotism as something particularly evil to the "sway exercised by the British press," which presented Nicholas to the world as "a stern, inflexible tyrant . . . destitute of integrity" after he got in the way of British policy in the East. In the reporting of the Eastern Question, therefore, "our Anglo-American press has, according to custom, pliantly lent itself as an instrument in echoing these spiteful effusions of any and all disappointed rivals and enemies." The *Review* thus considered it "an act of justice" to find out if the Tsar was actually at fault in the dispute over which the Crimean War was being fought.[75]

The proper conclusion, declared the "Young Americans," was that both the Tsar and the United States were victims of British and French rapacity. Russia's only goal was a free passage into the Mediterranean for its commerce, which the Allies unreasonably opposed. The parallel to an analogous dispute in the Western hemisphere was irresistible:

> In order to bring this question home to the people of the States, it is only necessary to observe that the Czar has the same, if not still stronger motives for his policy in relation to Turkey, and his desire to open the gate of the Black Sea, that the United States have for coveting the possession of Cuba. . . .
>
> The Czar believed, and had good reason to believe, that the Ottoman Empire was on the eve of dissolution; and that, in the approaching dismemberment, its possessions on the European, if not the Asiatic side of the Bosphorus and the Dardanelles, would, in all probability, pass into the hands of a great maritime power like England or France, whose policy it would be to shut Russia up for ever in the Black Sea. The United States have equal cause to believe that the island of Cuba, which, in possession of either of these powers, would command the commerce of the Gulf of Mexico, is in the hands of a government incapable of independent action, and ready to relinquish the real substance of sovereignty to any power able to aid her in retain-

ing the shadow. Thus it is, that the press of England and France had placed the United States and Russia in the same class of delinquents, and cited them before the bar of the civilized world for no other reason than that they present insuperable obstacles to the accomplishment of their vast schemes of ambition not only in the East but the West.[76]

While Tsarism was held to be a doctrine innocuous enough to permit close political ties, Islam was considered by the *Review* as a contaminant to all who dealt with it. This enabled the editors, for good measure, to denounce the Allies for the additional sin of supporting a heathen and decadent Moslem state. As opposed to the Ottomans, "old and exhaustive and exhausted," Russia was "still in its earliest years of manhood, progressive, expansive. . . ." The outcome, later if not at that time, was inevitable, for "what special providence of Mohammed can oversway such odds?" [77] And despite its weakness, Turkey was also responsible for the outbreak of the war, since "for many years past, the Porte, moved by the most inveterate animosity, has eagerly embraced every opportunity of embittering her relations with Russia." [78] By such ideological and historical legerdemain it could thereby be claimed that Russia was the injured party and the upholder of civilization's highest values.

In conclusion, then, the journal's editors could "frankly confess our sympathies as between [the Tsar] and England and France, are all on the side of Russia." With the United States, the Northern autocrat presented "an insuperable obstacle to the great scheme of the *entente cordiale* for regulating the balance of power in the new as well as the old world. . . ." [79] The *Review* could do little else but wish the Russians success in the unequal and unjust conflict into which they had been forced:

England, clothed in all the show of sanctity, and France, impelled by the domineering nature of her national character, and directed by an upstart of the

darkest treachery and most shameless perjury, have
at length succeeded in forcing Russia into a war, which
they desire the world at large, and more especially the
United States, to believe a holy crusade. But it is for
power, and power alone, that these two hitherto hostile
nations have taken each other by the hand. They already give a foretaste of how they would exercise it,
if their sway, by destroying Russia, should become
firmly established. Let us hope that the calm, quiet
self-reliance with which Nicholas accepted the challenge
of the allies, may indicate a speedy and successful
termination to a war which has been thrust upon him.[80]

Southern opinion during those years put much hope in
expansion as a guarantee for the extension and stabilization
of slavery, and Southerners therefore were generally hostile
to those powers opposing the further acquisition of territory
to the south by the United States. The most influential organ
of Southern opinion—*De Bow's Review,* published by James
D. B. De Bow of New Orleans—as well as leading newspapers
such as the *Richmond Enquirer* and the *New Orleans Picayune* thus expressed the same attitude toward the Crimean
War as did the *United States Review.* Apologizing to its
readers for the slightly anti-Russian tone of an article on
Danubian commerce in 1854, *De Bow's* announced: "Our own
sympathies, in the matter of Russia and the allied powers,
are in accordance with the general public voice in this country—with neither particularly, with the former if at all." [81]
*De Bow's* also joined the detractors of the only non-Christian
power in the war, calling attention to its stagnation and
weakness.[82] But the clearest indication of its position throughout the conflict was made soon after the Allied declaration
of war. In a long article on the Eastern Question by William
Henry Trescot, the diplomatic historian from South Carolina
who served for a few months during this period as a minor
diplomatic official in the Pierce administration.[83]
    Trescot began with the interesting assumption that "with
the exception of the United States, it may safely be said that

Russia is the only power in the world with a fixed policy, and a constant progress." Proof of this was found in Russia's policy toward the independence of Greece and her support of Schleswig and Holstein against Danish pressure. It was true that the Tsar had "systematically" encroached on Turkey, but this was justified by Russia's need of a commercial outlet and the theory that "the history of the world is the history of encroachment, of invasion, of wrong, if you so will." [84]

After an involved exposition of the background of the conflict, Trescot concludes that "Russia did not provoke this crisis." The Russian proposals for the partition of Turkey were, in his eyes, eminently reasonable. To the argument that the Tsar would misrule any additional territory, he countered that the autocracy "has built splendid cities, created a wide and rich commerce . . . and as far as possible ameliorated the condition of her people," at the cost of maintaining centralized power but without destroying any of the component nationalities of the empire. Trescot argued that the increase of Russian influence was not necessarily a threat to the balance of power or to Great Britain, which could maintain its full strength whatever the outcome of the Eastern Question.[85]

He added that the power of Britain and France was dangerous whereas Russia's strength was not, and the implications of this were not limited to the Eastern hemisphere:

> We think there is, however, this difference between them: England has already touched that point beyond which any *increase* of her power is dangerous to the world, while Russia has not yet developed the matured proportions of that influence which she can fairly use for the world's benefit. . . .
> England has presumed too far in her pride of place. Of late, especially, she has interfered rashly, inconsequentially, and wrongfully, in every corner of the globe. . . . The natural growth, therefore, of any counter-balancing European power is a clear gain to the world at large, especially where such a development neither springs from nor necessitates a violent invasion

of England's present strength. In this light, the discom-
fiture of Russia, by the alliance of France and England,
will be disastrous to Europe, and dangerous to the
world, for it increases the power, and stimulates the
ambitious activity, of the two most restless kingdoms of
Europe—kingdoms whose natural jealousy has hitherto
served as a mutual check.

But passing by all such speculations, the alliance
of England and France for joint action, according to
Lord Clarendon, *in both hemispheres,* is a baleful
phenomenon in politics. It bodes no good anywhere;
but the Tripartite Convention as to Cuba illustrates
fully its consequences in this country.[86]

In conclusion, Trescot declared that the United States
had "a noble, but difficult" task to fulfill. While maintaining
an "honest, determined, neutrality," the United States government needed a more extensive diplomatic organization so that
it could "at any moment comprehend the whole scope of
European politics, and give each separate event its true significance," and it also needed "a navy commensurate with its
rank, to support its decisions." In short, the country was
"somewhat like the old neutral and trading republic of Ven-
ice." The neutrality envisioned by Trescot was clearly not
passive or isolated; like most of his contemporaries he viewed
neutrality as a policy that could be maintained to advantage
only through an active and informed diplomacy.[87]

The more vigorous expansionist elements in Southern
politics were, if anything, still more antagonistic to Great
Britain (and thus more sympathetic to Russia). Dr. Samuel
Cartwright of New Orleans, an extreme advocate of slavery
who propagated "biological" theories of the natural hierarchy
of human races, expressed such a viewpoint when he wrote
the filibustering General Quitman on May 21, 1856:

The Clayton-Bulwer Treaty, the preposterous claims
set up to a large portion of Central America, and the
Africanization of tropical America, are parts and

parcels of the same policy that led Great Britain into
the late war with Russia—the policy being to preserve
and extend her East India and Asiatic conquests against
American competition in the West and Russian progress
in the East.[88]

Southern credulity regarding Russo-American ties was sometimes extreme. J. H. F. Claiborne, in his biographical sketch
of Quitman, claimed that "had the war in the Crimea continued, and had Spain sent a contingent to the Allies, as was
anticipated, Russia, in all probability, would have furnished
means for the invasion of Cuba." According to Claiborne's
imaginative account, only the lack of money at the critical
moment prevented the "liberation" of the island.[89]

Of course any broad movement of opinion, such as public sympathy for Russia in the Crimean War, will have extreme manifestations. These manifestations may not be useful
as a guide to the general trend of thought, but they help to
indicate the farthest reaches of public opinion and its various
tendencies. In this category would fall many of the statements
made by Southern expansionists such as Cartwright and
Claiborne. Others reacted to the "Anglo-French menace" less
dramatically, but with greater attention to the long-term
aspects of the situation. Charles Boynton, an Ohio minister,
wrote that "hand in hand, Russia and America are coursing
the threshold of the new era, the Great Powers of the future,
while Western Europe is plotting against both, and threatens
and fears them." [90]

Boynton, who later became chaplain in the U.S. House
of Representatives and taught in the Naval Academy, reacted
to the Crimean conflict by warning his countrymen that "the
interest of the United States in this struggle is second only
to that of Russia, and to a great degree is evidently identical
with hers." The British and French attack on Russia, said
Boynton, was not the result of any honorable motive but was
simply "the unrighteous design of checking the growth and
hindering the prosperity of a neighboring nation, which might
dispute with them their commercial supremacy. . . ."

For Boynton, as for the great number of Americans who looked with favor on the Tsarist side, the real root of the problem was the similarity between Allied policy toward Russia and their policy of opposition to the further expansion of the United States. Cooperation between the two nations was thus made inevitable by the common opposition of the Western powers:

> The fact will not much longer be concealed from the world, that the true question involved in this war is whether France and England shall be the joint dictators of the world, domineering over all oceans with their navies, and prescribing limits to the growth of nations; whether they shall be permitted to say to Russia, "You shall advance no further eastward," or to say to the United States, "You shall neither have the Sandwich Islands, nor Cuba, nor Mexico, and you, and all other Powers, shall dwell within the limits which we think proper to allow." This is the real significance of the Eastern war, to which the United States will do well to give heed in time. . . .
> The batteries of Cronstadt and Sebastopol are ranged in front of American as well as Russian rights, and the interests of the United States in the preservation of the Russian navy is second only to that of Russia herself. The last war for American independence is yet to come, if Russia can be humbled.
> The United States and Russia sustain almost precisely the same *general* relations to France and England, and to the main objects of their Alliance. Both are animated by a vigorous life, seeking on all sides room for expansion. . . .
> Both are seeking to secure for themselves a share of the commerce of the East, and meet alike the opposition of France and England. . . . Both stand confronted by the Anglo-French Alliance—the one in the Baltic and at Sebastopol, the other in the Gulf of Mexico, in the Sandwich Islands, and in Central America, ready to say "No" to our progress when "Russia is settled." [91]

Just as sympathy for the Russian cause was found particularly among pro-expansionist, pro-Southern, and pro-administration sources, sympathy for the Allies was common among those who opposed expansionism, the extension of slavery, and the anti-British policy of the Pierce administration, which they considered a shameless appeal to emotion in general and to certain ethnic minorities in particular. In 1854 such feelings were characteristic of Northern Whigs and anti-Nebraska Democrats, especially those elements of each group that were beginning to join together in the new Republican party. And despite the pro-Russian sentiment then prevalent, British and French sympathy remained strong among these factions.

Very few Americans would probably have gone as far as the *American Whig Review* article of December, 1850, entitled "Russian Ambition," which predicted a war between Russia, the champion of despotism, and Britain, the champion of freedom. The author then asked: "When the war shall lie between the Europe of freedom and the Europe of the Vandal and the rehabilitation Hun,—when the English people themselves shall gird up their loins for the Holy War,—think you we can turn deafly away, or look on quiescent?" [92] It might be noted that while this plea is at wide variance with the subsequent policy of the Pierce administration, it is clearly no more isolationist than the latter.

During the Crimean War, many Whigs came to share the prevalent anti-British feeling. Even Daniel Webster, a noted Anglophile, threatened war over the fisheries question (above, p. 36). In spite of the supposed conservative bent of the press, pro-Allied sentiments were not expressed as frequently as the opposite viewpoint. But when they *were* expressed, they came almost exclusively from convervatives, opponents of slavery, and those opposed to the Pierce administration.

The aristocratic *North American Review*, which had even defended Austria during the Hungarian uprising of 1848 and 1849,[93] was quick to take up the cudgel against Russia in 1854. The average Russian believes, said the *Review,* that "the great race of which he is a part will fulfill its magnificent mission by conquering the world and stamping its own nationality on all the inhabitants of the globe, and that the leader in this final crusade is he to whom his political allegiance is due,—the CZAR." [94] A similar viewpoint was expressed by *Harper's,* whose antipathy to the aggressiveness of the Pierce administration was well expressed in its reaction to Marcy's "dress circular": "If it is foolish for a Court to require a certain dress and etiquette, it is certainly more foolish to lose the advantages of foreign social intercourse for no more serious reason than the color of a cravat." [95] From the first days of the war, *Harper's* editor George William Curtis, writing in the "Editor's Easy Chair," left no doubt about his sympathies. The main issue of the war, he argued, was "Russian aggression." The real contest was between England and Russia, since the latter power was taking the first step toward India. Accordingly, "there can no doubt upon which side American sympathy will be." The issue was not expansion, but ideals: "England is our friend, when the question is against Russia; for who does not see that Russia represents that spirit of life and government which is diametrically opposed to our own?" [96]

Although eventually forced to admit that the general public did not accept the importance of such considerations, throughout the course of the war *Harper's* continued to emphasize the principles of government involved:

> Thus in the Crimean War, on the one hand, England fights for her interest, for the integrity of her empire, and dreads to see Russia advancing upon India. But, on the other hand, England and France, representing the principle of constitutional government, are opposed to Russia which represents dead Asiatic despotism. . . . It is this conviction that secures to the Western Powers the sympathy of all truly thoughtful minds.

Going a step beyond this, *Harper's* ultimately arrived at the conclusion that "the great, and final, and formidable foe of Russia is America," and that consequently any democratic or semi-democratic nation fighting Russia was "really upon the American side." [97]

Boston clergymen, among the leading abolitionists in the United States, were also among the leading Allied sympathizers. William R. Alger, a noted Unitarian minister and pacifist, wrote a pamphlet upon the Crimean War in which he mixed a strong abhorrence of war with a special antipathy to the Tsar:

> On the part of the Muscovite was a passion of miserable bigotry, and a policy of grasping injustice. . . .
>
> Had there been a little less bigoted obstinacy and insolence, and a little more forbearance or human sympathy, in the cold autocrat of the North,—there would have been no war. . . .
>
> Another fact of benignest import, a broad sign of the times, is brought into strong light by the union of France and England. The cooperative friendship of these ancient foes and pitted rivals reveals a grand progress of the deepest social force in the modern world. . . .
>
> The first obvious result of the war is a partial and temporary crippling of the aggressive power of Russia. Her external advance has been checked, her bristling frontier dismantled, her military pride rebuffed and, by the salutary lessons of experience, an evident and most powerful directive impetus given to the development of her internal resources—a prudent peace policy, nursing all her domestic industries, prosperities, and improvements.[98]

George Perkins Marsh, conservative Whig and noted New England man of letters, was an Anglophile, like most men of his background and tastes.[99] His views are particularly significant in view of his service as Ambassador to Turkey during Fillmore's Whig administration and until his successor was appointed in late 1853. In general Marsh believed the English were too timid in opposing Russia; in one despatch he sent Marcy a strong warning of the impending absorption of the Ottoman Empire by Russia.[100] After his return to the United States, Marsh wrote a long article in which he outlined his view of the Crimean struggle. The main issue, he said, was "the realization of that long-cherished Muscovite dream, the establishment of a Russian *suzeraineté* throughout Christian Europe," and the resultant loss of liberty on that continent. Civilization in its advanced form would be replaced by "a new form of associate life developed from a Tataro-Slavic germ." If she had been victorious in the Crimean War, Marsh believed, she would have commanded "the direct communication between Europe, Asia, and Africa," and, in so doing, "who can doubt that the Emperor of Russia, once seated on the throne of the Constantines, would . . . dictate the policy and control the action, of every government belonging to the European political system?" [101]

The pro-Russian trend in American opinion seemed entirely perverse to Marsh. In his eyes, it was based upon a false understanding of American interests. Stemming from American fears of Anglo-French policies:

The federal administration suddenly gave unmistakable indications of strong Russian tendencies, which were immediately responded to by the Democratic organs throughout the North, as to oracular utterances from the party tripod, while the South found in the close analogy between the "domestic institutions" of Russia and its own, an additional motive for obeying the signal-orders exhibited by the government press. The attention of the public was diverted from the real issues, both direct and collateral, and the American journals were almost unanimous in viewing the Anglo-Gallican alliance as a consipiracy between Louis Napoleon and the Aberdeen Ministry, the objects of which

were, first, to curtail the power of the Czar, and secondly, in the spirit of Lord Clarendon's bravado, to
"regulate" the affairs of this continent, and especially
the relations of the United States with the independent
Hispano-American republics and the colonial possessions of the European powers.[102]

Concluding that "the integrity and independence of the
Ottoman empire are absolutely necessary . . . to the free
enjoyment of human rights in any part of that continent
[Europe]," Marsh could only hope that, in the next stage
of the contest between Russia and the forces of civilization,
the United States would be better aligned: "The contest . . .
will probably assume a character which will more directly
appeal to our political sympathies, if not to our material
interests; and it is earnestly to be hoped, that our moral
influence at least may be thrown into the scale of human
liberty and human progress." [103]

A similar voice heard among the public was that of Francis J. Grund, Philadelphia journalist and diplomat, who charged
that Russia, as the dominant power in Europe, had stymied
all liberal movements on that continent prior to the Crimean
War. The emotional and ideological appeal used by those who
sought a more conservative foreign policy is summed up in
his words: "Whatever fate may have in store for us—whatever vicissitudes may befal [sic] us as a nation, we shall
never forget that we are the children of England . . . and
that France was our first ally." [104]

But whatever ideological arguments or justifications
were used in favor of one side or another in the Crimean
War, the division of public opinion corresponded to something more than an intellectual debate over the comparative
virtues of different governing systems. There was a consistent
correspondence between those who favored an active foreign
policy, along the lines of that pursued by the Pierce administration, and those who saw the virtues of the Russian position in the war. Conversely, the opponents of an active expansionism, who sought accommodation with Britain, saw in

the Tsarist regime the enemy of humanity. Behind the ideological debate there lurked differing conceptions of America's
existing or desired political relations with the major world
powers, and according to these conceptions the ideological
arguments were shaped. Thus the Young Americans dwelt
on the virtues of Muscovite autocracy, while the Whigs silently
passed over Napoleon III and found the religion of the Turks
unimportant. The majority of the public apparently felt,
however, that the enemy of their enemy was by definition
their friend. Public opinion on the Crimean War, like the
attitude of the Pierce administration, was basically shaped
by considerations of how the national interests of the United
States were affected by that conflict.

# NOTES

1. Marcy to Buchanan, March 12, 1854, Instructions to Great
Britain, NA, RG 59.
2. Seymour to Marcy, March 31, 1854, Despatches from Russia,
NA, RG 59.
3. See the reports later submitted by members of the commission:
Major Richard Delafield, *Report on the Art of War in Europe in 1854,
1855, and 1856* (Washington: George W. Bowman, 1860); and Major
Alfred Mordecai, *Military Commission to Europe in 1855 and 1856*
(Washington: George W. Bowman, 1861). Neither document contains
any relevant political observations.
4. Seymour to Marcy, June 2, 1854, Despatches from Russia, NA,
RG 59.
5. Seymour to Marcy, April 13, 1854, *ibid.*
6. See Evfrosina Dvoichenko-Markov, "Americans in the Crimean
War," *Russian Review*, XIII (April, 1954), 137.
7. Ministry of Foreign Affairs to Alexander Bodisco, July 30, 1837,
cited by Golder, *Guide to Materials for American History in Russian
Archives* (Washington: The Carnegie Institute, 1917), p. 63.
8. Autobiography of Andrew Dickson White, I (New York: The
Century Co., 1905), 450.
9. Benjamin Perley Poore, *Reminiscences of Sixty Years in the
National Metropolis*, I (Philadelphia, Chicago, Kansas City: Hubbard
Brothers, 1890), 479.
10. *Washington Union*, May 10, 1853.
11. Hülsemann to Buol-Schauenstein, May 27, 1853, cited by Curti,
*Austria and the United States*, p. 148.
12. Poore, *op. cit.*, I, 429.

13. Mrs. Roger A. Pryor, *Reminiscences of Peace and War* (New York: The Macmillan Company, 1924), p. 26.

14. Brown to Marcy, June 25, 1853, Despatches from Russia, NA, RG 59.

15. Seymour to Marcy, September 15, 1854, Despatches from Russia, NA, RG 59.

16. Spence to Marcy, June 20, 1885, Despatches from Turkey, NA, RG 59.

17. Rush to Marcy, March 9, 1854, quoted in Robert L. Scribner, "The Diplomacy of William L. Marcy" (unpublished Ph.D. Dissertation, Department of History, University of Virginia, 1949), pp. 169-170.

18. Marcy to Buchanan, March 12, 1854, Instructions to Great Britain, NA, RG 59.

19. Marcy to Spence, March 27, 1854, Instructions to Turkey, NA, RG 59; Scribner, *op. cit.*, p. 528; Spencer, *op. cit.*, pp. 289-90.

20. Buchanan to Marcy, January 19, 1854, Despatches from Great Britain, NA, RG 59.

21. See, for example, *The Times* (London) (April 28, 1854, March 17, 24, 1855).

22. Buchanan to Marcy, March 17, 1854, Despatches from Great Britain, NA, RG 59.

23. Foster Rhea Dulles, *The Road to Teheran* (Princeton: Princeton University Press, 1944), p. 53.

24. Marcy to Stoeckl, April 14, 1854, Notes to the Russian Legation, NA, RG 59.

25. Marcy to Seymour, May 9, 1854, Instructions to Russia, NA, RG 59.

26. Only the two Sicilies, Hawaii, Nicaragua, Peru, and Bolivia signed similar agreements with the United States. David Hunter Miller, ed., *Treaties and other International Acts of the United States of America*, VI (Washington: United States Government Printing Office, 1942), 800-812.

27. Count Karl Nesselrode to Bodisco, November 28/December 10, 1853, cited by Frank A. Golder, "Russian-American Relations during the Crimean War," *American Historical Review*, XXI (April, 1926), 462.

28. Catacazy to Nesselrode, February 14/26, 1854, cited by Golder, *American Historical Review*, XXXI, 363.

29. Stoeckl to Nesselrode, January 5/17, 1854, quoted *ibid.*, p. 465.

30. Nesselrode to Stoeckl, March 20/April 1, 1854, quoted *ibid.*

31. Blumenthal, *op. cit.*, p. 71.

32. *Ibid.*, pp. 465-66; Stoeckl to Nesselrode, April 19/May 1, 1854, Nesselrode to Stoeckl, April 10/22, 1854, quoted *ibid.*

33. Nesselrode to Stoeckl, May 26/June 7, 1854, quoted *ibid.*, p. 469.

34. *Ibid.*, pp. 467-69.

35. B.V. Struve, *Vospominaniia o Sibiri* (St. Petersburg, 1889), pp. 155-56, quoted in Hallie M. McPherson, "The Interest of William Mc-Kendree Gwin in the Purchase of Alaska, 1854-61," *Pacific Historical Review*, III (March, 1934), 30.

36. *Ibid.*, p. 32.
37. Stoeckl to Nesselrode, March/April, 1854, cited by Golder, *American Historical Review*, XXXI, 467.
38. Hülsemann to Buol-Schauenstein, August 7, 1854, quoted in Curti, *Austria and the United States.* . . , p. 148.
39. Clarence A. Manning, *Russian Influence on Early America* (New York: Library Publishers, 1953), p. 160.
40. Benjamin Platt Thomas, *Russo-American Relations, 1815-1867* (Baltimore: The Johns Hopkins Press, 1930), p. 110; Manning, *op. cit.*, p. 162.
41. McPherson, *Pacific Historical Review*, III, 33-34.
42. Stoeckl to Gorchakov, December 23, 1959/January 4, 1860, quoted *ibid.*, p. 34; Thomas, *op. cit.*, pp. 110-11; Manning, *op. cit.*, pp. 162-65.
43. U.S., Congress, *House Executive Documents*, No. 107, 34th Cong., 1st Sess., 1856, pp. 5-44.
44. *Ibid.*, p. 101.
45. Dvoichenki-Markov, *Russian Review*, XIII, 139-40; E. White, *op. cit.*, p. 454.
46. Dvoichenki-Markov, *Russian Review*, XIII, 141; E. White, *op. cit.*, p. 455.
47. See, for example, Eddie William Schodt, "American Policy and Practice with Respect to European Liberal Movements, 1848-1853" (unpublished Ph.D. dissertation, Department of History, University of Colorado, 1951), p. 540.
48. John Gerow Gazley, *American Opinion of German Unification, 1848-1871* ("Studies in History, Economics and Public Law," Vol. XCCI, No. 267; New York: Columbia University, 1926), p. 88.
49. *Ibid.*
50. *Ibid.*, pp. 88-89; L. Jay Oliva, "America Meets Russia: 1854," *Journalism Quarterly*, XL (Winter, 1963), 65-69.
51. Gazley, *op. cit.*, p. 89.
52. Olivia, *Journalism Quarterly*, XL, 65.
53. Howard R. Marraro, *U.S. Opinion on the Unification of Italy: 1846-1861* (New York: Columbia University Press, 1932), p. 193.
54. Dulles, *The Road to Teheran*, p. 52.
55. *New Orleans Picayune* (November 9, 1854).
56. *New York Herald* (December 17, 1854).
57. *Portland Transcript* (November 4, 1854); *Brownson's Quarterly Review* (July, 1854, January, 1855).
58. Oliva, *Journalism Quarterly*, XL, 65-66.
59. Laurence Oliphant, *The Russian Shores of the Black Sea* 3rd ed. (New York: Redfield, 1854), pp. 253, 255.
60. *Autobiography of Andrew Dickson White*, I, 465.
61. Bailey, *America Faces Russia*, p. 63.
62. Gazley, *op. cit.*, p. 94.
63. *Portland Transcript* (January 5, 1856).
64. *Richmond Enquirer* (November 15, 1855).
65. Bailey, *America Faces Russia*, p. 64.
66. Ivan Golovin, *Stars and Stripes or American Impressions* (Lon-

don, 1856), pp. 147, 149, quoted in Max M. Laserson, *The American Impact on Russia* (New York: The Macmillan Company, 1950), pp. 158-59.
67. Gazley, *op cit.*, p. 90.
68. *New York Herald* (February 28, 1854, October 17, 1856). See also issues of September 26, 1854, and March 28, 1855.
69. *Richmond Enquirer* (November 11, December 27, 1855, March 28, 1856); *New Orleans Picayune* (April 19, June 18, November 22, 1854).
70. *New York Atlas* (December 19, 1854), quoted in E. White, *op. cit.*, p. 144.
71. See, for example, *Brownson's Quarterly Review* (July, 1854, January, 1855); *Portland Transcript* (November 4, 1854).
72. "Russia and the Anglo-French Alliance," *United States Review*, XXXV (April, 1885), 245.
73. *Ibid.*, p. 244.
74. "Our Transatlantic Cousins," *ibid.*, XXV (April, 1855), 285.
75. "The Czar of Russia," *ibid.*, XXV (January, 1855), 1, 3, 4.
76. *Ibid.*, pp. 7, 8, 9.
77. "Christianity-Islamism," *ibid.*, XXVI (November, 1885), 380. See also "Sultan Abdel Medjid," *ibid.*, XXV (May, 1855), 394-98.
78. "A Few Facts in Regard to Nicholas of Russia," *ibid.*, XXV (March, 1885), 233.
79. "The Czar of Russia," *ibid.*, p. 13.
80. "A Few Facts. . . ," *ibid.*, p. 233.
81. "Russia and the Mouths of the Danube," *De Bow's Review* (August, 1854), p. 172. The article itself is an example of the bias that many claimed was inherent in American sources on Russia. It was lifted, without credit, from Oliphant, pp. 242-51.
82. "Turkey—Its Commerce and Its Destiny," *ibid.*, XVI (February, 1854), 109-28.
83. William Henry Trescot, "The Russo-Turkish Question," *ibid.*, XVI (March, April, 1854), 277-300, 329-350. In the first installment of the article (p. 285) De Bow described the author's point of view as "just and wise."
84. *Ibid.*, p. 289.
85. *Ibid.*, pp. 329, 337-38, 340-41.
86. *Ibid.*, pp. 346-47.
87. *Ibid.*, pp. 349-50.
88. Quoted in Claiborne, pp. 229-30.
89. *Ibid.*, p. 209.
90. C. B. Boynton, *English and French Neutrality and the Anglo-French Alliance in their Relations to the United States and Russia* (Cincinnati: C.F. Vent & Co., 1864), p. 6.
91. *Ibid.*, pp. 103-06; these selections are taken from a passage quoted by Boynton from his own earlier work. *The Russian Empire: its Resources, Government and Policy* (Concinnati: C.F. Vent & Co., 1856).
92. *American Whig Review*, VI, 632, quoted in Bailey, *America Faces Russia*, pp. 53-55.

93. Gazley, *op. cit.*, p. 550.

94. *North American Review*, LXXVIII (April, 1854), 534, quoted in Bailey, *America Faces Russia*, p. 55.

95. *Harper's New Monthly Magazine*, VIII (April, 1854), 700.

96. *Ibid.*, VIII (January, 1854), 271.

97. *Harper's New Monthly Magazine*, XI (September, 1855), 557. See also *ibid.*, XI (November, 1855), 849, 851.

98. William R. Alger, *An American Voice on the Late War in the East* (Boston: John P. Jewett and Company, 1856), pp. 11, 13, 28, 35.

99. Marsh wrote a friend in 1855: "Don't be too hard on poor old England. In spite of the misconduct of her *rulers*, the existence of her *people* is the sole source of light and hope to European civilization and Christianity. All else is devilish." Marsh to Francis Markoe, August 5, 1855, quoted in Lowenthal, p. 157.

100. Marsh to Marcy, August 14, 1853, Despatches from Turkey, NA, RG 59.

101. [George Perking Marsh], "The Oriental Question," *The Christian Examiner*, CCVII (May, 1858), 394, 416-17.

102. *Ibid.*, p. 406.

103. *Ibid.*, p. 420.

104. Francis J. Grund, *Thoughts and Reflections on the Present Position of Europe* (Philadelphia: Childs & Peterson, 1860), pp. 98, 244-45.

# Opportunity Knocks

## CHAPTER FOUR

> Engaged in a war which is almost certain to become a
> continental war in Europe . . . it seems to me that Great
> Britain is now under bonds to keep the peace with our
> Government on this question. . . . We know, and the
> world knows, that this is regarded by some as the favored
> time to strike at the interests of Spain in Cuba, and at
> the interests of Great Britain.[1]

## THE "BLACK WARRIOR" AND CUBA, 1854

Of all the opportunities that the distraction of Britain
and France in Crimea presumably opened up to the United
States, none seemed more immediate or more hopeful than
the chance to acquire Cuba, which had figured as one of the
prime goals in the Pierce administration's expansion program
of early 1854 (see above, page 51). It was also one of the
areas where the influence of that conflict was first felt. Fully
one month before the Allied declaration of war, William H.
Robertson, United States Consul in Havana and a man who
exhibited a keen appreciation of the benefits United States

foreign policy could expect to derive from the Eastern entanglements, had written Marcy that:

> A few months since . . . I remarked that the serious
> position of the Eastern question had prevented a large
> French and English fleet from assembling at this point.
> . . . When the Eastern question is settled, [this force]
> will not be long in making its appearance—As to the
> French fleet . . . I think it was four months ago, that
> it was expected here; I obtained the information from
> no less Authority than the French Consul General him-
> self—and the expectation of an English fleet I learned
> from equally good Authority.[2]

There was another explanation for the high degree of
concern that Americans evidenced toward British and French
policy in Cuba in early 1854. At this time the country, and
especially Southern expansionists, had been troubled by the
rumor that Spain, under British and French encouragement
and guidance, was planning to free all the slaves on Cuba
and otherwise to "Africanize" the island in order to make it
"indigestible" to the United States. Whatever the truth
behind this story, American statesmen took the possibility
seriously enough, and Robertson himself felt that the first
duty of any French and British fleet in Cuba would be to
support these changes in the island's social and economic
structure.[3] The threat of "Africanization" attracted wide
attention during these months and was widely regarded as
a logical and likely policy for the Spanish to adopt in order
to forestall American moves; Senator Stephen Mallory of
Florida, for example, expressed the conviction that "Spain
had deliberately entered on the policy of retaining possession
of Cuba herself, of course in the first instance, and to Africanize it if she cannot do that. . . ." Such a development might
well succeed in stymying American designs on the island and
invalidating the axiomatic belief that Cuba would come to
the United States "just as certainly as an apple parted from

the parent limb gravitated to the earth." [4] If Spain were intent on pursuing the one course of action that might stop the United States from annexing Cuba, the act of seizure had to be consummated before the Spanish policy could succeed.

Knowledge of French and British intentions regarding Cuba was obviously an essential factor in American policy-making. After Clarendon's disturbing speech in the House of Lords during this period, one of the main points in Marcy's instructions to Buchanan had been for the latter to determine how far England and France would support Spain in the island; meanwhile, under his own initiative, Buchanan had ascertained that no formal commitment had been made.[5] Marcy had written Soulé on almost the same day as he had given his instructions to Buchanan, and had asked him to offer his assessments of the intentions of the two countries, further commenting that

> The prompt interference of Great Britain and France in behalf of Spain in the late disturbances in regard to Cuba, may have emboldened her to experiment upon the patience of this country, but I am not prepared to believe that these Powers, whatever be the schemes embraced in their joint policy as to this hemisphere, will sustain her in such a causeless aggression upon our commerce and national rights.[6]

The greater the involvement of the two powers elsewhere, of course, the better the chance for the United States to act with a free hand in any conflict involving Cuba. The conjunction of French and British entry into the Eastern war with the "Black Warrior" affair thus tended to shed a new light upon Cuban affairs and, from the Spanish point of view, to underline the dangers inherent in such confrontations.

The "Black Warrior" was an American steamship engaged in the carrying trade. On February 28, 1854, Spanish authorities in Havana confiscated a cargo of cotton which the ship's owners had failed to declare that it was carrying, in violation of port regulations that had been previously unenforced. Though technically justified, the Spanish action was certain to raise loud protests in the United States as another substantiation of the threat that Cuba constituted to American interests under the existing state of affairs. The demand for strong and forceful action was vociferous.[7]

According to a probably apocryphal story told by the Spanish Chargé d'Affaires in Washington, Pierce, upon hearing of the incident, exclaimed: "Good, good. Here is a fine bit of political capital!" According to the same source, Marcy had told the Russian Chargé that he would have sent a suitable naval force to Havana immediately upon hearing of the Spanish action, had it been available. After recounting the "diatribes" in the American press against the Spanish authorities in Cuba, along with other evidence of American intransigence, the Chargé advised the Cuban Captain General that "from the President down, all are disposed to take advantage of any opportunity to get possession of Cuba, whether it be by attacking the island directly or by lending aid to the revolutionaries." The fact that England and France were becoming embroiled in the Eastern war would undoubtedly help to insure Spain's isolation in any conflict, and the influence of this calculation in Washington was apparent. As the Spanish Chargé reported: "The situation in the Orient they believe to be as favorable to this as they have for some time desired; and they will have it understood that the preoccupation of France and England in those regions will prevent these nations from lending aid to us and that they can work more freely." [8]

The crisis quickly came to a head. As early as March 15 Pierce had transmitted a Presidential message to Congress preparing it for the worst in the dispute:

> I shall not hesitate to use the authority and means which Congress may grant to insure the observance of our just rights, to obtain redress for injuries received, and to vindicate the honor of our flag.

In anticipation of that contingency which I earnestly hope may not arise, I suggest to Congress the propriety of adopting such provisional measures as the exigence may seem to demand.[9]

Soulé's instructions for presenting American demands were drafted two days later, and they were severe. Marcy directed the American Minister in Madrid to insist on $300,000 indemnity and to enter into no further discussion on the matter, but merely to "obtain as early a reply as practicable to your demand." The official view of the United States government was that "neither the views of this government nor the sentiments of the country will brook any evasion or delay. . . ." Marcy further added that the messenger bearing his despatch would remain in Madrid until Soulé had obtained a reply, for which "a very few days it is believed will be sufficient." [10] The Pierce administration would obviously be perfectly willing to face the denouement, if any; such instructions hardly seem intended for redress alone.

Soulé, furthermore, was not the man to carry out these instructions timidly. Upon presenting his strongly worded demands, he exceeded his instructions by giving the Spanish government forty-eight hours to respond favorably. The Spanish were, of course, unwilling to submit to such ignominious terms before even receiving an account from their own officials in Cuba; neither Marcy nor Soulé had thought it necessary to allow for the time required to make such communications. Soulé thus received only a promise of investigation before the expiration of his ultimatum, and this he considered entirely unsatisfactory.[11] The Pierce administration failed to support his extreme truculence, however, and instead of receiving the expected instructions to demand his passports, Soulé was "left to cool his ardour at Madrid." [12] This change of heart in Washington was due not to a reassessment of the "Black Warrior" affair, but to a change of tactics necessitated by an even more ambitious project.

Marcy, before he learned of Soulé's conduct in the matter, had already drafted further instructions to the latter, broadening the aims of the United States. The moment was considered suitable for another attempt to obtain one of the treasured aims of American expansionism. Soulé's attention was called to the way in which the constant irritations over Cuba disrupted "amicable relations" with Spain, and the hope was expressed that the "enlightened statesmen" of that country would see the advantage of removing this source of "annoyance and injury." Soulé was authorized, therefore, to "enter into a convention or treaty for the purchase of Cuba." The unsettled political conditions in Spain, as well as domestic problems within Cuba, thought Marcy, would further "open the way to the accomplishment of the object so much desired by the United States." But what if Spain should fail to evaluate her own interests as they were evaluated for her in Washington, and should cling obstinately to the troubled isle? In this case, Marcy told Soulé, in a passage that was suppressed in all public versions of the instructions until long after the event, to:[13]

> direct your efforts to the next most desirable object, which is to detach that Island from the Spanish dominion and from all dependence on any European power. If Cuba were relieved from all transatlantic connection and at liberty to dispose of herself as her present interest and prospective welfare would indicate, she would undoubtedly relieve this government from all anxiety in regard to her future condition.[14]

The outcome of this campaign the Pierce administration recognized, depended in great measure upon the extent to which Britain and France were deflected by events in the Near East. Marcy was well aware of their continuing interest in Cuban affairs; the Spanish Chargé, for one, reported a long conversation between French Ambassador Sartiges and the Secretary of State in his note of March 20. The former, he told his government, had tried to convince Marcy that the affair was purely a "commercial question" in which the United

States government ought not to take any political interest. Marcy had obviously been unimpressed. He had reportedly suggested to the English Minister upon another occasion that in return for American suppression of privateers the British and French should be so satisfied that "said powers would put no obstacles in the way of the annexation of the island." [15]

Soulé, in response to Marcy's earlier inquiries on British and French support for Spain, bragged that he was pursuing the "divide and rule" maxim with favorable results: "Should I be successful in widening the breach now existing between this government [Spain] and the governments of France and Great Britain, an almost certain opportunity would occur of my being placed in a position to effect something important and eventually to carry my point." [16] Later letters were not so uniformly optimistic. Soulé felt that in any event the British would not support Spain in Cuba, reporting that in informal conversations the British representative in Madrid had declared that "Great Britain would give no material aid to the Spaniards to maintain their dominion over the Island of Cuba against the U. States. . . ." The French, however, presented a different problem, and Soulé believed that the French Minister (with whom he had duelled) was "all for resistance." He later told Marcy that the French had offered to defend Cuba if Spain would contribute to the Allied effort in the Near East, but that Spain had balked at this arrangement. Even the British Minister "was not so sure about the intentions of the French government." But while Soulé discounted the likelihood of Allied support for Spain, he attributed the Spanish resistance to American demands to belief in this support: "Spain is not perhaps encouraged in her stubbornness by either England or France, but there is little doubt that she derives much confidence from the conviction that those two powers will eventually uphold her in any struggle against us." [17]

The effect of the Crimean War upon the British and French position in the New World was difficult to gauge, and not all of Pierce's advisers were of the same opinion. Soulé was more optimistic than most. The advice from London, for example, was less certain about the restraining influence of the conflict upon Anglo-French behavior elsewhere; for one thing, the war might draw the two countries closer together. And while Buchanan recognized that "the French alliance will not last forever," he also recognized that "John Bull is a pugnacious animal and is ever ready for a fight," having been somewhat taken aback by the enthusiasm with which the country had entered the war with Russia. He believed that the British government was playing a dangerous game by refusing to come to terms with the United States over Central America while engaged in the Eastern conflict, and thought that if the British public could be made aware of this fact, "public opinion would operate powerfully in favor of a prompt, fair and peaceful settlement of the questions in dispute." He was particularly taken aback by the long-awaited Clarendon note in response to his statement of the issues in Central America. Characterizing this paper as "rambling and inconclusive," he commented that it seemed "to put to an end any reasonable hope of arriving at a satisfactory understanding with the Government of Great Britain . . . or even of effecting any compromise of the Central American questions which the United States could with honor accept." [18]

The British position appeared to be one of maintaining a watchful eye on the new world and keeping the United States uncertain as to its intentions. A month later Buchanan reported an inquiry from Lord Clarendon on the progress of the "Black Warrior" question, in which he indicated concern for its peaceful settlement. But Buchanan could gather no further information on British intentions beyond his previous assurances that there was no formal commitment to defend Cuba.[19] In his next despatch he cautioned that the French Emperor was probably more hostile than the British in this regard, which might lead to problems: "Should the Union of the two powers be successful in humbling Russia, then there might be serious danger of an alliance between them to preserve Cuba to Spain." [20]

The pressure for forceful action in Cuba continued unabated in May, particularly after the receipt of a report from the special agent the Pierce administration had sent to Cuba to investigate the Africanization rumors. The opinion of the agent, although by no means indisputable, was that Africanization was indeed imminent.[21] As many American politicians of both parties were convinced that, in view of the Russian war, the United States had nothing to fear from the Allies in Cuba, the clamor for action grew louder. On May 24, 1854, Senator Seward, a leading Whig, observed that many thought the time ripe "to strike at the interests of Spain in Cuba, and at the interests of Great Britain," reasoning that the likelihood of continental war in Europe put Britain "under bonds" to keep the peace.[22]

Under these circumstances, it became more important than ever for the Pierce administration to ascertain the much-disputed intentions of the French government, which according to most accounts, was closely committed to Spain. Minister Mason had at last come to believe that the Eastern conflict was not likely to be solved in the near future, all diplomatic efforts having accomplished nothing more "than to complicate the question." [23] But this did not clear up the main point of uncertainty, the importance of which was emphasized by Marcy in a directive to Mason later in the month:

If there be any Treaty embodying such a provision or any explicit understanding to that effect [that France would protect Cuba] between France and Spain it is quite important that this Government should get at that fact. I hope you will do what you can to get reliable information on that subject.[24]

Mason's reply gave the government some comfort. He began by stating the obvious regarding the aims of British and French policy: "I have no doubt that both France and England will use all the influence which they can bring to bear, to prevent a sale of the Island to the United States." And Mason could put his finger directly on the motives behind this policy: "It is because its possession will so strengthen the United States that they would not desire it. . . ." But after explaining the fears of the Allies from military, commercial, and political standpoints, Mason turned to the basic issue and came to a succinct conclusion on it: "The question remains will France and England, or either of them, engage in war as allies of Spain if the United States shall resort to the declaration of war in vindication of its national rights and honor. My opinion is that they will not."

Great Britain, said Mason, was too dependent upon trade with the United States to go to war against the latter at that time. France had a greater interest in Spain, but had the same commercial ties with American industry upon which it depended heavily. Two other obstacles faced the French. The bad state of finances in the country could not stand the strain of a second war. But, more importantly,

It is well known that success in the war with Russia is regarded as essential, perhaps, to the continuance of the Imperial Power. . . . Adverse fortune in this war would impair if not destroy his [Napoleon's] prestige, and endanger his throne itself—and no one yet sees a prospect of peace. . . . The power of the western allies, is very great, but they obviously have their hands full and the necessity of directing undivided energies to the prosecution of the war with Russia . . . renders it scarcely possible that there shall be a disposition to engage in war with a new enemy whose power in war, though latent, is appreciated to its full extent. . . .[25]

The Pierce administration had therefore received assurances from a number of sources that British or French intervention in a conflict between Spain and the United States was unlikely. The opportunity presented was not, however, fully utilized, at least insofar as a test of arms was concerned. There is general agreement that "war between Spain and the United States was only avoided by the narrowest of margins." [26] But other and simultaneous pressures on the Pierce administration dictated greater prudence, leaving the bellicose actions and words of isolated individuals such as Soulé unsupported. Foremost among these pressures was the Kansas-Nebraska bill, which passed the Senate on March 4 and reopened the bitter question of slavery in the territories. Under severe attack in the North for supporting this measure, Pierce could ill afford a war over Cuba which would have branded him even more strongly as a friend of slavery, and would not have the broad public support it might have commanded before the slavery issue was revived.[27] The aggressive mood in which the government had initially responded did not therefore, bring about the expected results when its extreme—and presumably unnegotiable—demands were not met.

The ultimate question of British and French intentions was not put to the test either. The actual policy of the two countries during the crisis was to encourage Spain to make enough concessions to insure a peaceful settlement and thus avoid having to face the difficult choice between a double war or an embarassing retreat in Spanish America. The Spanish government did, in fact, give compensation to the owners of the "Black Warrior," after direct negotiations, and while this did not satisfy all American demands, it helped to reduce war fever. In any event, the three nations *did* maintain a united diplomatic front; Soulé's insolent correspondence to the Spanish government, for example, was passed on by it to the British and French. Had Britain and France not been involved in war elsewhere their support of Spain might well have extended much further.

Soulé's temporarily dashed hopes were revived again by the Madrid insurrection of the summer of 1854, in which the American Minister, it was later discovered, had definitely been involved with the republican forces. It was Soulé's hope that a republican government in Spain would sell Cuba to the United States.[28] Moreover, the occupation of the Spanish authorities with domestic troubles would undoubtedly handicap their powers of resistance; as Soulé hinted very broadly to Marcy: "What a moment for taking in our own hands that question of Cuba, which it seems almost impossible we may hereafter be able to adjust in any other way than by force of arms!" [29] In London, the more conservative Buchanan felt that the Spanish revolt might lead to Cuban unrest, and he advised that "under these circumstances, it will be for the Government at Washington to decide whether they ought to take any steps to give a direction to the impending Revolution in Cuba." [30] But the Spanish insurrection did not grow to the expected dimensions and this additional ray of hope was soon extinguished.

Though the "Black Warrior" affair was gradually eclipsed by domestic problems, it was not completely resolved for some time. Pierce sent a second message to Congress on August 1, before the final settlement had been made, advising that measures of precaution were still in order. But the new tone of relative moderation in Washington was also established in the same message, when Pierce issued a stern warning to the filibusterers that the country's laws prohibiting private expeditions against foreign countries would be enforced.[31] The possibility of officially tolerated, if not officially supported, attempts to launch a "private" invasion of Cuba had been one of the chief sources of concern to Spain and her Allies during the tense days of the crisis. Such a development would have enabled the United States to protest its own innocence while blocking British or French intervention (in the name of "nonintervention"). And the forces being organized for such expeditions were of a strength and determination to be taken seriously. John A. Quitman, former governor of Mississippi, was openly gathering such a force to "liberate" Cuba. The philosophy of the filibusters, as expressed by Quitman at the time of the "Black Warrior" affair, recognized the Anglo-French "containment" policies as the chief threat to the United States:

The great question of our age and generation is the question whether American or European policy shall prevail on this continent. Of this great question, Cuba

is the battleground for its solution. The erection of a
strong negro or mongrel empire opposite to the mouth
of the great outlet of the commerce of the Southwestern
States, an empire included within the European scheme
of the "balance of power," would forever put a stop
to American progress and expansion on this continent,
and very probably eventually crown their scheme by
bringing about a dissolution of this Union. We are a
strong people when united, but weak whenever the
slavery question is started. Spain and her allies, by the
possession of Cuba, have it in their power at all times
to distract the United States with this question. We
must disarm them of this power to injure us. How shall
we do it? I say by encouraging a revolution in Cuba.[32]

Though unwilling to go this far, the Pierce administration clearly shared this same basic concern over the European
"balance of power," and the hostile intentions of the Crimean
Allies. Summarizing what he had learned of the British and
French attitudes, Marcy wrote to Soulé during the same
month that he thought it unlikely that Great Britain would
forcibly intervene to prevent the acquisition of Cuba, though
she might oppose it as she had the annexation of Texas. The
French, however, had "indicated a tendency to intermeddle in
the affairs of the American continent." [33] A more comprehensive judgment, expressed in a communication to Seymour
three months later, again indicated an appreciation of the
temporary relief afforded the United States by the conflict of
these powers with Russia:

Thus far during the present contest, the Western
powers have shown a kind of feverish desire to cultivate friendly feelings with our Country. It requires no
great degree of sagacity to perceive that much of it
is assumed rather than felt, and that, like their recent
concessions on the subject of Neutral Rights, the feelings they now manifest for us, are produced by present
circumstances rather than by anything which points

to the future. When they have humbled the power of the Czar, as they expect to do, and domineered perhaps over the rest of Europe, they will have leisure to turn their attention to American affairs and meddle with a continent which neither asks for their laws or will submit to their interference.[34]

# PROPOSALS FOR MEDIATION BY THE UNITED STATES IN CRIMEA, 1854-1855

The summer of 1854 was the high point of both the "Black Warrior" affair and of speculation concerning American mediation in the Crimean conflict. Just as the former was affected by events in the Black Sea, so the latter may have reflected certain issues raised by the American-Allied confrontation in the Western hemisphere. The idea of American mediation, at first glance a rather harmless form of wishful thinking, later seems to follow the general tenor of relations between the powers of the old and new worlds.

The British and the French were, indeed, quite unreceptive to the idea that the United States might be suggested, or might even propose its own services, as a mediator in their war with Russia. As a neutral and presumably far-removed power in the war, the United States could logically pose as an impartial arbitrator. But just as the claim of being so far removed from the war was subject to qualification, mediation by the United States was viewed by the Allies as anything but impartial. It never became, therefore, a serious possibility, since the British or French would probably have rejected it. But such rejection might have been embarrasisng if it became necessary to refuse such an offer openly, and for this reason the two states may well have had a certain interest in seeing that the offer was not made.

The thought that the United States might be able to avert armed conflict through its friendly offices had occurred to many Americans almost from the beginning of the dispute.

Minister Ingersoll had written Marcy, shortly before the Russian occupation of the provinces, suggesting that the United States government might make "an effort on its part to averting the threatened catastrophe." Pointing out that Austria was not suited to the role of mediator, and that "it might greatly illustrate our country to make the offer," he pointed to the opportunity created by lack of concrete interest in the Eastern question: "Aloof from the scenes of controversy as well as the questions involved, might we not utter a voice of friendly suggestion that would lead to mediation, or arbitration, or some other peaceful mode of adjustment?" [35] In the 1850s there was apparently less fear of "impartial" involvement to preserve the peace of Europe than there was to be three-quarters of a century later.

Part of the impulse behind the American movement for mediation came from genuine pacifist sentiment, of course. The leaders in this cause included George C. Beckwith and William R. Alger, both Massachusetts clergymen, and William H. Allen, President of Girard College. The best known advocate of peace, however, was Elihu Burritt, "the learned blacksmith," a talented linguist who devoted his life to the pacifist gospel. The leading pacifist organization was the American Peace Society. The pacifists, while usually free of political motives, were a noisy minority who believed that American ideals should be promoted on a universal scale. As one student of the subject has expressed it, the American peace movement, which dated back to 1815, arose "from the conception that it was the duty of America to uplift common men everywhere." [36]

American pacifists were naturally opposed to the generally aggressive tone of the Pierce administration, with its "Young America" elements. They condemned the policy of the United States in Cuba, Central America, and other areas where the government had pursued its strong anti-British program. Elihu Burritt, nevertheless, succeeded in making personal contacts with a large number of important officials in the administration, and was even invited to dinner with President Pierce on one occasion. According to Burritt's own account, the President listened with sympathy to his pleas for international arbitration, especially in the European war then being waged.[37]

But although the Pierce administration might cite humanitarian arguments and cultivate the support of pacifist circles, it was clearly influenced more by political motives than pacifist sentiments. The attitude of the United States government toward the idea of American mediation, and the European reaction to the same proposal, indicated that the move was designed to force France and Great Britain either to retire gracefully in the Western hemisphere or to openly reject the proffered services of an "impartial and uninvolved" mediator. Marcy first mentioned the idea casually at a diplomatic dinner on April 21, 1854, but serious promotion of the proposal was apparently sparked by Seymour's assurance, a month later, that Russia would accept it.[38]

Sometime in early July, Marcy approached Stoeckl and told him that, as Russia had offered mediation in the War of 1812, the United States would be willing to return the gesture of good will in the war being waged. He reported that the Cabinet had approved the plan in principle and that the scheme would be proposed to all belligerents in ten days or two weeks. According to Stoeckl's report, he asked Marcy whether the well-known partiality of the United States for Russia might not lead England to reject the idea, to which Marcy answered, "Let her do so. It will be one more count against her in our eyes. You surely can not object to that." [39]

As might have been expected, Stoeckl advised his government to try the idea. From the Russian point of view, it would result either in mediation by a friendly power in a difficult war or in refusal of the proposal by Russia's enemies, who would then bear the onus of rejecting a peaceful settlement. But, at the same time, Stoeckl called attention to the ulterior motives underlying the offer. The plan was designed, he thought, to forestall Allied intervention in the Cuban dispute then raging. It also was undoubtedly an appeal to the Irish vote. Caleb Cushing, the leading Anglophobe in the Cabinet, was thought to be the moving force behind the idea.[40]

Nesselrode's reply, written in September, expressed perfect willingness to have the United States mediate the war, since he was certain of the "impartiality" of the American government. But, he added, England and France would never accept mediation by the United States, since they did not believe the latter was impartial, and thus Russian acceptance of the plan would be viewed as a sign of weakness unless the Allies could somehow be brought to accept the plan. Russia would wait, therefore, until the United States could get some encouragement from the Western powers. In the meantime, his country appreciated the attempt of the United States to serve the cause of humanity by bringing an end to the bloody conflict.[41]

But by this time the plan had already been dealt a death blow. Marcy had unveiled his proposal to the Allied powers in June, and the response was negative to the point of bitterness. Sartiges had transmitted the offer to his government with some very caustic remarks.[42] Drouyn de Lhuys, the French Foreign Minister, advised him to "elude it politely," adding that "the United States can hardly hope to solve the Eastern Question for which the European powers have been unable to find a solution during the last twenty-five years." [43]

In addition to the complete lack of enthusiasm among the Allies, the plan was frustrated by some second thoughts that had occurred to the Pierce administration. Marcy wanted nothing to detract from his efforts at that time to secure a neutral rights convention. It was recognized that continuance of the war was favorable to this as well as other aims of United States foreign policy. Finally, the offer of American mediation might be used to support the British argument that there was no clear division between the Old World and the New World in international politics. In early August Marcy advised Stoeckl that his government was dropping its offer to mediate.[44]

But even after the final rejection of the idea by the Pierce administration, and the absorption of the United States government with a new set of disputes involving Britain and France in late 1854 and early 1855 (see Chapter 5), mediation

in the Crimean War continued as an issue in American politics. Despite Russian evacuation of the Danubian provinces
in July, 1854, which met the demands made of Russia by
Britain and France when they entered the war, the Western
powers had invaded the Crimean peninsula in September, cap-
turing the port of Balaclava on the twenty-sixth of that
month. On October 17 the bombardment of Sebastopol began,
and the battle of Inkerman on November 5, though presumably an Allied victory, made it clear that the struggle over the
Crimean peninsula would be long and bloody. It was largely
American pacifist sentiment, however, combined with increasing anti-British feelings, that kept the movement for American intervention alive, the political motives that had provided
much of the initial momentum having lost much of their force.

On December 21, 1854, Senator Charles Sumner of Massachusetts submitted a Congressional resolution calling for an
offer of American mediation in the war.[45] Sumner and Elihu
Burritt, who were in close communication, had of course both
suspected that political considerations were dominant in the
Pierce administration's initial proposal of mediation as well
as its final rejection of the idea, and they sought to keep the
project alive with or without official support.[46] In the following months Congress was indeed flooded with petitions, me-
morials, and resolutions supporting the rôle of the United
States as a peacemaker in the Crimea.[47] One strong Congressional advocate of mediation, Representative T. C. Cling-
man of North Carolina, actually denied that the continuation
of the war benefitted the United States in any way; and in so
doing revealed the existence of a body of opinion subscribing
to the opposite view:

> A gentleman over the way said, the other day,
> when I first brought up this proposition, that he hoped
> that the war between Russia and the allied powers
> would continue for fifty years. I take it for granted
> that he did not express this benevolent wish from any
> opinion that it was advantageous to the parties en-
> gaged in it; but he must have made the remark to

carry the impression that the United States would derive some advantage from it. It will be conceded, on all hands, that it will give us no glory and no additional territory.[48]

According to one historian, the principal sources of the petitions sent to Congress and of the strength of the mediation movement were New York and Southern commercial interests, whose trade had been interrupted by the war.[49] Such varied sources as Austrian Chargé d'Affaires Hülsemann, the *London Economist*, and the *New York Evening Post* all agreed on this fact.[50] But whatever the sources of mediation sentiment— pacifist, political, or commercial—the question itself formed part of the political background upon which recurring dramas such as the "Black Warrior" affair were played out. The support of the idea by many prominent public men, and the quiet opposition of France and Great Britain to American interference, were the subject of continuing public discussion.[51] The Crimean War, in one way or another, was very much on the minds of American politicians.

# NOTES

1. Senator William H. Seward, May 24, 1854. *Congressional Globe*, 33rd Cong., 1st Sess., XXVIII, Part 2, 1300.
2. Robertson to Marcy, February 14, 1854, Despatches from Consulate at Havana, NA, RG 59.
3. *Ibid.*
4. *U.S. Congressional Globe*, 33rd Cong., 1st Sess., 1854, XXVIII, Part 2, 1260. See also pp. 1298-1300.
5. See page 58.
6. Marcy to Soulé, March 11, 1854, Instructions to Spain, NA, RG 59.
7. For a full account of the controversy see Henry L. Janes, "The Black Warrior Affair," *American Historical Review*, XII (January, 1907), 280-98.
8. Fernando Magallon to Juan de la Pezuela, March 16, 20, 1854, quoted *ibid.*, pp. 292-94. Magallon pointed out that the "chivalric and independent" *National Intelligencer* had sought to stem the tide by calling for caution and moderation in the response of the United States to the Spanish action. The *Intelligencer* was the organ of the Whig

party and thus the leading voice of opposition to much of the extreme anti-British expansionism in the Pierce administration.

9. Richardson, V, 235.

10. Marcy to Soulé, Instructions to Spain, March 17, 1854, NA, RG 59. For collected documents on the "Black Warrior" affair see U.S., Congress, *House Executive Documents*, No. 76, 33rd Cong., 1st Sess., 1854.

11. Soulé to Marcy, April 13, 1954, Despatches from Spain, NA, RG 59.

12. R. B. Mowat, *The Diplomatic Relations of Great Britain and the United States* (London: Edward Arnold & Co., 1925), p. 145; Janes, *op. cit.*, 290-91.

13. Learned, *op. cit.*, p. 193.

14. Marcy to Soulé, April 3, 1854, Instructions to Spain, NA, RG 59.

15. Magallon to Pezuela, March 16, 20, 1854, quoted in Janes, *op. cit.*, pp. 292-93.

16. Soulé to Marcy, April 7, 1854, Despatches from Spain, NA, RG 59.

17. Soulé to Marcy, April 22, May 3, 10, 1854, *ibid.*

18. Buchanan to Marcy, April 7, 14, 25, 1854, Despatches from Great Britain, NA, RG 59.

19. Buchanan to Marcy, May 19, 1854, *ibid.*

20. Buchanan to Marcy, May 23, 1854, *ibid.*

21. C. W. Davis to Marcy, May 22, 1854, in William R. Manning, ed., *Diplomatic Correspondence of the United States, Inter-American Affairs, 1831-1860*, Vol. XI: *Spain* (Washington: Carnegie Endowment for International Peace, 1939), pp. 768-95.

22. *Congressional Globe*, 33rd Cong., 1st Sess., XXVIII, Part 2, 1300. For full quote see first page of this chapter.

23. Mason to Marcy, June 22, 1854, Despatches from France, NA, RG 59.

24. Marcy to Mason, June 27, 1854, Instructions to France, NA, RG 59.

25. Mason to Marcy, July 20, 1854, Despatches from France, NA, RG 59.

26. Mowat, *op. cit.*, p. 145.

27. The Spanish Chargé had believed earlier that the reemergence of the slavery issue would favor rather than hinder a bellicose foreign policy: "Internal questions have so divided the Democratic party that it will not be strange if this government utilizes this or any other excuse to create a national question, with the purpose of unifying the party on it." Agallon to Pezuela, March 20, 1854, quoted in Janes, *op. cit.*, p. 291. As events turned out, this was apparently not the case. See, for example, Mowat, *op. cit.*, p. 145.

28. Soulé to Marcy, June 28, 1854, Despatches from Spain, NA, RG 59; Ettinger, *op. cit.*, pp. 336-37.

29. Soulé to Marcy, July 18, 1854, *ibid.*

30. Buchanan to Marcy, July 21, 1854, Despatches from Great Britain, NA, RG 59.

31. Richardson, *op. cit.*, V, 245-46.

32. Quitman to Thomas Reed, August 24, 1854, in J. F. H. Claiborne, *Life and Correspondence of John A. Quitman* (New York: Harper & Brothers, 1860), p. 207.

33. Marcy to Soulé, August 16, 1854, Instructions to Spain, NA, RG 59.

34. Marcy to Seymour, November 20, 1854, Instructions to Russia, NA, RG 59.

35. Ingersoll to Marcy, July 22, 1853, Despatches from Great Britain, NA, RG 59.

36. Rippy, *op. cit.*, p. 42.

37. Merle E. Curti, *The American Peace Crusade* (Durham, N.C.: Duke University Press, 1929), pp. 130, 208-09.

38. Spencer, *op. cit.*, pp. 294-95; Seymour to Marcy, May 26, 1854, Despatches from Russia, NA, RG 59.

39. Stoeckl to Nesselrode, July 2/14, 1854, quoted in Golder, *American Historical Review*, XXXI, 471.

40. *Ibid.;* Spencer, *op. cit.*, p. 295.

41. Nesselrode to Stoeckl, September 10/22, 1854, cited by Golder, *American Historical Review*, XXXI, 473.

42. Sartiges to Drouyn de Lhuys, June 26, 1854, cited by Spencer, *op. cit.*, p. 296.

43. Drouyn De Lhuys to Sartiges, July 20, 1854, quoted in Blumenthal, *op. cit.*, p. 70.

44. Stoeckl to Nesselrode, July 29/August 10, 1854, cited by Golder, *American Historical Review*, XXXI, 472; Spencer, *op. cit.*, pp. 296-99.

45. *Congressional Globe*, 33rd Cong., 2nd Sess., 1854, XXX, 105.

46. Curti, *American Peace Crusade, 1815-1816*, pp. 208-09.

47. See for example, U.S., Congress, *House Journal*, 33rd Cong., 2nd Sess., 1854-55, pp. 63, 75, 146, 162.

48. *Congressional Globe*, 33rd Cong., 2nd Sess., 1855, XXX, Part II, Appendix, 60.

49. Curti, *American Peace Crusade* . . . , p. 210.

50. Hülsemann to Buol-Schauenstein, December 31, 1854. *The Economist* (January 13, 1855). *New York Evening Post* (December 26, 1854). All quoted *ibid.*

51. Golder, *American Historical Review*, XXXI, 473-74.

# Pushing the Advantage: American-Allied Rivalry in the New World from Greytown to Ostend

## CHAPTER FIVE

> But, if it were otherwise, if it is to bring upon us
> the calamity of a war, let it be now, while the great
> powers of this continent are engaged in that stupendous
> struggle which cannot but engage all their strength and
> tax all their energies, as long as it lasts, and may before
> it ends, convulse them all.[1]

## THE PATTERN OF OPPOSITION, 1854-1855

The end of the Crimean War seemed distant in late 1854. After the Allied landings on the peninsula, fighting had fallen into a costly stalemate. The possibilities for a peaceful solution had been temporarily exhausted, and the arrival of winter postponed any military solution for several months. The problems of supply and reinforcement for the Allied armies were serious ones, and the British government in particular was subject to a good deal of criticism for the way in which they were met. As hopes for a quick end to the conflict faded, and as the demands of the war grew more urgent, British and French policy reflected increased pressures from the North American republic. Because they were unwilling to concede all the disputed points to the Americans in order to avert a second conflict at such an unpropitious time, the Allied powers' task of maintaining a tenuous balance between conciliation and opposition was made more difficult. Allied statesmen could not risk an actual war with the United States, but at the same time they had to avoid creating the impression of unwillingness to act or of powerlessness in the Western hemisphere, which they assumed would only encourage American aggressiveness. Conflicts had to be played down or drawn out if possible, and compromises made quietly if necessary. British Prime Minister Aberdeen advised Clarendon, his Foreign Secretary, to "carefully avoid quarreling" with the United States, but said at the same time that "I would contrive to hang up all matters in dispute by means of civil negotiations for some indefinite period, and would make no concessions at this moment, if it could be avoided." [2]

Thus, by the latter half of 1854, the Crimean Allies were meeting the increased American pressure with a quiet but constant counter-pressure, seeking to prevent the expansion of American influence by peaceful means and making concessions only when pressed to the danger point. From the American viewpoint, the most effective response to such a strategy would have been to force the issues, on the reasonable assumption that the Western powers would avoid a second war. The Pierce administration was aware of its advantageous position and indeed sought to push its advantage, but in most cases did so in too uncertain a manner to force a British or French retreat. While antagonizing the Allies by its assertiveness and thereby precluding accommodation, the United States lacked the perserverance or determination to pursue a successful policy of intimidation. This was due to several factors: internal division, domestic pressures, lack of clear plans, and imperfect administration control. But the end result was a foreign policy that forfeited the major opportunities presented to it for attaining its objectives, not through lack of awareness of these opportunities but through inconstancy in policy implementation.

The constant jockeying over Cuba, which was dramatized in the "Black Warrior" affair, and American overtures regarding mediation in the Crimean war were but two elements in the general rivalry between the United States and the Western powers. From this mosaic of incidents, all seemingly inconsequential, one can gradually discern an overall design with several distinctive motifs. In Santo Domingo, Ecuador, and throughout Latin America, Americans quietly opposed the Crimean Allies. In Canada and Central America the British sought to alternately resist and appease American pressure.

Another important area of contention was Hawaii. The islands, with their large American population and strategic location, were a natural objective for the expansionists of the Pierce administration. The first flurry of excitement over the possibility of adding the Hawaiian kingdom to American soil was created in late 1853 when Marcy was informed by the American representative in Honolulu that the recent appointment of an American to advise the king might be a prelude to a request for annexation.[3] The rumors of such a possibility had immediately evoked loud protests from the British and French Ministers.

Sartiges, upon delivering such a protest in a November interview with Marcy, had been asked if he would not prefer American control of the Hawaiian Islands to English or Russian. This justification for American expansion was deflated by his response: "You know very well that Russia cannot, France will not, and Britain has declined to annex Hawaii."[4] But preventing the dominance of other powers in Hawaii was not, of course, the only motive of American policy. Marcy had made it clear, in answer to one of Crampton's protests, that the American desire to annex Hawaii was no passing fancy to be airily waved aside: "If the present Government of the Sandwich Islands [Hawaii] must fall, and their admission to this Union be desired, I will not conceal from you that it is highly probable that the Government as well as the Congress and People of the United States would be disposed to receive them." [5]

Even before British and French entrance into the Crimean War, Marcy had not believed that the two Allied governments would resort to war in defense of Hawaii. But he had considered it likely that they would oppose American annexation by all means short of war, and had made some efforts to find out what their precise response would be. He had written both Buchanan and Mason on December 16, asking them to inquire discreetly into the most likely policy to be pursued by both governments in the event of an American move in Hawaii. As French activity in Hawaii worried Marcy more than British moves, he was more elaborate in his instructions to Mason. After explaining to the American Minister the nature of French and British protests over the contemplated annexation, as well as the inevitability of United States acquisition of the islands, Marcy added:

> Their language to me leaves it doubtful in my mind how far Great Britain and France intend to go in preventing such a transferrence of them to this country. I am satisfied that these powers will do what they can short of a resort to actual force to defeat that object. Their Ministers, particularly the Minister of France, labored to impress me with the belief that such a transfer would be forcibly resisted; but I do not believe that these Governments would go to that extreme length. . . .
>
> The object in addressing you at present is to request you to look into this matter, and ascertain if possible without making it a matter of direct discussion, what would probably be the course of France in case of an attempt on the part of the United States to add

these Islands to our territorial possessions by negotiation or other peaceful means.[6]

The replies received in response to these questions emphasized the determination of the two powers to oppose such
an attempt, and the possibility that France, at least, might
risk an open conflict over the issue. This advice was given, of
course, before the actual outbreak of war in the East.[7] Marcy
next referred to the subject in his letters of March 11, 1854,
which he wrote to ascertain the meaning of Clarendon's speech
on the Crimean alliance (see above, page 57). At this time
the outbreak of war between the Western powers and Russia
was imminent, and Marcy warned Buchanan that the United
States was preparing to press the acquisition of Hawaii:

> The last advices from the Sandwich Islands render
> it probable that the Hawaiian rulers with the very
> general acquiescence of the people will tender the sov-
> ereignty of that country to the United States.
> Though this Government has done nothing to pre-
> cipitate such an event yet when it perceives that the sov-
> ereign power cannot be any longer retained in the fee-
> ble hands of the native rulers, and that the people desire
> to come under our control, the United States will prob-
> ably regard it to be their duty to accept the sovereignty
> of these Islands, though the act should be antagonistic
> to the schemes of the world-embracing policy of Eng-
> land and France.
> Should it be one of the objects of their "happy
> accord" and united policy as I apprehend it is, to pre-
> vent our acquisition of these Islands with the consent
> of the rulers and the people, there is reason to appre-
> hend that a collision before long may arise on this
> subject between those powers and this country.[8]

The American government was, therefore, willing to risk
a collision on the matter—at least after the onset of war in

the East. The combination of circumstances, including the propitious developments in Hawaii itself, was considered highly favorable to a successful conclusion of the affair. The plan collapsed, however, for several reasons. First of all, though the Pierce administration was willing to arouse British and French suspicion of American activity, it was unwilling to force events in the manner expected. Instead, the United States government waited upon events, which it assumed would bring Hawaii into its hands. As it turned out, the Hawaiian government was not serious about annexation, and in the absence of strong American pressure at the critical moment, the scheme failed of adoption.[9] But Marcy did not lose hope, and in fact continued to lay the groundwork for the acquisition he felt to be inevitable. Accordingly, later in the same year he asked the Russian government, through Stoeckl, what the Tsar's reaction would be. Nesselrode told his Minister to encourage any move that would create antagonism between Britain and the United States, declaring that from the Russian point of view no other legal or political considerations were important.[10]

Negotiations between the American Consul in Hawaii and the native government continued, and by late 1854 there were again rumors that an annexation treaty was about to be concluded.[11] The British and French, in response, moved a combined naval force into Hawaiian waters,[12] which did not fail to impress the American government, for once again no direct steps were taken to insure annexation. From London, Buchanan advised caution despite the presumed reluctance of the British to fight over Hawaii:

And here it is my duty to observe that I fear the annexation of these Islands, at the present moment, may result in serious consequences. After having been a close observer for more than a year in England, I am now convinced that both this Government and People earnestly desire to preserve peaceful and friendly relations with the United States. They would make many sacrifices rather than go to war with us.

In my opinion, Louis Napoleon is not inspired by similar sentiments. As a despot, he regards the existence
and the rapid advance of the Republic of the United
States as a standing censure upon his usurpation and
his tyranny.[13]

There is no clear indication whether Pierce and Marcy
would have been willing to put the matter to a test at this
time, since the outcome of the negotiations was again unfavorable—which many attributed to British influence. The
annexation treaty that was finally drawn up called for immediate statehood for the islands, a physical and political impossibility. It was felt in some quarters that this provision,
and another calling for an annuity of $300,000 to the Ha-
waiian government, were purposely added in order to make
the treaty unpalatable to the United States. This was done, it
was thought, either because the native government was only
using the negotiations to head off possible filibusters, or because the British agent in Honolulu was able to exert his
influence at the proper moment.[14] In any event, Marcy was
forced to write his Hawaiian representative that "there are
in his [Pierce's] mind strong objections to the immediate in-
corporation of the Islands in their present condition into the
Union as an independent State," and to insist that any treaty
drawn up must conform to the conditions laid down previously
by the United States.[15] But at this juncture the Hawaiian king
died, and his successor, a declared enemy of annexation, ended
the scheme for peaceful annexation of the islands. The aims
of the British and French policy of blocking American expansion were thus achieved—at least in Hawaii.

In other areas, too, American activities were met by quiet
but often effective opposition from the British and French,
and resentment of the Crimean allies was kindled as a result.
The United States and France were confronting each other in
Santo Domingo, for example. French agents in that country
had been accused earlier by American residents of plotting to
overthrow the Dominican government and install a man of
their preference in power. Marcy had instructed Mason, be-

fore he arrived at his post, to make an inquiry into the matter.[16] When Mason relayed the accusations, originally made by the American commercial agent in that country, Drouyn de Lhuys had denied any French interference in the internal affairs of Santo Domingo and declared that his government supported the status quo there. Any agent acting outside his instructions, he had added, would be recalled.[17]

The American government, could not, however, be described as a supporter of the status quo in Santo Domingo, for both the United States and France had long competed for Samana Bay, a natural harbor on the island that was potentially an excellent site for a naval base.[18] In July, 1854, the Pierce administration despatched William Cazneau as a special agent to the Dominican Republic, with orders to conclude a commercial treaty and, if possible, to buy or lease the bay. Cazneau succeeded in negotiating the treaty, including the cession of Samana Bay, in October. But under French and British pressure the Dominicans removed the article ceding the bay from the treaty before it was signed, and the Dominican Senate also added to the agreement provisions on racial equality for Dominican Negroes in the United States that were clearly unacceptable to the Southern-oriented Pierce administration. In the end, Cazneau refused to submit the mutilated document to his government, and Marcy recalled him in December.[19] But American hopes of expansion in this area continued, as did fear of French activity in the Caribbean. The *Richmond Enquirer*, for example, cited French activity in Santo Domingo during 1854 as one of the aggressive actions of the Allied powers that proved their intent to wage a war with the United States in order to destroy its power.[20]

The pattern of opposition was much the same elsewhere in Latin America in 1854. American agents in Chile and Peru complained of British and French efforts to implant "monarchistic" ideas in these countries as a prelude to expansion of their influence.[21] Both sides competed for the favor of the Brazilian Empire, and the French Chargé in Ecuador warned that government not to cooperate with the United States, which would be properly humbled after the end of the Crimean War.[22] The rivalry between the two sides was both general and persistent—clearly not just the result of chance encounters.

One of the more interesting sidelights of the South American situation during these months involved Ecuador, which owned the Galapagos Islands. Formerly thought worthless, in the early 1850s these islands were discovered to possess large quantities of guano (bat manure), a source of lucrative trade due to its value as a fertilizer. Competition between the nationals of the Allied countries and American shippers was thus extended to this area,[23] and American newspapers spoke up for the "rights" of American citizens in the guano competition, as they had supported them in struggles for neutral rights and other important principles.[24]

Americans had gained the first advantage in the Galapagos by discovering and surveying the guano deposits there, and in late 1854, despite the competition and opposition of Britain, France, and other states, the American Minister in Quito succeeded in negotiating a commercial agreement with the Ecuadorian government that brought the trade from the islands largely into American hands.[25] This brought a storm of protests from Britain, France, Spain, and Peru, and was one of the chief motivations behind the later three-power and seven-power South American Continental Treaties of 1856, which were designed largely to resist the expansion of American influence.[26] But American guano traders persisted in the following years and Congress further aided them by the passage of the "guano law," on August 18, 1856, authorizing the government to claim any unoccupied island for the purpose of the fertilizer trade. This has been described in at least one place as the "first empire" of the United States.[27]

Numerous other minor incidents troubled the relations of the United States and the Crimean allies in the 1850s. British Foreign Office records for 1854 include references to a mysterious voyage of an American ship to St. Vincent Island in the British West Indies, to the aggressive behavior of an American naval officer in the Falkland Islands, and to the visit paid by an American naval vessel to San Juan Island.[28]

All of these events caused concern to Whitehall, which viewed them as further examples, however petty, of the aggressiveness of the United States. And they appeared even more threatening as the British were in no position to counter blow for blow.

In such an atmosphere, suspicions of American activity grew to fantastic lengths. Sartiges accused the United States of trying to make China into an "American India." [29] While American aims in the Far East were limited, at this time, to commercial equality, the comment indicates the Allies' deep suspicion of American motives and their apprehension of America's growing ability to interfere successfully in far-flung regions. The behavior of the British and French governments also showed indications of regret that the United States could enjoy such relatively great freedom from effective opposition due to her geographical position and the distractions of European powers who had interests in the same areas. And there was little doubt in their minds that the Pierce administration would not hesitate to take advantage of its opportunities.

# BRITISH CONCILIATION: THE RECIPROCITY TREATY AND GREYTOWN

In 1854 the British did not succeed completely in avoiding concessions to the United States. Their course of quiet opposition and delaying tactics was successful in many cases, but sometimes American pressure was too great. One issue on which a confrontation was inevitable without some sort of settlement was the fisheries dispute, which involved the whole question of the relations between the United States and Canada. Marcy had sent the British government a draft embodying American views in late 1853, and after six months of waiting for a response he told Buchanan that the outlook was not good, since the United States would insist on its own view of American fishing rights "at any hazard." He thought that open conflict was distinctly possible: "The fishery negotiation looks dubious. If the negotiation falls through and England insists upon excluding us from the open Bays, there will be trouble." [30] The British policy of postponement was clearly at work here; as the leading historian on the subject has remarked, the British "seemed in no hurry to conclude a treaty." [31] Involvement in the Eastern Question was used, as in the Central American dispute, to justify the long delays in answering American notes and proposals. But the nature of the question, aggravated by the ever-present danger of an actual armed clash in the fishing grounds themselves, limited the possibilities of shelving it through prolonged negotiations.

The British government had, by the middle of 1854, arrived at the unequivocable conclusion that it could not afford another war at that time, and recognized that at least some of the North American issues were too pressing to be indefinitely dragged out. It was considered essential to take some of the heat out of Anglo-American relations for the time being. The British therefore decided to settle the fisheries dispute by as good a compromise as could be obtained, realizing that "with the Crimean War impending, and Russia and the United States becoming friends, the time seemed to have come for a general settlement of the outstanding issues in North America." [32] They proposed, in short, to trade use of the fisheries and free American navigation of the St. Lawrence River for trade concessions to Canada. This, they hoped, would placate the United States while providing enough economic stability in Canada to squelch the annexationist movement there. James Bruce, Earl of Elgin—Governor-General of Canada—was sent to the United States in the summer of 1854, with instructions to conclude an agreement on the best terms acceptable to the United States. According to Marcy's biographer, "this was a reflection, of course, of Britain's desire to placate the United States, since the coming of the Crimean War; her recent statement on neutral shipping had been a comparable step." [33]

The Reciprocity Treaty of 1854 was signed by Lord Elgin and Marcy on June 5, 1854, and subsequently ratified by all parties. The United States received the fullest use of the fisheries, free navigation on the St. Lawrence River and Canadian canals, and the right to transport lumber on the St. John River. Canadian subjects, in return, were to be allowed to fish along the American coast as far south as the thirty-sixth parallel, and duties on trade between the United States and Canada in most natural products were abolished.[34] The treaty was greatly favorable to the United States; of all its provisions, the reciprocal trade "was really the only valuable one granted to the inhabitants of British North America. . . ."[35]

From a larger point of view, of course, the chief advantage of the pact to the British government was the fact that it settled an explosive issue that threatened to involve Her Majesty's government in an untimely armed conflict. It also, presumably, removed the temptation for Canadians to demand annexation to the Union by providing them with an economic union that accomplished many of the same ends. Buchanan reported to Marcy that

> Lord Clarendon is evidently very much gratified with the Treaty. . . . One cause of the favor with which it is regarded in this country, is the belief that Canada, having acquired by it a free trade with the United States in her most valuable productions, will feel no desire to change her allegiance and annex herself to the American Union.[36]

Some Americans, however, arrived at the opposite conclusion—that the reciprocal trade was greatly to the advantage of the United States; economic union with Canada would lead, they reasoned, to fuller forms of association. Pierce's personal secretary later recalled that "Pierce believed that if the treaty could be ratified . . . and be permitted to work its sweet will during the years to come, a peaceful merger [of Canada and the United States] . . . was, sooner or later, inevitable." [37] In any event, the Canadian Reciprocity Treaty of 1854 was a victory for United States foreign policy. And

the Crimean War, according to the leading accounts of the
episode, was an important factor in the British decision to
meet most of the American demands.[38]

While the British were striving to dispose of one set of
issues as peacefully as possible, relations in yet another area
were approaching the boiling point. The Central American
dispute, though perhaps less of an immediate danger to relations between the two states than the fisheries disputes, presented more difficult problems to British statesmanship, for
the question of influence on the isthmus was both less suscept-
ible to compromise and more important to the relative power
positions of the two countries. The delays in British responses
to American demands on Central America were probably due
to indecision as well as purposeful stalling, since the British
government had settled on no firm policy. Clayton had even
consulted Sir Henry Bulwer, co-signer of the disputed 1850
treaty, who advised him in March, 1854, that

> Central America is no longer what it was and is daily
> becoming the most important spot of earth in the
> whole world. . . . We cannot, we must not see it Ameri-
> can, I mean belonging to the U.S.[39]

Bulwer's advice to establish a "counterpoise" to American
influence in Central America was indeed the ideal long-range
aim of British policy. But British resources could not be
strained indefinitely, and it is apparent that by late July the
Aberdeen government had decided that a policy of graceful
retreat from the Isthmus was indicated. A third step in British conciliation was to follow the earlier concessions on the
neutral rights issue and the fisheries dispute. In this they
were undoubtedly influenced by the uncompromising stand
taken by the United States, which Buchanan had confirmed
again in his vigorous and lengthy rebuttal to Clarendon's inconclusive note in May. In this note the American government
allowed none of the British arguments, continued to insist

upon return to the status of 1786 in Central America, and called upon the British in strong terms to withdraw from the disputed territories.[40]

In response the British government prepared to execute a strategic retreat. Clarendon drew up a memorandum described by one scholar as "a sweeping concession to the American point of view." [41] The British government, in Clarendon's language, would "withdraw from the Mosquito Protectorate and from any political connexion [sic] with the Mosquito Indians," requiring only that Nicaragua provide some land for the Indians' use. Great Britain had no intention "to insist upon the claim to any portion of Central America or to its adjacent islands, with the single exception of the Belize Settlement with the limits and in the terms on which it was granted to her by the Treaties with Spain of 1783 and 1786. . . ." Clarendon clearly hinted in the note that British withdrawal would be carried on whenever some proper face-saving promises on use of the territory were obtained from Nicaragua and Honduras, and the United States was invited "to exert its good offices . . . in obtaining this purpose. . . ." The concessions were to be presented as the removal of obstacles to the operation of "the wise and liberal commercial policy" of the 1850 treaty.[42]

This document was prepared in late July or early August, 1854,[43] at a time when the British were already advising the Spanish government to pacify the United States in the "Black Warrior" affair, and were preparing for the invasion of the Crimean peninsula. The precise use for which it was intended is uncertain, but according to one scholar: "Quite probably . . . it was intended for immediate use. Faced with the Crimean War, the British may well have decided to resign their role in Central America." [44] But the memorandum was never delivered. British efforts to conciliate the United States in the Central American dispute were brought to a halt by a new incident in that region which reemphasized "Yankee aggressiveness" and put British honor to the test.

One of the chief points points of friction between the two countries in Central America had been Greytown, the port city occupied by Mosquito Indians and British subjects under British protection. An American settlement had been established at Punta Arenas, across the river from Greytown, and an American transit company was located there. The inevitable incidents followed. The Pierce administration was persuaded to send an American sloop-of-war, the U.S.S. "Cyane," to protect American property in the area, and the Captain, William Hollins, was told that "these people should be taught that the United States will not tolerate these outrages." [45] The United States government apparently intended to demonstrate to the British, who could not risk war, that the United States would insist on its interpretation of the Clayton-Bulwer treaty and that "complete abandonment of former [British] claims in Central America was essential to the preservation of friendly relations with the United States." [46] This could be seen as part of the American effort to make the British feel uncomfortable enough in the area to withdraw.

Hollins' action had the unintended effect, however, of stiffening British resistance. Upon arriving in the area, the American captain delivered an ultimatum to the residents of Greytown demanding reparation for damages to American property. When his conditions were not met, the town was bombarded and then burned to the ground on July 13. The unexpected violence of this chastisement met with stern censure not only in Britain but also in the United States, where such anti-administration papers as the *New York Times* attacked the deed severely.[47] Buchanan, upon hearing of the incident, even assured the British government that the United States would almost certainly disavow the action. But the administration was of a different mind, since Hollins had not exceeded his vaguely worded instructions, and it was felt that backing down would hurt the American negotiating position. Marcy expressed the view of the administration in comments to Buchanan:

The occurrence at Greytown is an embarrassing affair. The place merited chastisement, but the severity of the one inflicted exceeded our expectation. The Government will, however, I think, stand by Capt. Hollins.[48]

United States apprehension of the British reaction did cause the administration to refrain, for the time being, from defending its action publicly. In spite of British impatience over the delay in an official explanation of what Clarendon privately referred to as an outrage "without a parallel in the annals of modern times," the American government neither disavowed nor supported the bombardment.[49] Marcy did not believe, however, that the British government would dare to go to war over the issue. He asked Buchanan's opinion of the likelihood of British intervention, adding laconically that, should London seek redress by arms, "her course will tend to bring Central American affairs to a crisis." He apparently felt that armed conflict was extremely unlikely or no great threat to the United States, and that, as a consequence, a little pushing would serve the American cause well.[50]

But the Pierce administration underrated the British. Willing to concede disputed points when this was realistically necessary, Great Britain would not be forced to retreat under such crude pressure. The loss to national prestige would have been too great to bear, in the view of the Aberdeen government. Accordingly, the effort to conciliate the United States in Central America was, for the moment, abandoned. The British determined to hold to their position come what may, while still refraining from actions that might actually bring about war. Clarendon's conciliatory note was not delivered.[51] When Buchanan, in his next interview with Clarendon, suggested that the Central American questions be settled as the fisheries dispute had been, the Foreign Secretary remarked that "the burning of Greytown was not well calculated to lead to such a result," and reiterated the standard arguments for the British position.[52] The United States had overplayed its hand.

Buchanan, at least, sensed that American pressure on the British was too strong to serve its intended purpose. In one of his next despatches, he asked Marcy to tone down the anti-British attacks in the *Union*, which were "quite too belligerent." [53] Not all leading members of the American government understood, as did Buchanan, that the advantages of neutrality must be sought with finesse as well as determination. Otherwise, the British would renounce all effort, to keep the United States genuinely neutral and consider that country as an opponent, belligerent or not.

The attitude of some British leaders toward the diplomatic issues of the Crimean War was colored by their relations with the United States. Forced to retreat in the Western hemisphere at an unpropitious moment by unmerciful American pressure, the British looked upon American attitudes toward the war with Russia with ill humor. Their resentment over the way the United States was utilizing the Crimean War to embarrass the Crown cropped out, for example, in a note from Clarendon to Buchanan during this period:

> The United States profess neutrality in the present war between the Western Powers and Russia; but have no acts been done within the United States, by citizens thereof, which accord little with the spirit of neutrality? Have not arms and ammunition and warlike stores of various kinds been sent in large quantities from the United States for the service of Russia? Have not plots been openly avowed and conspiracies entered into, without disguise or hindrance, in various parts of the Union, to take advantage of the war in which Great Britain is engaged, and to seize the opportunity for promoting insurrection in Her Majesty's Dominions and the invasion thereof by an armed Force proceeding from the United States? [54]

Clarendon's accusations were undoubtedly exaggerated as a result of the generally poor state of Anglo-American relations. But it is significant that his natural reaction was to consider the Crimean War as an integral part of relations between the two states.

# ANGLO-ALLIED RIVALRY AND
# THE OSTEND MANIFESTO

Much as the Greytown bombardment in late summer of 1854 had created a temporary stalemate in Central America, so the withering and fading away of the "Black Warrior" affair had by that time exhausted American initiative in the Caribbean. As The United States had shrunk from exploiting the *casus belli* when it was available, and was able to make no diplomatic headway by using the incident as a counter in bargaining. As a result, it was left temporarily without a scheme for the acquisition of its most desired goal. But with Britain involved in the Crimea, under pressure in Central America, and already forced to retreat in the North American fisheries, American statesmen still felt that Spain's chances of obtaining support from the Allies were slight. Mason's previously mentioned dispatch of July 20 (see pages 119-120 above), advising that France would probably not help Spain to retain Cuba, arrived as Pierce and his advisors were casting about for a new means of pressuring Spain into disposing of the island. Daniel Sickles, new Secretary of the legation in London (the appointment of George Sanders, "Young American" had not been confirmed by the Senate), was in Washington, and exerted heavy pressure on the President to make renewed efforts in this direction. In a lengthy memoir, "On the State of Europe: Its Bearing on the Policy of the United States," Sickles vigorously promoted Mason's contention that the Crimean war would prevent the Western powers from defending Cuba from American acquisition.[55]

In the absence of a clear course of action, but in recognition of the propitiousness of the moment, the United States government decided to assemble the American Ministers to Great Britain, France, and Spain, in order to arrive at a common strategy for acquiring Cuba without causing interference from the first two of these states. Marcy accordingly wrote Soulé, on August 16, directing him to meet with Buchanan and Mason "to consult together, to compare opinions as to what may be advisable, and to adopt measures for perfect concert of action in aid of your negotiations at Madrid." The main problem, Marcy said, was to determine British and French intentions concerning the annexation of Cuba. He believed that Great Britain would refrain from any hostile action but that the British government would undoubtedly try to obstruct American expansion as she had during the annexation of Texas. The government of France, moreover, "is less responsible to public opinion than that of Great Britain; it is not checked by any effective parliamentary influence and it has already indicated a tendency to intermeddle in the affairs of the American continent." Marcy concluded that "these and other considerations . . . suggest that much may be done at London and Paris either to promote directly the great object in view, or at least to clear away impediments to its successful consummation." [56]

The notorious Ostend Manifesto was the result of the conference called primarily in order to gauge the policies of Britain and France with respect to Cuba. It constitutes a recognition of the importance of events in Europe for American policy in the Caribbean, and likewise of the unecertainty about the best American policy to adopt under the prevailing circumstances.

More than one approach suggested itself for neutralizing Britain and France on the Cuban question, and even the three Ministers who were to assemble at Ostend in response to Marcy's instructions were not of the same mind. For this and other reasons, the value of the conference itself was not clear at all. As Buchanan commented to Marcy, "I can not for myself discover what benefit will result from a meeting between Mr. Soulé, Mr. Mason, and myself." [57] The intentions of the Allied powers might be judged just as effectively without such a consultation, it was reasoned, and a meeting of this sort might only arouse the suspicions and hostility of those powers whose animosity it sought to control.

Even in Soulé's own command the councils of war, while

reasonably united in their evaluation of aims and circumstances, were divided on the question of tactics. Horatio
Perry, secretary of the Madrid legation, took advantage of
Soulé's absence to go over his superior's head and warn Marcy
of Soulé's ineffectiveness in Spain. Comparing the latter's
actions in Madrid to Menshikov's in Constantinople, Perry
warned that they might have the same disastrous consequences. He denied that the United States had anything to
fear from Britain and France, who would not "risk a war
with us for the purpose of keeping Cuba out of our hands,
when fairly and peaceably offered to our embrace," but who
might very well go to war if the American government tried
to use force to gain the island. The United States, warned
Perry, should not "wantonly throw away the fair fruits of
peace and those incalculable benefits which must accrue to
neutrality on our part during the tempest of war in Europe
which has only as yet begun, in exchange for . . . bloody and
interminable war with Spain and her allies." [58]

The three diplomats who assembled at Ostend, however,
were dominated by Soulé's forceful personality and arrived at
somewhat different conclusions as to the best method for reap-
ing the advantages of neutrality. The joint communication
they drew up on October 18, supposedly confidential but soon
leaked to the world at large, asserted that "if Spain, actuated
by stubborn pride and a false sense of honor, should refuse
to sell Cuba to the United States, then, by every law, human
and divine, we should be justified in wresting it from Spain if
we possess the power." [59]

This "Manifesto" was clearly aimed at deterring European interference in the Cuban question by exhibiting the
strong determination of the United States on the issue at a
time when the Western powers were not likely to pick up the
challenge. In his letter conveying the document to Washington, Soulé argued for a forceful solution of the Cuban issue on
the grounds that the Crimean War would keep Britain and
France from aiding Spain in any war over the island. "Now is
the moment," he declared, "to be done with it; for if we
delay its solution we will certainly repent that we let escape

the fairest opportunity we could ever be furnished with, of bringing it to a decisive test." If there was to be war, he continued, "let it be now, while the great powers of this continent are engaged in that stupendous struggle which cannot but engage all their strength and tax all their energies, as long as it lasts, and may before it ends, convulse them all." With "no inducement to assume the burthen of another war," it seemed clear to Soulé that "neither England nor France would be likely to interfere with us." [60]

The repercussions of Ostend in Europe were considerable. Rumors of the conference and of its findings "sent shivers throughout the chancelleries of Europe, [and] provoked hurried consultations between the heads of the French and British admiralties." [61] But even while the stir over the Ostend Manifesto was gathering momentum on the heels of the Greytown incident, yet another controversy was to be added to the problems entangling the United States and the Crimean allies. This new quarrel involved, not surprisingly, Pierre Soulé.

The irrepressible Louisianan sought to return to Madrid from Ostend through his native France. Upon landing at Calais, however, he was denied passage through the country by the French government. While Louis Napoleon's antipathy to the republican emigré was understandable, the United States could not recognize a distinction between native-born and naturalized United States citizens. While Soulé awaited the outcome of the affair in London, Mason lodged vigorous protests in Paris.[62]

Mason reported to Marcy that the outcome of the dispute might not be peaceful, particularly if the United States insisted on a complete reversal of the action and an apology, as he thought it should. Marcy indicated full approval of his Minister's proposals.[63] The American press, especially the elements antipathetic to the Allies, was violently hostile to the action. The *New York Herald* and the *Richmond Enquirer* considered it was just another example of the French threat to the United States, which this country should seek to humble with the greatest despatch.[64] The *New Orleans Picayune* added that hatred of Napoleon was practically unanimous in the United States: "There are very few Americans who do not entertain these sentiments." [65] Even Horace Greeley's *New York Tribune* called for a suspension of diplomatic and commercial relations with France.[66]

The French government, however, backed down at the first signs of an unfriendly reaction. Drouyn de Lhuys sent a note to Mason on November 1 apologizing for the original "misunderstanding," and permitting Soulé to pass through France.[67] This eliminated the main point of contention, and the affair began to fade away even before news of it reached American shores. The British, in particular, were anxious for this to happen, and were highly critical of their Crimean allies for publishing an official explanation of its actions a week later (this move, wrote Cowley, the British Ambassador in Paris, would only revive a controversy that "may yet entail disagreeable results").[68]

If the British were afraid that French truculence might drag them into an American war, they had other cause for concern besides the Soulé affair. French-American relations in late 1854 were further embittered by an incident involving the French consul in San Francisco, Patrice Dillon. The Dillon affair had grown out of the earlier Raousset expedition in Mexico (see pages 37-38 above). In violation of an existing treaty with France, the Consul had been compelled to appear in court as a witness at a trial that had resulted from the ill-fated adventure. Although he was released as soon as the judge was informed of the terms of the consular treaty, Dillon demanded an apology for the outrage, and Sartiges took up the matter with Marcy in a number of heated interviews. At one point he advised Marcy "not to let the question slip from our diplomatic and friendly hands into the robust arms of our two peoples." [69]

During a November interview with Marcy, Sartiges finally erupted with the complaint that "you have brought us to the point where we question your good will by your constant pleas in favor of the Russian cause." Marcy justified the American attitude with a reference to the pronouncement made ten months earlier by Clarendon, "who made our people incline toward Russia by proclaiming in full Parliament that, with the end of the war in the East, England and France would come over to us to resolve questions still pending. . . ." [70] The French statesman concluded, not without reason, that the United States was using the Crimean war as a support for its unwillingness to compromise on the disputed issues.

In any event, Marcy refused to be threatened into compliance. Taking a calm attitude, he tried to transfer the Dillon dispute to Paris, where it would be considered by French statesmen with a "world-wide view of French interests." The affair was further complicated when Dillon himself was arrested, in mid-1854, for violation of the neutrality laws. Arguments and counter-arguments dragged on into 1855, with the American government willing to admit the violation of the consular treaty but unwilling to submit to Sartiges' idea of proper atonement.[71] The French government did not press the matter, even after Dillon's arrest, beyond the area of legal argument. Dillon was acquitted by a hung jury, and eventually, in late 1855, the French settled for a token salute to a French warship in San Francisco.[72] But as long as the affair persisted it was another source of irritation in the troubled relations between the United States and the Crimean allies.

In the face of these numerous problems—the Ostend Manifesto and Cuba, Central America, Hawaii, Santo Domingo, the Soulé and Dillon affairs, and a number of petty annoyances—British and French policy-makers had a difficult time in their dealings with the United States. As time went on, moreover, their reluctance to arouse American ire became more marked, especially in London, due to domestic criticism of any step tending to distract from the war effort against the major foe: Russia. Several British government leaders were particularly apprehensive over the dangers of drifting into a second war at a time when their conduct of the Crimean war was coming under heavy fire from opposition leaders. By late October and early November, the seriousness of the problem created another serious internal debate and policy review within the British government—the second such debate in three months. Lord John Russell, President of the Council in the Aberdeen government, was "tormented by the shadow of war with the United States," and urged that Clarendon's conciliatory memorandum, still undelivered after three months, be sent to Washington immediately along with a conciliatory mission to settle outstanding questions.[73] Sir James Graham, First Lord of the Admiralty, was equally disturbed by the trend of events but was less fearful of the outcome:

> We are fast "drifting" into a War with the U. States; and I am afraid that on the Grey Town and Central America Question we shall not have France on our side; whereas with respect both to Cuba and St Domingo, France will be disposed to make common cause with us, at least up to a point just short of War. But a rupture between us and the United States is the diversion which Russia anticipates in her favor and anxiously desires.
>
> In these circumstances we must be on our guard; and if a quarrel be inevitable, the St Domingo and Cuba Ground is better and safer than Grey Town and the Mosquito Protectorate. . . .[74]

Other members of the government recognized the danger but felt, particularly after the Greytown experience, that conciliation would be the surest method of encouraging American aggression. British policy, they argued, should do nothing to show that the Crimean engagement made them fearful of conflict elsewhere, or the results would be fatal. Granville Gower, Earl of Granville, government leader in the House of Lords, made a clear statement of the virtues of standing firm:

> As long as the Govt. of the United States think it necessary to strengthen themselves at home by showing their teeth abroad, all unsettled questions are dangerous, and may lead unexpectedly to fatal results. A war arising out of the protectorate of the Mosquitos be-

tween America and England would be a frightful calamity.

Nothing would lead so infallibly to such a result as to show at a moment when we are engaged in a European struggle the slightest dread on our part of the bullying disposition of President Pierce and his party. Our tone must be firm. . . .[75]

The last word belonged to Prime Minister Aberdeen, who, after weighing the alternatives carefully, finally rejected Russell's proposal for a conciliatory mission. While recognizing that Britain could not afford another war, Aberdeen continued in the general line set in August after the Greytown affair, rejecting further conciliatory moves at the moment, on the grounds that retreat would demonstrate weakness. The best policy, so long as Britain was faced with the war in the East, was still one of delay:

My great objection to the Mission is the time at which it will take place. We cannot send Carlisle, and allow him to return *se infecta*. Now, we dare not quarrel; and the alternative is concession. In ordinary times, I should not object to Carlisle's making a graceful concession of the matters in dispute; for I believe our right to be very questionable and the importance of the subject to be much exaggerated; but under the pressure of the present moment, our motives would be intelligible to the whole world. . . .

This is not the moment to abandon these claims; for it is very clear that the concession is made to Russia, and not to the United States alone. . . .[76]

The veto of Russell's conciliatory mission left British policy with the problem of effecting the right balance between quiet opposition and nonprovocation. It was important, while attempting to contain American expansionism, to avoid any additional inflammatory issues and to arouse the American government as little as possible in the disputes that were unavoidable. When, immediately after the Ostend gathering, Spain sought French and British backing for ridding themselves of Soulé, for example, the Allied governments urged the Spanish to drop the idea. Cowley told the Spanish Minister to France that Spain would make a grave mistake by raising more issues with the United States at that time. The French government also communicated to Madrid its opposition to any action that would further embitter American relations with the three Western European countries. Spain decided to follow the counsels of her sponsors and endure Soulé; the British Minister in Spain was able to tell his government in late November that "the Spanish Government will act as you wish, and do nothing about Soulé at this moment." [77]

The trend of British policy was also reflected by Buchanan's reports of his interviews with Clarendon toward the end of the year. The discussions covered the same points of tension again and again, with the two statesmen sparring over the legal questions, and sometimes touching on broader political implications, but inevitably accomplishing little. During Buchanan's first meeting with Clarendon following the Ostend conference, for example, the conversation covered Cuba, Hawaii, and Santo Domingo, among other matters. In each case Buchanan defended American policies in these areas, arguing that the acquisition of Cuba was a necessity, that the Hawaiians had the right to ask for annexation if they so chose, and that the naval base at Samana was needed for American security. Clarendon challenged all these points, without making any definite statements on what British policy would be if acquisition of any of the three became imminent. Buchanan thought, however, that "we might acquire Cuba with far less danger of serious consequences than would result from the acquisition of the Sandwich Islands," which, he added, "may result in serious consequences." The greater danger of armed interference, he continued to believe, was from France, not Britain. [78]

The arguments over the Central American question

dragged on, with interminable legalistic quibbling over the interpretation of the Clayton-Bulwer Treaty. Clarendon avoided any conclusive actions. When Buchanan suggested that the dispute should be settled so that construction of a trans-isthmian railroad or canal could begin, the Foreign Secretary replied that he did not believe such a project was of much importance. The good understanding of the two countries, he added, was of much greater significance. He also admitted, in Buchanan's words, that "their existing war with Russia was a good reason why they should feel at the time doubly anxious to cultivate the best relations with the United States." [79] But judged by Clarendon's actions, British conciliation for the moment was limited to verbal assurances of friendship and willingness to discuss the issues; it did not include the surrender of a solitary point of substance.

The Crimean War came up more than once in these discussions. When Clarendon hinted at the possibility of arbitrating the Central American question, Buchanan had "playfully observed that it would now be difficult to find an impartial umpire, as they had gone to war with our arbitrator, the Emperor of Russia." The "playful" reference to American-Russian friendship was but a prelude, however, to more serious and far-reaching discussions of the connections between events in the Old and New Worlds. In the same despatch Buchanan reported that "the balance of power in Europe,—the resistance which we would make to the application of this doctrine to America—the threats thrown out in some of the British Journals that England and France would regulate us after they had done with Russia . . . are topics upon which I often comment." [80] American public sympathy for the Tsarist cause continued to serve as a topic of discussion also, and one apparently taken seriously by the British, for Buchanan reported in late 1854 that: "We do not stand as well with the popular element in England as we did six months ago." [81] When Clarendon broached this subject later, Buchanan's reply was no less frank than British statements on the matter:

In regard to the sympathy expressed in the United States for Russia, I told him that . . . the true cause was the belief that England and France were disposed to interfere with the rights of the United States on the other side of the Atlantic. . . . I referred . . . to the recent conduct of the British and French Consuls acting in concert to prevent the United States from concluding a Treaty of Commerce with the Dominican Republic; and observed that on all occasions in which the United States were interested, the officials of the two Governments appeared "to hunt in couples," and to be ever ready to do us injury.[82]

# THE RECOIL FROM OSTEND IN AMERICAN POLICY

Greytown and Ostend led both the British and the Americans to a reappraisal of their policies in the struggles between the two powers. Just as the British and French faced the problem of dealing with American expansionism while occupied elsewhere, American policy-makers had to determine the best use of the advantages provided by the war. By late 1854 and early 1855 the Pierce administration was reassessing its aims and methods. Some of its schemes had failed, the outcome of others was still uncertain. The question of where, and how hard, to push, was a constant problem. The most difficult decisions to be made were those concerning American plans for the annexation of Cuba.

Although the Central American talks dragged on and the issues involved lost some of their immediacy, the Ostend meeting, which might be viewed realistically as a temporary substitute for a Cuban policy, sharpened the vital question of what policy the United States should adopt with regard to the island. Would the United States follow up its policy of verbal belligerence with a more forceful effort to obtain the cession of Cuba, or would it again choose the alternative of waiting for events to occur which would bring about the acquisition it considered inevitable? As opposed to Soulé, Marcy felt that as long as Cuba would gravitate to the United States in time, why engage the country in another war fought on flimsy pretexts so soon after the Mexican conflict? He also hoped that British and French suspicions might be moderated, and even their acquiescence obtained by a less boisterous posture.

It was Marcy who won the day in the administration councils. In his first instructions to Soulé after the Ostend conference, he rebuked the American Minister for his lack of conciliatory efforts in Spain, which had ruined chances for the purchase of Cuba, and flatly declared that, contrary to the impression created by the Ostend Manifesto, the United States would not go to war to obtain it.[83] Soulé resigned his post soon after and returned to the United States.[84] Marcy made quite clear his view as to how the island might be acquired in a letter to a friend, "Cuba would be a very desirable possession if it came to us in the right way, but we can not afford to get it by robbery or theft." [85]

Having appeared sufficiently belligerent to arouse the European powers thoroughly and discourage their conciliatory efforts, the Pierce Administration then left itself in an anomalous position by stopping short of the actual belligerence that would have gained its ends. This can be clearly seen in Pierce's second annual message of December 4, 1854. While still taking a moderate position on the Cuban and Central American questions, the American President startled his own country and Europe by a lengthy and violent defense of the Greytown bombardment, which had occurred five months earlier. He defended Hollins' action on the grounds that "justice required that reparation should be made for so many and such gross wrongs. . . ." [86] Much of the benefit that might have been derived from the new moderation in American policy was thus dissipated in a defense of past history. European suspicions were not allayed.

Pierce also delivered another ringing defense of the right of the United States to expand without interference from Europe:

Some European powers have regarded with dis-
quieting concern the territorial expansion of the United
States. This rapid growth has resulted from the legitimate exercise of sovereign rights belonging alike to
all nations, and by many liberally exercised. Under
such circumstances it could hardly have been expected
that those among them which have within a compara-
tively recent period subdued and absorbed ancient
kindoms, planted their standards on every continent . . .
would look with unfriendly sentiments upon the acquisitions of this country, in every instance honorably
obtained, or would feel themselves justified in imputing
our advancement to a spirit of aggression or to a pas-
sion for political predominance.[87]

Reaffirming the American belief in the insulation of the New
World from the Old, the President sought to define the limits
of French and British interference on the basis of this principle. The United States, he warned, would not accept the
European concept of a balance of power. The Crimean War
had not affected the United States, which observed the separation of hemispheres:

Although our attention has been arrested by pain-
ful interest in passing events, yet our country feels
no more than the slight vibrations of the convulsions
which have shaken Europe. . . .
The wise theory of this Government, so early
adopted and steadily pursued, of avoiding all entangling
alliances has hitherto exempted it from many complications in which it would otherwise have become involved. Notwithstanding this our clearly defined and
well-substantiated course of action and our geographical position, so remote from Europe, increasing disposition has been manifested by some of its Governments to supervise and in certain respects to direct
our foreign policy. In plans for adjusting the balance
of power among themselves they have assumed to take

us into account, and would constrain us to conform our conduct to their views.[88]

While many of its foreign policy decisions demonstrated an instinctive appreciation of the effects of the Crimean War on the American position, the Pierce administration was also blinded to other implications of the war by its own ideological assumptions. American statesmen sometimes displayed a seeming unawareness of what, judging from the reactions of their opponents, was the most effective weapon in their arsenal. In the first place, the American government could not decide between a policy of gentlemanly pressure and one of open belligerence, thereby losing the advantages to be gained by following either course. Second, the President and his administration never had a clear understanding of how to exploit the advantage offered by the Crimean War, in part perhaps because of their own stated belief on the irrelevance of European embroilments for Western hemisphere affairs. By the beginning of 1855, however, there was less internal division over foreign policy, and the government could still hope for the fulfillment of at least a few of its far-reaching aims. The same opportunities and the same preoccupations that had shaped the past year would continue to guide the events of 1855.

# NOTES

1. Soulé to Marcy, October 20, 1854, Despatches from Spain, NA, RG 59.
2. George Gordon, Earl of Aberdeen, to Clarendon, November 5, 1854, quoted in Van Alstyne, *American Historical Review*, XLII, 498.
3. Luther Severance to Marcy, September 5, 1853, Despatches from Hawaii, NA, RG 59.
4. Sartiges to Drouyn de Lhuys, November 27, 1853, quoted in Blumenthal, *op. cit.*, pp. 63-64.
5. Crampton to Clarendon, November 20, 1854, quoted in Spencer, *op. cit.*, p. 390.
6. Marcy to Mason, December 16, 1853, Instructions to France, NA, RG 59. See also instructions to Buchanan of same date.

7. Buchanan to Marcy, January 28, 1854, Despatches from Great Britain, NA, RG 59. Mason to Marcy, February 9, 1854, Despatches from France, NA, RG 59. Spencer, *op. cit.*, p. 390.

8. Marcy to Buchanan, March 11, 1854, Instructions to Great Britain, NA, RG 59.

9. See Spencer, *op. cit.*, p. 391. British sources confirm the suspicions of American diplomats that the British and French agents in Hawaii influenced this result. Silverstein, *op. cit.*, p. 72.

10. Nesselrode to Stoeckl, November 4/16, 1854, quoted in Golder, *American Historical Review*, XXXI, 467.

11. Marcy to David L. Gregg, April 4, 1854, Instructions to Hawaii, NA, RG 59; Spencer, *op. cit.*, p. 392.

12. Blumenthal, *op. cit.*, p. 64.

13. Buchanan to Marcy, October 31, 1854, Despatches from Great Britain, NA, RG 59.

14. Spencer, *op. cit.*, p. 393; Silverstein, *op. cit.*, p. 72.

15. Marcy to Gregg, January 31, 1855, Instructions to Hawaii, NA, RG 59.

16. Marcy to Mason, December 22, 1853, Instructions to France, NA, RG 59.

17. Mason to Marcy, April 22, 1854, Despatches from France, NA, RG 59.

18. Blumenthal, *op. cit.*, p. 49.

19. Nichols, *Franklin Pierce*, p. 397.

20. *Richmond Enquirer* (November 16, 1854; October 11, 1855).

21. W. R. Manning, *op. cit.*, V, 241-46; X, 749-53.

22. Blumenthal, *op. cit.*, p. 30.

23. For the complete story of this chapter of American foreign policy, see Roy Franklin Nichols, *Advance Agents of American Destiny* (Philadelphia: University of Pennsylvania Press, 1956), pp. 157-201.

24. See *New Orleans Picayune* (November 18, 1854,; March 30, 1855).

25. Philo White to Marcy, November 24, 1854, Despatches from Ecuador, NA, RG 59.

26. Gustave A. Nuermberger, "The Continental Treaties of 1856; An American Union 'Exclusive of the United States,'" *Hispanic American Historical Review*, XX (February, 1940), 33.

27. Nichols, *Advance Agents of American Destiny*, pp. 184-85.

28. Cited by Van Alstyne, *Journal of Modern History*, XI, 171-72; Spencer, *op. cit.*, pp. 315-16.

29. Sartiges to Drouyn de Lhuys, July 3, 1854, quoted in Blumenthal, *op. cit.*, p. 65.

30. Marcy to Buchanan, March 11, 1854, Instructions to Great Britain, NA, RG 59.

31. Charles Tansill, *The Canadian Reciprocity Treaty of 1854* (Baltimore: The Johns Hopkins University, 1922), p. 62.

32. John Bartlett Brebner, *North Atlantic Triangle* (New Haven: Yale University Press, 1945), p. 156.

33. *Ibid.*; Spencer, *op. cit.*, p. 303.

34. Miller, *op. cit.*, VI, 667-72.

35. Tansill, *op. cit.*, p. 81; See also Spencer, *op. cit.*, p. 307.

36. Buchanan to Marcy, August 18, 1854, Despatches from Great Britain, NA, RG 59.

37. Sidney Webster, "Franklin Pierce and the Canadian Reciprocity Treaty of 1854," *Proceedings of the Grafton and Cooe County Bar Association* (1892), p. 380, quoted in Nichols, *Franklin Pierce*, p. 344.

38. For confirmation of the importance of the Crimean War on the British position in the fisheries-reciprocity negotiations, drawn from British sources, see Silverstein, *op. cit.*, pp. 72-73.

39. Bulwer to Clarendon, March 1854, quoted in Van Alstyne, *American Historical Review*, XLII, 495.

40. Buchanan to Clarendon, July 22, 1854, in Moore, *The Works of James Buchanan*, IX, 216-41.

41. Van Alstyne, *Journal of Modern History*, XI, 175.

42. "Memorandum by Clarendon on the Clayton-Bulwer Treaty," quoted in Van Alstyne, *American Historical Review*, XLII, 496-97.

43. The memorandum is not dated, but was almost certainly written between July 22 and receipt of the news of the Greytown incident in early August. Van Alstyne estimates a date of August 1 for its composition. *Ibid.*, 496; Van Alstyne, *Journal of Modern History*, XI, 176.

44. *Ibid.*

45. U.S. Congress, *House Executive Documents*, No. 126, 33rd Cong., 1st Sess., pp. 2, 19-20; Spencer, *op. cit.*, p. 311.

46. Williams, *op. cit.*, p. 177.

47. Williams, *op. cit.*, pp. 178-80; Spencer, *op. cit.*, p. 313; *New York Times* (August 1, 1854).

48. Buchanan to Marcy, August 18, 1854, Despatches from Great Britain, NA, RG 59; Marcy to Buchanan, August 8, 1854, Instructions to Great Britain, NA, RG 59.

49. Williams, *op. cit.*, pp. 181-82; Clarendon to Crampton, August 31, September 21, 1854, quoted *ibid.*, pp. 180, 182.

50. Marcy to Buchanan, August 8, 1854, Instructions to Great Britain, NA, RG 59; Spencer, *op. cit.*, p. 313.

51. Van Alstyne, *Journal of Modern History*, XI, 175-76; Spencer, *op. cit.*, p. 317.

52. Buchanan to Marcy, August 18, 1854, Despatches from Great Britain, NA, RG 59.

53. Buchanan to Marcy, September 1, 1854, *ibid.*

54. Clarendon to Buchanan, September 27, 1854, in Moore, *The Works of James Buchanan*, IX, 412.

55. Edgcumb Pinchon, *Dan Sickles* (Garden City, N.Y.: Doubleday, Doran and Company, Inc., 1945), p. 46; Nichols, *Franklin Pierce*, pp. 357-58.

56. Marcy to Soulé, August 16, 1854, Instructions to Spain, NA, RG 59.

57. Buchanan to Marcy, September 1, 1854, Despatches from Great Britain, NA, RG 59.

58. Perry to Marcy, September 6, 1854, Despatches from Spain, NA, RG 59.

59. The Ostend papers are collected in U.S., Congress, *House Executive Documents*, No. 93, 33rd Cong., 2nd Sess., 1854.

60. Soulé to Marcy, October 20, 1854, Despatches from Spain, NA, RG 59.

61. Pinchon, *op. cit.*, p. 48.

62. U.S., Congress, *House Executive Documents*, No. 1, 33rd Cong., 2nd Sess., 1854, pp. 20-28.

63. Mason to Marcy, October 25, 30, November 11, 1854, Despatches from France, NA, RG 59; Marcy to Mason, November 14, December 13, 1854, Instructions to France, NA, RG 59.

64. *New York Herald* (November 13, 14, 1854); *Richmond Enquirer* (November 16, 1854).

65. *New Orleans Picayune* (November 18, 1854).

66. *New York Tribune* (November 13, 16, 1854).

67. Drouyn de Lhuys to Mason, November 1, 1854, quoted in Blumenthal, *op. cit.*, p. 83.

68. Cowley to Clarendon, November 8, 1854, quoted in Ettinger, *op. cit.*, p. 424.

69. Spencer, *op. cit.*, p. 327. Sartiges to Marcy, July 31, 1854, Notes from the French Legation, NA, RG59. Blumenthal, *op. cit.*, pp. 80-81.

70. Sartiges to Drouyn de Lhuys, November 26, 1854, quoted in Ettinger, *op. cit.*, p. 435.

71. *Ibid.* Marcy to Mason, May 30, June 8, July 14, September 11, 29, October 23, December 13, 1854, Instructions to France, NA, RG 59. Mason to Marcy, June 26, July 15, 1854, Despatches from France, NA, RG 59.

72. Marcy to Mason, January 18, September 10, 1855, Instructions to France, NA, RG 59.

73. Van Alstyne, *Journal of Modern History*, XI, 176; Russell to Clarendon, November 4, 1854, quoted *ibid.*

74. Graham to Clarendon, October 24, 1854, quoted in Van Alstyne, *American Historical Review*, XLII, 497-98.

75. Granville to Clarendon, October 18, 1854, quoted *ibid.*

76. Aberdeen to Clarendon, November 5, 1854, quoted in *ibid.* George William Frederick Howard, Earl of Carlisle, was then rector of the University of Aberdeen.

77. Ettinger, *op. cit.*, pp. 450, 453; Drouyn de Lhuys to Turgot, November 25, 1854, John Herbert Carodoc, Baron Howden to Clarendon, November 24, 30, 1854, quoted *ibid.*

78. Buchanan to Marcy, October 31, 1854, Despatches from Great Britain, NA, RG 59. See also despatch of November 1, in which the argument over Cuba is enlarged.

79. Buchanan to Marcy, December 30, 1854, *ibid.*

80. Buchanan to Marcy, November 21, 1854, *ibid.*

81. Buchanan to John Forney, December 14, 1854, in Moore, *The Works of James Buchanan*, IX, 284.

82. Buchanan to Marcy, January 19, 1855, Despatches from Great Britain, NA, RG 59.

83. Marcy to Soulé, November 13, 1854, Instructions to Spain, NA, RG 59. Blumenthal, *op. cit.*, p. 57. Ettinger, *op. cit.*, p. 396. Spencer, *op. cit.*, pp. 326-27.

84. Soulé to Marcy, December 17, 1854, Despatches from Spain, NA, RG 59. Soulé typically tried to make his departure from Spain appear as a recall by his government and a rebuke to Spain. The Spanish government apparently was not fooled by the trick, and failed to give the reaction that Soulé probably expected. Soulé to Claudio Anton de Luzuriaga, Spanish Minister of Foreign Affairs, January 28, 1855, in W. Manning, *op. cit.*, XI, 834; Perry to Marcy, February 6, 1855, Despatches from Spain, NA, RG 59.

85. Marcy to Lorenzo Shepard, April 15, 1855, quoted in Learned, *op. cit.*, p. 215, and Spencer, *op. cit.*, p. 339.

86. Richardson, *op. cit.*, V, 280-84, especially p. 282.

87. *Ibid.*, 274-75.

88. *Ibid.*, 273-74.

# Repeat Peformance, 1855

## CHAPTER SIX

England and France are destined to be the salvation of the world, which is threatened by Russia and her allies on the East, and by the United States on the West.[1]

## THE RENEWAL OF HOSTILITY

"History," said the American Minister to Turkey, "presents no example of such unpardonable imbecility, combined with such gross ignorance on the part of a general, his staff and the commissariat department of his army." The object of this contempt was the British army in Crimea, suffering through its first winter of the war. Spence claimed that the French military effort showed great energy and organization in contrast, and that therefore "our country has more to apprehend from an intervention on the part of France with our foreign policy, than from England." [2]

Winter was the main enemy of all the Crimean belligerents in the first two months of 1855. Fighting was difficult, and both sides were marking time until the opening of the

169

Vienna Conference in March. This latest attempt at a peaceful solution to the conflict was the result of Russian acceptance of the "four-point" proposal made by the Allied powers and Austria. Except for the frequently expressed belief that France had proved her aggressive intentions and abilities to be greater than previously thought,[3] recent developments in the Crimea itself had brought about little significant change in the war's effect on American foreign policy.

There were, however, other important developments in European politics that were closely followed by American policy-makers. Two of the three leading belligerents had a change of government early in 1855. The accession of Tsar Alexander II, after the death of his father Nicholas I on March 2, brought about no immediate marked changes in the personnel or policies of the Russian regime. But the fall of the Aberdeen government, and the appointment of Henry John Temple, Viscount Palmerston, as Prime Minister, meant more than a stiffening of the British attitude toward the Crimean War. Palmerston, a statesman long noted for his belligerence, was determined to curtail the expansionist tendencies of both Russia and the United States by whatever means were required. The new Prime Minister promised a vigorous prosecution of the British war effort in Crimea, which he and a majority of the House of Commons had characterized as weak, inefficient, and lacking in determination. Regarding Britain's disputes with the United States, Buchanan noted laconically, "The change will not be for the better so far as our Country is concerned." [4]

In later despatches the American Minister gave his government a more complete appraisal of the background and probable policies of the new British leader. Stating his belief that the Central American dispute would have been settled had Aberdeen remained in power a few weeks longer, he remarked that "the accession of Lord Palmerston, should he retain his often expressed opinions, will render this impossible." [5] Palmerston, he noted, was really "the author of the modern Mosquito Protectorate," having been Minister for Foreign Affairs during the important periods of its occupation by Britain in 1841 and 1848. "I might refer," he added, "to other acts and declarations of his Lordship at different periods indicating his aggressive policy in regard to Central America, but this would be wholly unnecessary." The United States, therefore, could have little hope "that he will ever carry into execution the Clayton and Bulwer Treaty according to what we firmly believe to be its true construction." [6] The outlook for relations between the United States and Britain was, to say the least, inauspicious.

It is no surprise, therefore, that Americans' sympathy for the Russian position in the Eastern war was not diminished by Palmerston's approach to Anglo-American affairs. And their appreciation of the value of Britain's preoccupation in Crimea was, if anything, increased. Not all public figures, of course, were as frank as Alexander Stephens, the Georgia expansionist, who thought the Pierce administration far too timid in its push outward:

> I have seen for near twelve months that our people were deceived and *bamboozled* by this administration upon the subject of Cuban acquisition . . . . You are right sir—now is the time to act . . . while England and France have their hands full in the East.[7]

Even the relatively moderate Buchanan, who often expressed his admiration for Anglo-Saxon institutions and culture, showed little sympathy for the British attitude toward Russia. After the breakdown of the Vienna Conference over Russia's refusal to demilitarize the Black Sea, for example, he asked rhetorically: "What would be thought by the Government [Great Britain] if an attempt were made on the part of a Foreign Power to limit the number of British vessels of war in the English Channel?" A Russian offer to open the Black Sea to all nations was, he thought, the only effective and honorable solution.[8] Like most Americans in public life, he tended to view British demands in areas remote from England with an abiding suspicion.

Marcy echoed these views in his reply, commenting that "in its true aspect," the Crimean War "appears to be a war against Russia, justified by a suspicion that the Emperor intended to do what she has been in the practice of doing for a century and a half—encroaching upon, absorbing, the territories of other nations." [9] His instinctive sympathy for the Tsar was clearly founded, to some extent, upon the similarity of this situation to the situation in the Western hemisphere (as he saw it). The United States sympathized with Russia, in other words, because it faced the same type of "obstruction" to its growth from Britain and France. As Marcy explained the issue, such sentiments should cause no surprise to anyone:

> In looking over a file of the "London Times," I observe in one of them a complaint against the United States for want of sympathy for the allies. . . . The allegation is, to some extent, true. It is a matter of some surprise that the British Ministry, and persons so well informed as the editors of the "Times," should not be aware of the cause of this phase of public sentiment in this country, regarding Great Britain as well as France, since the "entente cordial," has placed herself in our path, and attempted to obstruct us in whatever direction we have attempted to move. . . .
>
> The want of good faith on the part of Great Britain in regard to the Clayton and Bulwer treaty, and the constant succession of offensive articles in the British press against the Government and people of this country, are well calculated to extinguish all sympathy in our people with England in her present cause. . . .[10]

Hostile comments in the Allied press and by the government leaders in the Allied countries helped to keep mutual suspicion and animosity alive. One remark that caused particular bitterness in early 1855 on the American side of the Atlantic, was the warning of the *London Times,* considered

the organ of the British government, that the British fleet
"which can winter in the Baltic can summer in the Gulf of
Mexico." [11] But an even greater stir, equivalent in impact
to that created by Clarendon's speech a year earlier, was
caused by Louis Napoleon's address to the French Legisla-
tive Chambers on December 26, 1854:

> What firmer bonds can there in fact be, than those
> bearing the names of victories belonging to the two
> armies, recalling a common glory? Than the same
> anxieties and the same hopes, agitating the two coun-
> tries? Than the same views and the same intentions,
> animating the two Governments in every corner of the
> globe [*sur tous les points du globe*]? [12]

The strongest reaction to these remarks of the French
Emperor was registered in the chambers of the Senate on
February 20, 1855, when Lewis Cass, the Michigan war-
horse, took the floor. Napoleon's words, which he quoted,
confirmed in his eyes the intentions denied by Clarendon
with regard to his own speech in 1854:

> The language here used, with respect to this
> union of policy is identical in its meaning with that
> employed by Lord Clarendon, and it was used at the
> first legislative convocation after the British Secretary
> of State had publicly proclaimed the same sentiments.
> And it is a significant fact, that the address of the
> Emperor must have been under consideration at the
> time Lord Palmerston visited Paris, and when the
> British statesman was reported to be in the habit of
> daily intercourse with the French ruler. I suppose, that
> among the strong points of Lord Palmerston's char-
> acter, there is none stronger than his bitter aversion
> to this country. . . .
> Restricting the inquiry to the period of the new
> relations of confidence, which have recently sprung up
> between France and England, it will be found, on

examination, that these powers have acted in concert, in opposition to every measure of our foreign policy, which could excite their jealousy; and, I may add, but too successfully. They seem to have followed us over the world, watching, counteracting, and opposing, from the loading of a cargo of guano, to the acquisition of a kingdom. At the Sandwich Islands their influence has been in constant operation, openly used, and pertinaciously exerted. In Dominica they tracked us, and frustrated, it is said, a very reasonable arrangement, to which there could be no proper objection, unless that it was acceptable and useful to the United States, and was disapproved by the two great American regulators. And so at the Gallipagos [sic] Islands, where interests far more reasonable than any views of acquisition were struck down by the same interposition. . . .

If we were to regulate our conduct by their examples rather than by their precepts, and interpose ourselves between them and the accomplishment of the projects of aggrandizement, forming combinations with other Powers for this purpose, we should have occasion for action from the rising to the setting of the sun, in mighty continents, as well as in the smallest isles. . . .

Cass also noted the reaction of the Spanish to Napoleon's declarations. He quoted the *Diario de la Marina,* newspaper of the Spanish government, which declared on January 28, 1855, that "all civilized Europe" was supporting the alliance against the Tsar. The British and French accord held no dangers, *Diario* continued, for powers respecting international law, and American sympathy for Russia was viewed as evidence of the rapacity and greed of the American government: "For the advocates of the celebrated Monroe Doctrine . . . who . . . would wish to imitate the conduct of Russia, and appropriate a whole continent, without obstacle, there is no doubt but that this European system must be exceedingly disagreeable." Such an outlook suggests a conception of world bipolarity, more imagined perhaps than real, but

nevertheless a reflection of the events affecting Spanish interest in both the New and Old Worlds.

American interpretations of the world situation reflected
the same phenomena from, of course, a different point of
view. Admitting American partiality for the Tsar, Cass referred to a natural "process" clearly related to the prevailing
American attitudes toward Britain and France. Defending
the shift of opinion away from the Allies to support of
Russia, he noted:

> Far beyond the work of any Administration is
> this alteration in the views of the American people.
> For that it has taken place no one doubts. I have felt
> the process going on in my own mind. . . .
> It is a subject of vehement reproach against us
> in England, that we exhibit such national ingratitude,
> by not sympathizing with the "noble conduct" of France
> and England, as the Courier calls it, who are now
> fighting the battles of the world, "the battles of Chris-
> tianity and civilization," protected, as the Courier also
> says, by this combination.
> Now, sir, I do not believe one word of all this. I
> believe France and England are fighting their own
> battles, just as Russia is fighting hers. And each for
> its own purposes. This charge of ingratitude against
> our country is not a new one.[13]

Cass was followed on the Senate floor by Senator James
M. Mason of Virginia, Chairman of the Foreign Relations
Committee, who had been "armed with data" from administration files on the united obstructist tactics of Britain and
France. The Pierce administration, humbled in the 1854 elec-
tions and facing a growing crisis in the slavery question,
was thus trying, as Pierce's biographer expressed it, "to
make capital out of the foreign situation." [14] Pierce, according to this account, "still hoped that a vigorous foreign

policy might retrieve the fortunes of the Democratic party, in spite of the Cuban failure." [15]

Mason outlined the pattern of British and French opposition to American policies, documenting his account. Britain, he said, had violated the Clayton-Bulwer treaty and the Monroe doctrine by encroaching on Central American territory; the bombardment of Greytown was the result of British policy. French agents plotted against the United States in Santo Domingo and Haiti. The two powers together were guilty of countless acts of obstruction and aggression throughout Latin America and elsewhere. They had pressured Guatemala on European claims, interfered with American plans for the annexation of Hawaii, thwarted the commercial treaty with the Dominican government, and attempted to obstruct the American agreement with Ecuador on the guano trade in the Galapagos Islands. They had apparently united to prevent the advance of the United States in any corner of the world, and Americans, declared Mason, should take cognizance of the situation:

> I have, Mr. President, given the proofs. Taken by themselves, detached one from the other, they might not amount to much to impress the public mind; but collect them and collate them, and who can shut his eyes to the fact that, from reasons undisclosed, but which we have a right to conjecture while they are undisclosed, the two great maritime Powers of Europe consider themselves entitled of right to interfere here upon our coasts and on our borders with matters purely of American policy?

Mason, too, extended his comments to the Crimean War and the lessons that could be learned from that conflict regarding Allied policy:

> What is the present war about? The Western European Powers declare that it is to prevent the

aggrandizement of Russia at the expense of Turkey.
. . . They assume and exercise the right, by curbing
here and retrenching there, to take care that one
Government does not grow too strong for another.
And here, if we are capable of reading the signs of
the times—disavowed, not admitted, disclaimed inoffi-
cially [sic]—we find that for some undisclosed purpose,
they are at their work on this continent; and they
have done it effectually, seriously to the detriment of
the maritime interests of this country, in the case of
St. Domingo and Ecuador, if not at the Sandwich
Islands. We cannot shut our eyes to the fact they they
have such a policy. Is it to be submitted to? [16]

Another season of contest was underway. The Pierce
administration clearly considered the "Crimean coalition"
the chief obstacle to its foreign policy, and expected further
confrontation with those powers. And one of the major tasks
of American diplomacy, inevitably related to this, was chart-
ing a reasonable and effective course as a neutral in the
Crimean War itself.

# "EL DORADO": CUBA AGAIN

The renewed animosity of American-Allied relations,
and the failure to work out a peaceful solution to the Crimean
War, occurred almost simultaneously with yet another incident involving Cuba. In early 1855 Spanish authorities on the
island unwittingly gave American statesmen another opportunity to interfere in Cuba, similar to the "Black Warrior"
seizure of the year before. (The settlement of that affair
ironically had just been approved by Pierce.) An abortive
revolt on the island, in early March, had set the stage for
the controversial incident. On March 6 a Spanish vessel of
war, engaged in enforcing the state of siege declared by the
authorities, had fired upon the American steamer "El Dorado."
Following receipt of this news, on March 14, American
opinion was further outraged by the arrest of the United

States Consul at Sagua la Grande, I. C. P. Thompson, for alleged participation in the revolt. Reaction to these incidents was, of course, violent. The United States home squadron of six naval vessels was sent, on April 10, to prevent any further Spanish attempts to interfere with American merchant marine vessels.[17]

Marcy had written instructions on the affair to Perry, Chargé d'Affaires *ad interim* in Madrid, on April 9. The settlement of the "Black Warrior" incident, said Marcy, would have quieted the Cuban question in the United States "had not the announcement of it been accompanied by the news of the unjustifiable attack upon the steamer "El Dorado" on the high seas while employed in transporting the United States mail, and the arrest of Mr. I. C. P. Thompson . . ." Perry was to convey to Spain a clear warning that "her pretension to visit and search our vessels upon the open sea in the vicinity of her West India possessions, will not be acquiesced in." Thompson's treatment, Marcy maintained, was "a case of the violation of personal rights which calls for prompt and ample redress." He told Perry to inform Spain further that "if their conduct [i.e. of the Cuban authorities] is approved and upheld by the home government and a change of policy in this respect is not manifested, a rupture of the peace between the two countries will be very likely to ensue." [18]

Again the United States had to gauge the reactions of the British and French to the possibility of war with Spain. As before, events in Europe provided a certain margin of comfort. Perry, in anticipating the importance of this question, had already written Marcy that the United States would undoubtedly be free of Allied interference in any "well directed effort . . . for the just and honorable arrangement of all our diffculties with Spain. . . ." Since Spain had refused to lend support in the fight against Russia, he believed that the Allies would not feel obligated to support Spain in a war over Cuba. Furthermore, they were busy: "England and France are both too much occupied in the contest against Russia to be desirous of undertaking anything on the side of

Spain having for its object more than the maintenance of tranquillity here, let her go where she may." [19]

Marcy had apparently decided in the meantime, however, to rely on political pressure and other peaceful methods to force concessions from Spain. He first instructed Augustus Dodge, the new American Minister to Spain, to press for the establishment of direct contacts with the Cuban authorities and for an increase in commerce between the United States and Cuba. Dodge was also to seek assurances that the internal policy of the Cuban authorities would be in accord with the interests of the inhabitants of Cuba, "and as such calculated to tranquillize the people of the United States." The possibility of war was not, however, dismissed; Dodge was told to exert himself to the utmost to attain these objectives, "fully prepared, if you find no correspondent sentiments entertained by the Spanish Government, to be summoned at any moment to relinquish your mission and return to the United States." [20]

As might have been expected, the Spanish proved unwilling to entertain the idea of American ties with Cuba in any form, either as an atonement for the "El Dorado" affair or for any other reason. They succeeded again in dragging out the talks until the controversy was no longer heated and the war fever had abated. As it was unwilling to make Spanish procrastination or refusal of full satisfaction a *casus belli*, the Pierce administration gained little from the chance offered by the attack on the "El Dorado." The affair faded from public memory; by July, Marcy could remark to Dodge that "you are aware that the firing at and detention of the mail steamer El Dorado occasioned at the time considerable sensibility in this country." [21] Over a year later, Marcy was still rejecting Spanish explanations of the all-but-forgotten incident as "unsatisfactory" and explaining that the views of the American government were unchanged.[22]

The Pierce administration was able in fact, to gain nothing from Spain during the remainder of its tenure. Spanish suspicion of the North American republic had grown to such proportions that Madrid would not even contemplate

a mutually beneficial commercial treaty. The Spanish chapter
of United States foreign policy during this period has been
characterized as a "futile one, and very discreditable to the
United States." [23] American actions had so increased the
hostility of Spain that no advantages could be gained by
any means short of war, and again, despite the opportunity,
Pierce and Marcy would not resort to an open conflict to
accomplish their ends.

# OTHER SCHEMES

The diplomatic records quoted in these pages have borne
adequate testimony to the feeling in the Pierce administration
that the Crimean War presented an excellent opportunity
for the accomplishment of its aims in foreign policy. Why,
then, were so few of these goals achieved? As shown above,
the answer lies in the use made of the opportunities. In
addition to a lack of clear foresight and planning, the Pierce
administration also was badly handicapped by the domestic
strife over slavery, so that all of its diplomatic moves, whatever their actual motive, were ultimately measured in terms
of their relevance to that issue. Cuba, for example, could not
have been acquired without arousing Northern anti-slavery
forces, for it would have become slave territory.

Another part of the explanation for the fitful course
of United States policy was undoubtedly the divided counsel
given to Pierce. While most government officials appeared
to support the expansionist aims of American foreign policy
and to share the same appreciation of the opportunities presented by the European conflict, they proposed very different
methods to achieve these ends. Marcy clearly preferred a
more cautious approach, respecting certain conventional limits
in order to avoid arousing open opposition from other powers.
Others in the State Department (the Young Americans) and
in the Cabinet (Jefferson Davis and Caleb Cushing) were less
restrained and urged a more direct approach. Pierce vacil-
lated between the two points of view. Thus the United States

government often gave the appearance of extreme bellicosity
in its declarations without gaining the benefits of belligerence
in practice. This self-paralysis is typified by the way in which
the United States handled the question of the Hawaiian
islands.

The possibility that Hawaii might be acquired, by some
act of revolt or informal invasion, was still considered highly
favorable during 1855. Suspicion of American designs on
the islands had led the British and French to maintain a
naval force in the area. At the same time, however, Marcy
managed to wring from the Cabinet a declaration forbidding
"unlawful" expeditions to Hawaii, despite "objections of the
most lively sort" from Jefferson Davis and others. Marcy
argued that such expeditions were not the only or even the
best method of acquisition, maintaining that annexation would
come inevitably through natural developments and ought not
to be achieved dishonorably. But suspicions of American
intentions to use force made acquisition by "natural developments" an impossibility, just as Marcy's defeat of these intentions eliminated the chance of acquisition by violence.[24]

The same situation prevailed elsewhere. In Mexico, Gadsden's outrageous behavior had increased British influence
in the country. Notes from the American Minister were
routinely sent by Santa Anna's government to the British
legation, and the Mexican Minister in Washington was instructed to act in concert with the British and French representatives there. Under these conditions Gadsden found his
proposals ignored and his threats unavailing. Yet his advice
to the Pierce administration to support the overthrow of
the Santa Anna regime led to no decisive action. Despite
the overwhelming superiority of American strength, United
States policy in Mexico was impotent.[25]

Sometimes the United States could not attain even the
minor objectives of its foreign policy. The Crimean War
presented it with a promising, though hardly major, opportunity, to gain greater commercial privileges in Persia. Russian influence in the court of the Shah was at this time
strong, and in view of the friendship between the United

States and Russia it was not a great surprise when in early
1855 the Pierce administration received information from
United States Minister Spence that the Persian Minister
in Constantinople had suggested a commercial treaty between
his country and the United States. The American diplomat
observed: "I am induced to believe that our attempt to make
a treaty in 1852 was defeated by the influence of England
at the Persian Court and I am inclined to think that the Shah
has been instigated by the Czar, to renew negotiations with
us." [26]

Marcy immediately raised the subject with Stoeckl. He
hinted to the Russian Minister that the United States would
like to compete with English commerce in Persia, adding
that "it is in your interest to put us more and more in contact with the English." [27] Soon thereafter he authorized
Spence to begin negotiations with the Persian representatives,
but warned him to keep the talks quiet in view of the probable British and French reactions:

> Both England and France have shown a readiness
> to intermeddle with nearly all the negotiations we have
> recently attempted, and it is apprehended they would
> do the same thing in this case if they were aware of
> our intentions to open a negotiation with Persia. If you
> deem it necessary, you will impress upon the Persian
> Minister at Constantinople the embarrassment and dan-
> ger which will be likely to arise if the agents of these
> powers should ascertain that the negotiation was on
> foot.[28]

At the same time the United States attempted to obtain
direct Russian support in the undertaking. Writing to Seymour, Marcy warned again of British and French interference and instructed him to ask the Russian government to
exert what influence it could over the Shah:

> This government is about to open negotiations
> with that of Persia for a commercial treaty, and from

its experience in other instances, it may meet with
opposition in this. England and France have on several
occasions interfered with, and embarrassed, our negotiations with foreign powers. . . . The Representative
of Russia at the Court of the Shah might have it in
his power to contribute in some way to the success of
the undertaking, if he were induced to believe that his
Government were favorable to it.

The President desires that you would converse con-
fidentially with Count Nesselrode on the subject. . . .[29]

Seymour, in reply, reported that Nesselrode seemed to
be familiar with the matter already. Furthermore, he had
unhesitatingly promised "that Russia would do all she could
to further the object of our Government." [30]

Despite the auspicious signs, however, conclusion of
a commercial treaty was again stymied, in this case in a
rather unusual manner. The Persian representative suddenly
insisted, as a condition of the treaty, that the United States
protect all Persian merchant ships and fight a war with
the Iman of Muscat to restore certain Persian Gulf islands
to the Shah. These provisions the United States could not,
of course, accept, and the negotiations temporarily foundered.
The reasons behind the sudden imposition of such clearly unacceptable demands were never ascertained, though British
influence was inevitably suspected.[31]

The Persian government offered a slightly modified ver-
sion of its proposals in mid-1856, but this was also declined
forthrightly by Spence, without even the formality of obtaining advice from his home government.[32] It was not until
late 1856, after the end of the Crimean War, that a satisfactory treaty was finally signed by both parties. The Persian
representative reopened discussions in September, dropping
the extravagant demands made previously. With these difficulties removed, terms were quickly agreed upon and the
document was signed on December 13, 1856. The sudden
shift of the Persian government back to its original policy
was probably a result of the crisis in British-Persian rela-

tions during that year, which led to actual hostilities in
November. Spence, at least, subscribed to the view that the
United States owed the eventual conclusion of a treaty to this
turn of events.[33]

If the United States could not benefit directly from
the Crimean War as far as its trade with Persia was concerned, it was thought by some that it might at least gain
an advantage in Russia itself. Seymour had been the principal champion of this possibility. During the first year of
the war he had observed:

> Our trade with Russia being pretty much cut off,
> if not extinguished for the present, by the blockade
> of the Russian ports, there is very little to communi-
> cate of pressing importance. I may remark, however,
> that when the war which is now pending is brought
> to a close, we shall be able to carry on a greater amount
> of business with Russia than ever before.[34]

Such a surmise was based, in part, on political developments.
A few months later Seymour reported that, since "the best
feeling towards our government continues to prevail at St.
Petersburg," American trade would enjoy a great advantage
when the end of the war finally threw Russian ports open
again: "It will be an easy matter for our citizens to get
contracts for supplying Russia with machinery, ships, and
to some extent with coal. The trade in cotton also will be
thrown almost exclusively into American hands." [35]

The events of 1855 further strengthened these convictions
and led Seymour to envision an overall strengthening of
postwar Russian-American ties—not only commercial, but
cultural and political as well:

> For various reasons, which will readily suggest
> themselves to the sagacious statesmen and merchants
> of Russia, this circuity of trade [through Great Brit-
> ain] should be avoided, and direct intercourse between

the two countries extended. In other respects than the mere interests of commerce, is this intercourse important. The arts, inventions, and improvements of the one would be speedily communicated to the other. Between no two nations on the globe are the relations of peace and amity so likely to be enduring. It is scarcely possible that the political policy of the one would interfere with that of the other—Rivalries and jealousies could scarcely spring up between them.

The present war, terminate as it may, will leave deep wounds inflicted by the respective parties on each other which will not be healed in a long period. That consideration will naturally incline the government and people of Russia to receive with favor any suggestion you may make for a more intimate commercial connection between this country and Russia.[36]

At least one Russian hoped to reap some advantage from the friendship between the two countries while the war was still in progress. In 1855 the United States had been able to accomplish little from its privileged position of neutrality in a conflict involving its principal opponents. But Stoeckl had not given up dreams of fitting out American privateers to prey upon Allied commerce under the benevolent eye of the United States government. The Russian Minister was especially aroused by British plans to enlist soldiers in neutral countries (see Chapter 7), and after obtaining Marcy's agreement that this was substantially the same as outfitting privateers, he began to plan the best means of establishing such a fleet. He reported to his government a conversation with Senator Gwin, who had encouraged the scheme and recommended San Francisco as the perfect location for the formation of a fleet that would be a serious threat to British shipping in the Pacific. Stoeckl was ecstatic over the possibilities, and urged his superiors to send money for the project.[37]

The scheme was killed, however, by Nesselrode, who decided not to endanger American friendship for such a risky and undoubtedly illegal enterprise. Russian policy should be limited, he said, to informing Americans who asked about such activities that they might take ships to Eastern Siberia to be outfitted as privateers at their own risk. Marcy had already assured the Russian government that what American citizens did abroad was their own business. But to issue letters of marque in the United States was an unnecessary and unprofitable business, particularly as good relations with the United States were considered of the utmost importance in long-range Russian foreign policy.[38]

Russian policy, as well as American, had to deal with the problem of establishing the best means of utilizing the common opposition of both countries to the Crimean allies. American policy, in particular, was unsettled in its choice of methods and even in its definition of immediate aims. Yet the diplomatic relations between the United States and the Crimean belligerents continued, in 1855, to follow a pattern which indicated the indirect yet significant relationships between the conflict in the Old World and the unresolved tensions in the New World. Evidence of American antipathy to Britain and France, alternating between quiet diplomatic pressure and noisy, threatening public denunciation, again appeared in recurrent incidents in various areas of contact. In contrast, friendship between the United States and Russia continued to exert its influence. Thus linked by webs of interlocking or antagonistic interests, the various powers moved into the last stages of the Crimean War and a new set of problems.

# NOTES

1. Earl of Granville to Clarendon, April 12, 1855, quoted in Van Alstyne, *Journal of Modern History*, XI, 171.
2. Spence to Marcy, February 12, 1855, Despatches from Turkey, NA, RG 59.
3. In addition to Spence's despatches, see, for example, Buchanan to Marcy, March 9, 1855, Despatches from Great Britain, NA, RG 59.
4. Buchanan to Marcy, February 9, 1855, *ibid.*
5. Buchanan to Marcy, February 16, 1855, *ibid.*
6. Buchanan to Marcy, April 7, 1855, *ibid.*

7. Stephens to Quitman, February 24, 1855, quoted in Urban, *Louisiana Historical Quarterly*, XXXIX, 60.

8. Buchanan to Marcy, May 11, 1855, Despatches from Great Britain, NA, RG 59.

9. Marcy to Buchanan, May 28, 1855, Instructions to Great Britain, NA, RG 59.

10. *Ibid.*

11. *London Times*, March 1, 1855.

12. U.S., *Congressional Globe*, 33rd Cong., 2nd Sess., 1855, XXX, 826.

13. *Ibid.* pp. 826-27, 829.

14. Nichols, *Franklin Pierce*, p. 376.

15. *Ibid.*

16. U.S., *Congressional Globe*, 33rd Cong., 2nd Sess., 1855, XXX, 830-33.

17. Nichols, *Franklin Pierce*, pp. 394-96; Spencer, *op. cit.*, pp. 338-39.

18. Marcy to Perry, April 9, 1855, Instructions to Spain, NA, RG 59.

19. Perry to Marcy, March 21, 1855, Despatches from Spain, NA, RG 59.

20. Marcy to Dodge, May 1, 1855, Instructions to Spain, NA, RG 59.

21. Marcy to Dodge, July 7, 1855, *ibid.*

22. Marcy to Dodge, October 13, 1856, *ibid.*

23. Spencer, *op. cit.*, p. 343.

24. Spencer, *op. cit.*, pp. 395-96.

25. Doyle to Clarendon, January 2, May 3, 1855, cited by Garber, *op. cit.*, pp. 153-54; Gadsden to Marcy, September 5, 1854, October 4, 1856, Despatches from Mexico, NA, RG 59. Impotent or not, American policy in Mexico certainly alarmed the Crimean allies; the French Minister in Mexico City actually equated the Americans with the Russians and the Mexicans with the victimized Turks. Both Russians and Americans, he wrote his government on May 15, 1855, were characterized by "ambition, the abuse of strength, and aspirations toward universal domination." The differences were superficial: "Russia aspires to dominate in Europe in the name of despotism, and the United States to dominate in America in the name of liberty." France and her allies must, therefore, contain both halves of this double threat. Quoted in Perkins, *Hands Off. . .* p. 112.

26. Spence to Marcy, November 25, 1854, Despatches from Turkey, NA, RG 59.

27. Stoeckl to Nesselrode, March 7/19, 1855, quoted (in French) in Golder, *American Historical Review*, XXXI, 467.

28. Marcy to Spence, May 11, 1855, Instructions to Turkey, NA, RG 59.

29. Marcy to Seymour, May 16, 1855, Instructions to Russia, NA, RG 59.

30. Seymour to Marcy, June 28, 1855, Despatches from Russia, NA, RG 59.

31. Spence to Marcy, September 17, 1855, January 29, April 16, 1856, Despatches from Turkey, NA, RG 59.

32. Spence to Marcy, June 22, 1856, *ibid.*

33. Spence to Marcy, December 22, 1856, *ibid.*

34. Seymour to Marcy, August 19, 1854, Despatches from Russia, NA, RG 59.

35. Seymour to Marcy, October 1, 1854, *ibid.*

36. Seymour to Marcy, October 1, 1855, *ibid.* See also despatches of January 17 and February 4, 1856.

37. Stoeckl to Nesselrode, January 24/February 5, February 10/22, 1855, quoted in Golder, *American Historical Review*, XXI, 470-71.

38. Nesselrode to Stoeckl, May 31/June 11, 1855, quoted *ibid,* p. 471.

# The Lion's Tail, 1855-56

## CHAPTER SEVEN

The prompt measures taken in New York and other places, to break up the scandalous recruiting stations, for the foreign service of the Western powers, have been well received here. It is to be hoped, that the citizens of our country will have nothing to do with the Allied powers in any shape. The principles of our government forbid interference of any kind in the struggle which is going on at the present time. But if it would be right to show the slightest leaning towards one side instead of another, I see nothing to convince me that we should give our preference to the masters, for the present, of the Baltic and the Euxine.[1]

## THE RECRUITMENT CONTROVERSY

One of the expedients adopted by Great Britain during the first winter of the Crimean War was the Foreign Enlistment Act of December 23, 1854, designed to compensate for deficiencies in manpower by providing for foreign volunteers in the British army. The United States was obviously one of the most likely sources of recruits, and the British Cabinet was clearly influenced in drawing up the act by

189

reports from their consuls in the United States. George B. Mathew, consul in Philadelphia, claimed, for example, that a strong battalion could be recruited in that city within a week.[2]

The British Minister and consuls had in fact received numerous offers to enlist in or recruit for the British cause. Many of these proposals were made by German immigrants and revolutionary emigrés from Europe, but there were also as usual, the adventurers. Typical was E. V. Ruthven (Major-General, Tennessee militia), who offered to raise a division of 6000 men in return for $1,500,000.[3] Crampton, the British envoy in Washington, was faced with the problem of devising a plan that would take advantage of enlistment opportunities in the United States without violating the strict American neutrality laws. By early February he had settled on a scheme, which he communicated to his government for approval. Recruits would be transported by the British government to points in Canada, where they would enlist. Agents would be hired to make these arrangements, but there would be no written engagements, for this might violate United States law. This plan should only be viewed as an experiment, Crampton added, commenting that "the people we shall get, if any, will be principally Germans. . . ." [4]

The British government approved the program, but warned against giving cause for complaint to the United States government.[5] As an added precaution Crampton consulted his Washington legal advisor, J. Mandeville Carlisle, who pronounced the plan legal so long as passage money was not paid until the recruits had arrived in Canada.[6] The recruitment actually began on about March 10, the day after the operation was placed in the hands of Joseph Howe, a well-known Canadian political figure.[7]

Howe, who had been brought into the plan by the Governor-General of Canada, a close friend, was less circumspect than the British government might have desired. Between March and May he spent over £5000 of the British Embassy's funds on the scheme, setting up recruiting operations in the larger United States cities. The agents he hired in these

cities were to provide recruits with cards guaranteeing free
passage to Halifax, Nova Scotia, where they would enlist.
Handbills and advertisements were employed to attract volunteers. This raised another legal question: the expenditure
of British government funds in the United States for agents
and advertising. The first issue—the provision of free passage in spite of the legal injunction against "hiring or retaining" recruits within the United States—had presumably
been solved by the card of credit. Crampton was less certain
about the advertising, but after a conference with Carlisle
and Howe decided that the latter's actions "will do no more
than practically to test the matter. . . ." He also talked with
Marcy and gained the impression that the American Secretary
of State concurred in the British course of action.[8]

If Crampton actually desired a court test, he had not
long to wait. Preparations to prosecute the recruiting agents
had begun with the appearance of the first advertisements in
March.[9] As it became clear that public trials, especially in
Philadelphia, might stir up adverse American opinion, the
British government became less eager to determine the legal
limits to their activity by judicial combat. In early May
Crampton clamped down on Howe's activities, forcing him
to withdraw from the recruiting business.[10] The British Minister was undoubtedly relieved by the opinion handed down
on May 22 by District Federal Court Judge John K. Kane
of Philadelphia, who said, "I do not think that the payment
of the passage from this country of a man who desires to
enlist in a foreign port comes within the [Neutrality] Act." [11]
Since other causes for complaint had presumably been eliminated through Howe's resignation, British authorities undoubtedly believed that this opinion settled the key question
regarding the legality of their recruiting activities.

But by this time the American government had determined to make an issue of all such activities. Marcy addressed
a note to Buchanan on June 9, denouncing the continuing
enlistment of Americans in Nova Scotia as not only a violation of American law, but also an affront to a sovereign
state under international law. The British government was

to be asked pointedly whether this would not justify American interference in Cuba, the one sin presumably being no worse than the other. Marcy made it clear that he wanted a complete stop to all recruiting measures, arguing that quibbles over U.S. neutrality laws had no bearing on the larger question.[12]

Faced with this uncompromising attitude, the British Cabinet submitted, immediately and completely, to Marcy's demands. Orders to cease all recruiting activities had, in fact, already been sent to Washington, Halifax, and Quebec on June 22. Clarendon, in reply to Buchanan's protest, declared that the British had already "determined that all proceedings for enlistment should be put an end to, and instructions to that effect were sent out before the undersigned had the honor to receive Mr. Buchanan's note." [13]

Even before receipt of this reply, however, Marcy had addressed a stronger note of protest to Buchanan for delivery to the British government. Complaining about the continuing enlistment of volunteers in Halifax, he asked for the closing of all such recruitment posts, punishment of officers and agents involved in the scheme, and discharge of all men enlisted into the British army from American soil.[14] The British government, however, remained unaware of the full extent of American demands, for Buchanan inexplicably failed to submit this note to its intended recipients until November 2. As a result, the Palmerston Cabinet imagined the causes for dispute removed, while American demands were in fact left unsatisfied.[15]

Crampton was also slow in complying with the directive to stop all enlistment activities. Apparently believing that his more circumscribed operations of the previous two months were unquestionably legal, the British Minister allowed enlistment at Halifax to continue until early August. He acknowledged receipt of the June 22 order on July 10, reporting to his government a few days later that he had stopped "all fresh measures" of recruitment. At the end of July he was nervous enough about the continuing enlistment efforts to declare that "I think it is on the whole advisable to put a

stop to it." But it was not until after he had learned of
Clarendon's assurances to Buchanan on July 16, and apparently recognized the necessity of a complete halt to the program, that he reported having "immediately put a stop to
all proceedings in the business. . . . It is absolutely necessary
that no case, legitimate or illegitimate, of an attempt to go
on with that matter should be brought up as having occurred
*subsequent to your assurance to Mr. Buchanan . . .*" [16]

It was far too late, however, for the British to retreat
gracefully, even if Crampton had carried out his instructions
immediately. The Pierce administration was adopting a stance
of outraged innocence over the violation of American neutrality. As reports of the close ties between the hired agents
and British diplomats came in, Marcy took an increasingly
adamant stand. Addressing Crampton on September 5, he
declared that the evidence that was accumulating demonstrated beyond a reasonable doubt the involvement of the
British government, and demanded to know the extent to
which recruitment activities had been known and sanctioned.
The crucial point, of course, was to determine the source
of the financial support for the recruiting operations; in
Marcy's view the use of British funds would constitute a
clear and flagrant violation of American neutrality laws.[17]
Crampton had obviously believed that the use of British
money to hire agents and ships was legitimate, although
he had halted Howe's advertisements and handbills. Clarendon, in reply, reiterated that the British government had
knowingly sanctioned no violations of United States law.
He further condemned the American attempt to prosecute
British agents as the type of procedure "resorted to under
despotic institutions." But his most serious grievance was
American insistence on the observance of strict neutrality
while the United States itself failed to maintain an impartial
position:

> The United States profess neutrality in the present
> war between the Western Powers and Russia; but have
> no acts been done within the United States, by citizens

thereof, which accord little with the spirit of neutrality? . . . Her Majesty's government have been silent on
these matters, which they did not consider indicative
of the general feelings of the American people. . . .
But her Majesty's government think themselves entitled
to claim the same credit for sincerity of purpose and
uprightness of conduct which they readily allow to the
government of the United States. . . .[18]

British petulance over the American attitude toward
the Crimean War was understandable. The struggle in the
East was proving a difficult and costly affair. A bloody as-
sault on Sebastopol on June 18 had failed, and another in-
decisive but violent engagement had been fought on the
Tchernaya River in mid-August. It was not until early September that Sebastopol was finally seized, after a siege of
almost a year, and even this was offset by the collapse of
the Allied resistance at Kars, in the Caucasus, which finally
fell to the Russians on November 28. They had received little
comfort from their "trans-atlantic cousins," who on the contrary seemed perfectly ready to believe the stories of Allied
atrocities in the Straits of Kerch.[19]

The Russian war effort appeared to be holding up despite the reverses; the American Minister at St. Petersburg
assured his government that the Russian morale and determination were still high.[20] Seymour also gave a good description of the American attitude that troubled British and
French observers most:

There is no danger I think of our ever coming
into collision with this distant northern power. . . .
But there is more reason to expect interference in the
affairs of our Country from those who are in alliance
against Russia, than from any other source. . . . It
may be worth our while to mark the manner in which
they choose to conduct this war.[21]

The tension in British-American relations created by the
question of British recruitment was heightened by the coin-

cidence of the issue with a revival of the dispute over the future of Central America. The British were still bogged down militarily in the East in late 1855 and early 1856. The critical question of recruitment thus came to the fore at a time advantageous to the United States, which the Pierce administration realized, for it chose this moment to reactivate the Central American question.

After Buchanan had sent his second note on July 22, 1854, and the British had decided not to proceed with their conciliatory plans upon the heels of the Greytown affair, the Aberdeen and Palmerston governments had successfully followed a policy of delay and evasion in the dispute. Buchanan received no official reply to the second note, and "such casual and desultory conversation as he obtained with Clarendon were not conducive to a revival of the hope." [22]

In August, 1855, however, the Pierce administration, impatient at the long delay in British discussions, exacerbated by the other disputes with the Allied powers, and eager to divert the approaching session of Congress to foreign issues, decided to bring the affair to a climax.[23] It also must have been aware that the Crimean War would not last forever. Once the war came to a close, the British would be able to consider a more active policy on the Central American isthmus. In any event, Marcy made it clear to Buchanan that the United States was to allow no more delay in the settlement of the issue:

> The President is anxious to have the questions which have been raised on the Treaty between the United States and Great Britain of the 19th of April 1850 settled or at least brought to a distinct issue before you retire from your mission. . . .
> The President has been unwilling to manifest impatience at the delay which has attended this negotiation while Her Majesty's Government was engrossed by the war with Russia, but he deems it to be but reasonable that it should now be urged to a conclusion. It is important that the United States should know the positions Great Britain is determined to maintain relative to the Central American questions.[24]

Buchanan, as directed, submitted a note to the British government reopening the Central American question, calling attention to the long delay in discussions and commenting that "the President does not feel that he would be justified in any longer delay." [25] Clarendon's vague reply[26] was written one day after his somewhat hot-tempered answer to Marcy's charges of British complicity in recruiting activities within the United States (see pages 193-194 above). As one historian has remarked, "the appearance of the recruitment difficulty coincident with the more menacing attitude of the Central American question placed British-American relations in a much more serious light." [27]

Marcy addressed another blistering note on the recruitment question to Buchanan on October 1, without waiting for the replies on either question. The testimony of the trials in Philadelphia, which he enclosed, proved to his satisfaction that "Mr. Crampton and several other British officials are deeply implicated in the transaction," since they had financed the operation and consulted with the lesser agents. Judge Kane had, furthermore, reversed his previous opinion that free passage to Halifax was legal, and the British agents were convicted on this count as well as the charge of soliciting volunteers with British funds.[28] Buchanan was directed to present this evidence to the British government and to get a final statement as to whether it would stand by its agents or not. If Great Britain intended to support its officers, he said, "it is important that its determination in that respect should be known." [29] When he finally received Clarendon's reply of September 27, he immediately responded with a defense of the United States against the charges of partiality in the Crimean War and strongly repeated his previous demands for redress in the affair.[30]

Having simultaneously thrown down demands for settlements of two important disputes, Marcy was perfectly justified in commenting that "the prospect, to my provision, looks a little cloudy. . . ." Neither the sovereign rights of the country nor its faith in international treaties, he declared, "will be sacrificed for the sake of peace." The question now was whether the British would remain steadfast in their refusal to make substantial concession on either of the disputes that the United States was pressing: "From the course of the British Government on the Central American controversy and the recruiting scheme, I am inclined to conclude that it cares very little about maintaining cordial relations with the United States." [31] And if British suspicion of American intentions and activities was not already great enough, it was increased by William Walker's conquest of Nicaragua in October. While the United States officially gave no support to the filibuster, the attitude of the Pierce administration was watched closely in Latin America and Europe, since it was known that Walker sought the eventual annexation of all Central America by the United States. The similarity to the pattern of events in the Texas annexation, which had occurred only a few years previously, was more than a little disturbing.[32]

The most eloquent response of the British to American provocation during this period followed these events. Palmerston, ever the assertive statesman, announced plans to send an enlarged naval squadron to the West Indies. He further instructed Clarendon, on October 25, to be as adamant as possible with the United States without making definite threats and to explain frankly that the enlarged fleet was a reaction to the threatening attitudes of the American government and public.[33] The British papers generally thought to represent the policies of the Palmerston government, Buchanan noticed, all printed hostile articles justifying the move as a necessary answer to American belligerence.[34]

Buchanan's immediate reaction, without even waiting for instructions, was to demand an explanation from Clarendon. American sensitivity to British naval moves is apparent in his direct challenge to the British Foreign Minister: "You have sent a large naval armament to your West India and North American stations, and I desire in the spirit of frankness and friendship to request you to inform me the reason why so many vessels of war have been despatched to the vicinity of our coasts." Clarendon's reply avoided the direct response previously suggested by Palmerston, offering instead a patently weak excuse for what was intended as a strong action. As paraphrased by Buchanan, the reply was:

> The fleet has not been sent with the least un-friendly intention. We have learned from unquestion-able authority, and from affidavits, that a large, fast, and powerful steamer has been built at New York under the direction of a Russian Naval officer, and that she is now altogether or nearly ready for sea. That this officer is to take her out from that port as a Russian privateer, and that the object is to intercept our ships from Australia conveying gold to this coun-try. Besides, three or four other steamers are building in New York for the same purpose. We are also in-formed that it was intended to capture one of the Cunard steamers and make her a Russian privateer.

Clarendon added, further straining his credibility, that the British feared filibustering expeditions of Irish-Americans to free the Emerald Isle from British jurisdiction![35]

The American reaction to these excuses was as Buchanan predicted: "They well know that no reason ever existed in point of fact for apprehension on account of Russian priva-teers, and still less, if that be possible, for an expedition to Ireland; and they will not attribute the sending of the fleet to these causes."[36] The statements in the British press had underlined the relationship of the action to more serious Anglo-American difficulties. This conclusion was difficult to reject. Although the Russian government had, by subterfuge, placed an order for a single steamer in New York, its im-portance clearly did not justify the disproportionate British naval reinforcement. The rest of Clarendon's supposed fears were quickly shown to be unfounded,[37] and that he himself was genuinely concerned with Russian privateering from New York remains doubtful. (The issue is seldom mentioned, even in British sources, and the mention of the "Ireland expedition" fantasy indicates, perhaps, the lack of seriousness in his charges.)

Both Marcy and Buchanan knew that the naval demonstration was intended to influence the United States to proceed more cautiously in the two pending disputes. Marcy approved Buchanan's course and agreed that the British action would make the American public more, not less, belligerent. He again asked for British replies on the two questions in order that "final measures" could be decided upon quickly. The American government was not to be intimidated by British bluff:

> What bearing this threatening language and menacing exhibition of Naval force in this quarter has upon the Central American difficulty, you can form as correct an opinion as we can here.
>
> If the course taken by the British Government be intended, as I suspect it is, to influence our action in regard to the offenders, official and unofficial, in the British Recruiting scheme within our territories, it is, to say the least of it, illjudged. Despite menace and bluster, this Government will do in that matter what respect for our national character, and the vindication of our rights, shall, in our judgment require. If such be the covert intent of Her Majesty's Ministers, they have yet something to learn in regard to the character of the American People. The effect of the articles alluded to, coupled with the sailing of the large naval force to this region, produced upon the people of the United States will be perceived by the public press. . . .[38]

The belligerency of the American public's responses can be gauged from the remarks of the *Washington Union* on the possibility of a war between the United States and Great Britain: "We confidently believe that if such a war should occur, we could raise three hundred thousand men for the invasion of England with less trouble than she raises thirty thousand for the invasion of Russia." [39] The *Union's* lack of appreciation for naval logistics was never tested, however, partly because the British public had learned after two years to appreciate the difficulties of distant wars. Buchanan repeatedly noted the lack of popular support for another war in Britain and predicted that Palmerston would never find the necessary backing if he tried to use force in his disputes with the United States. As long as the United States did not make the question a test of national honor, he felt that Palmerston would be forced to yield to any reasonable American demands. Two years of warfare had been enough.[40] There were other contributing factors, too:

> The present unsatisfactory financial condition of Great Britain; the dependence of their manufactories on the markets of the United States; the strikes at Manchester for higher wages; the dreadful condition to which the laboring poor will be reduced during the present winter from the high price of bread, and the pressure of the existing war, would all seem to point out the madness of provoking hostilities with the United States.[41]

Throughout this period of tension, British statements reflected not only a certain degree of war-weariness, but also continuing resentment of the American attitude toward the war. The British complaint that the United States sympathized with Russia came up in discussions over the recruitment issue and Central America, as it had appeared earlier in other contexts. During an interview held in mid-November, Clarendon complained of the way in which published reports of the trial of a recruitment agent had been circulated by the Russian Legation in Washington. He claimed that Stoeckl had been informed in advance of Marcy's notes to Crampton in the controversy. He also denounced "the universal hostility of the American Press towards them, and especially of the *Union,* thus evincing the unfriendly feelings of the American people and their partiality for Russia."

Buchanan replied, as he and Marcy had before, that American sympathy for Russia was Britain's own fault: "I told him that the sympathies in favor of Russia which existed in the United States arose chiefly from the impression that France and England, after having finished the war with Russia, intended to interfere with our affairs on the other side of the Atlantic." In the same interview Clarendon revealed that the British government had decided to send only four naval vessels to the West Indies, which would go nowhere near the coasts of the United States. Whether this was in part due to the vigor of the American reaction is a matter of conjecture, but it does seem clear that American pressure had had a perceptible influence on British calculations and policy.

The British government proved obstinate, however, in the Central American dispute. Buchanan observed at the end of the year that:

Further negotiations on these questions, during the continuance of Lord Palmerston's administration could lead to no favorable result. This administration is too far committed in their answer to the President's ultimatum to do us justice.[42]

But this was not meant to imply that the questions could not be brought "to an issue" in one way or another. On the same day that Buchanan had set down this pessimistic view on the future of the Central American negotiations, Marcy had finished an answer to Clarendon's latest reply on the recruitment question, in which the British statesman had agreed to offer a discharge and free passage back to the United States to any volunteer enlisted in violation of United States law.[43] Marcy's lengthy and comprehensive review of the controversy, which conceded not one inch to the British position, terminated with a demand that the British could not evade, delay, or negotiate. He asked for the recall of Crampton and the British consuls in New York, Philadelphia, and Cincinnati.[44]

The intention of forcing a showdown with Great Britain was also apparent in Pierce's third annual message, delivered on December 31, 1855. In this address the President gave no sign of willingness to compromise on the recruitment issue, but with considerable force justified the American demand for the recall of the principal British diplomatic agents in the United States. He also spoke of the Central American question, and here as well sought to bring matters to a conclusion. The British could consider, along with the threatened break in diplomatic relations, his warning on the consequences of not reaching a settlement in the Central American dispute:

> There is, however, reason to apprehend that with Great Britain in the actual occupation of the disputed territories, and the treaty therefore practically null so far as regards our rights, this international difficulty can not long remain undetermined without involving in serious danger the friendly relations which it is the interest as well as the duty of both countries to cherish and preserve.[45]

As 1855 ended, the United States stood a fair chance of joining the ranks of the belligerents, thereby extending the field of combat to the New World. The outcome depended on the British reaction.

# CRIMEAN DENOUEMENT AND BRITISH WAR CRISIS

Thomas Seymour, America's impressionable representative to the Tsar, greeted the new year of 1856 with the following observation:

> The present is a painfully interesting crisis in the history of this country, of Europe, and of the world. Peace and War seem to be so nearly balanced just

now, in the estimation of some persons of good judgment, that the slightest weight, thrown into either
scale, will put a stop to further hostilities, or prepare
the way for greater carnage than ever.[46]

Seymour was referring, of course, to the Crimean engagement, and his description of the state of that conflict
was an accurate one. After the fall of Sebastopol to the Allies
and Kars to the Russians, both sides waited, exhausted but
not beaten, for the next move. Then, on January 16, the
Russians, who had certainly suffered most, accepted an Austrian four-point proposal for peace similar to the one they
had rejected almost a year earlier (because they had objected
to the Black Sea demilitarization provision). A protocol based
on the four points was quickly signed on February 1, and
after two years of undistinguished military skirmishing,
the dismal conflict was all but over.

Some thought, however, that peace in the East would
have an adverse affect on the chances for peace in the Western
hemisphere. Such was the opinion of James Buchanan, whose
view of the British public's attitude had undergone some
change by mid-January. To his oft-repeated declaration that
a peaceful settlement of Central American difficulties was
"a sheer impossibility" during Palmerston's tenure in office,
he added the following warning:

It is still my impression there will be peace in
Europe before the season for opening the next campaign; and this will leave England in such a state of
preparation for war as she has never been at any
former period. This may act as a stimulus to the reckless and arrogant propensities of Lord P., which have
been so often manifested by him in his intercourse
with other nations.[47]

Buchanan expanded this theme in following despatches,
as peace in Crimea loomed larger. Elaborating on the likelihood of war over the outstanding issues, he said

In this state of affairs, the British people being sore and disappointed and being better prepared for war than they have ever been, Lord Palmerston, whose character is reckless and his hostility to our country well known, will most probably assume a high and defiant attitude on the questions pending between the two countries. The British people are now in that state of feeling that I firmly believe they could be brought up to a war with the United States, *if they can be persuaded that the territory in dispute belongs to themselves.* This, absurd as it is, may be done through the agency of a press generally, if not universally, hostile to us. I make these remarks because you ought to know the truth and be prepared for the worst. *Certainly not with a view of yielding one iota of our rights to Great Britain or any other power. Most certainly not.*

I understand from friends that it is now stated by British individuals in conversation, how easy it would be for them in their present state of preparation, and with our feeble navy, to bring a war with us to a speedy and successful conclusion. In this they would be woefully mistaken.[48]

The American Minister later added the thought that "the pride of the British people recoils from the idea of terminating the war without having acquired equal glory with the French." Since there had been no Waterloo or Trafalgar, he suggested that the British might look elsewhere for military glory.[49] The end of the Crimean war caused, in sum, a striking change in the views of the American Minister in London regarding the danger of war involved in pressing American demands against the interests of the Crown.

But Buchanan had misread the state of British opinion. The Palmerston government was actually under great pressure to moderate its American policy, for many leading British political figures felt that Crampton and the Palmerston Cabinet were to blame in the recruitment controversy.[50] When

Parliament met, on January 31, the government was criticized severely by Edward G. G. S. Stanley, Earl of Derby, opposition leader in the House of Lords, for running the danger of a war with the United States which he claimed would be disastrous. Clarendon, in reply, pointed out that he had offered to arbitrate the Central American question, and, while the United States had declined the offer, he still had hopes of settling the issue amicably. In the House of Commons, Palmerston was challenged by Richard Cobden, the noted free-trader and pacifist, who declared that the government was leading the country into a horrible calamity and asked for the Central American correspondence. John Arthur Roebuck, usually a Palmerston supporter, also pressed the Prime Minister on the recruiting question and asked for Crampton's instructions.[51] The tone of the British press underwent a decided change, with the appearance of friendly articles in such previously hostile papers as the *Times* and the *News*.[52]

Clarendon's mention of arbitration offers, calculated to convince Parliament of the government's reasonableness in the Central American dispute, came as a surprise to Buchanan and his government. Clarendon's only references to arbitration in his interviews with the American Minister had consisted of general hints thrown into the conversation, which Buchanan had not regarded as formal offers.[53] Commenting on Clarendon's claim to have offered arbitration, Buchanan subsequently reported to Marcy that:

> I have reported to you, in the most faithful manner, every conversation which has passed between Lord Clarendon and myself on the subject of a reference of these questions to a friendly power. As I have never learned that the British government has made any such offer to the government of the United States through Mr. Crampton, I infer that his lordship must have referred to the general conversations between him and myself, which would by no means justify the broad terms of his statement. Thus much merely to vindicate the truth of history.[54]

When Buchanan raised the matter with Clarendon, he was informed that the passing remarks of November, 1855, had been intended as an offer of arbitration, and that Crampton, furthermore, had been directed on the 10th of that month, to suggest the possibility of arbitration to Marcy. It soon became known that Crampton had misunderstood his instructions and neglected to relay the message to Marcy. Thus, while it is difficult to consider these hints and suggestions as the formal offer of arbitration which Clarendon, under pressure of Parliamentary debate, implied that he had made, it does appear that in early November, 1855, the British government had attempted to sound out the Pierce administration on this possibility. Such a move, made during the period of tension when the British fleet was moved to the West Indies, may well have been designed to facilitate an honorable British retreat. The fact that Clarendon now represented this gesture as a full-fledged arbitration proposal signalled another shift in British policy. Her Majesty's government was again showing signs of accommodation to avoid a second, and more unpopular, war right after the Crimean engagement.[55]

While the offer of arbitration on Central America was appreciated as a conciliatory gesture, the Pierce administration continued to insist on complete British withdrawal from all but the original Belize settlement, arguing that there was nothing to arbitrate.[56] Tension also remained at a high level in the recruitment controversy, while the United States waited for an answer to its demand for the recall of Crampton and the British consuls. The day after Clarendon made his speech on Central American arbitration, Buchanan observed to Marcy that "there can be no doubt but that the British Government will refuse to recall Mr. Crampton and the Consuls; and that your request to this effect will produce much excitement and ill-feeling in this country." He also noted an article in a pro-Palmerston paper containing "some atrocious suggestions in regard to the mode of carrying on war against our country, in the event of hostilities." [57] The demand for Crampton's recall was viewed by the Pierce administration as a direct challenge to the British government and a test of British determination.

Buchanan felt alternately pessimistic and optimistic about the outcome. In one despatch he repeated his warning about unfulfilled British ambitions in the Crimean War, indicated by comments in the British press that victory over the unprepared United States was certain, and concluded that the two countries "seem to be approaching a diplomatic, if not belligerent rupture; and I deem it almost certain that as soon as the news shall arrive in this country, that you have sent Mr. Crampton his passports, I shall receive mine from Lord Clarendon." One week later he noticed "a favorable change" in public opinion, brought about by fear of an unwanted war at an unpropitious moment, and reported a new "friendly tone" in Lord Palmerston's public attitude.[58]

The Pierce administration and the dominant forces in Congress, however, proceeded on the assumption that "if the American government stood firm Great Britain would avoid war by retreating from her position." [59] War would be accepted if the British chose that course, but the prevalent view was that Britain could ill afford such a conflict. After transmitting correspondence on the recruitment question to the Senate, the President had sent a message to Congress asking for a special military appropriation of $3,000,000.[60] The dominant attitude expressed in the debates on this request was that the United States should press its full demands even at the risk of war. It was generally doubted that the British would or even *could* fight a successful war against the United States.[61] The note of defiance was sounded in the remarks of such spokesmen as Lewis Cass:

It is not long since this feeling [of hostility] was indicated by a distinguished review, the North Briton, which observed by way of warning, or of threatening, or probably both, that the same fleet which passes the summer in the Black Sea may pass the winter in the Gulf of Mexico. It was at no time improper to look at our means of attack and defense, but it is our especial duty to do so as the affairs of the country become more critical. . . . This exaltation of their own power extends beyond us to the other nations of the world; for but a few short months have passed away since Petersburgh [*sic*] and Moscow were to fall, and the Czar to be driven back to the primitive inheritance of the Russian ruler in Asia. But Moscow, and Petersburgh, and Russia, have survived the power and the threats of England.[62]

In this discussion the Crimean War was considered as more than a test of military competence. The legislators recognized the fact that British willingness to fight a war with the United States was related to the outcome of the Eastern war and its impact on the British public. Typical were the comments of Senator Alfred Iverson of Georgia:

I believe that the British Ministry are hostile to this Government, and that there is but one possible manner in which war between that Government and this can be avoided. She would not be willing to come in collision with the United States if the peace conferences at Paris should end fruitlessly—she would have her hands full with Russia; but if peace should be established with all her present means of offensive and aggressive warfare in her hands, with the hostility of the British Ministry exhibited as it has been exhibited against this country, there is but one hope of peace between the two nations, and that is, that the popular voice in Great Britain may control the British Ministry.[63]

From the American point of view, then, the signing of the peace ending the Crimean War, on March 30, was indeed inauspicious. With relations between the United States and Great Britain still at a low ebb, the British had been freed from their military commitments in the East. The American government had not received satisfaction, in its own view, on either the Central American or recruitment question. The demand for Crampton's recall was still unanswered, and despite some favorable signs in Britain, American statesmen took an apprehensive view of Palmerston's intentions.

No one was more apprehensive of the future of American relations with Great Britain than George M. Dallas of Pennsylvania, who replaced Buchanan in mid-March at the Court of St. James (the latter having returned to the United States to campaign for the Presidency). Dallas, who shared the anti-British, expansionist views held by the majority of his party, immediately perceived the dissatisfaction of the British public over the conclusion of the Crimean War and accordingly took it for granted that he would receive his passports as soon as the British government was informed that Crampton had received his. He extended congratulations to the British on the end of the Crimean War, he reported, only in order to "quietly and respectfully imply a perfect and cool contempt for the idea that our government could in the slightest degree be affected in their pursuit of right by the powerful attitude in which that Peace left England." In concert with Mason, he recommended the strengthening of the United States Mediterranean squadron in order to protect American commerce there in case of a sudden outbreak of hostilities. He believed that the strongest deterrent to war lay in the assaults being made on the Palmerston government by many leading members of Parliament; he even dared to hope that "Lord Palmerston will be unable to sustain himself." But, he warned, even this hope might well prove illusory:

> The Premier is a man of great adroitness in extremities, and may yet, by sudden movement, twist round upon his tight rope, and dance off, with Parliament blinded and in tow, and in another direction. Pray observe how, in the distribution of the immense land and naval forces on hand, he is sending a larger force to Canada than they have ever yet had there; other troops to Bermuda; a most extraordinary supply of many millions of ball-cartridges, etc., etc.[64]

Dallas informed his government in late April that the long-awaited reply to demands for Crampton's recall was finally about to be delivered. According to his information, "this reply will be calm and moderate in tone, but definitive in declining to do what you have asked." [65] The British response was as he had predicted. While indirectly refusing to recall the British envoys, Clarendon's note was temperate in its defense of Crampton and the consuls; Dallas remarked that the document was "more than commonly conciliatory in tone, and its concluding paragraphs are thought to evince a sincere desire to avoid a breach." [66]

The British government was seeking to avoid an open conflict but was retreating as little as possible in doing so. It was up to the American government to throw down the gauntlet. Dallas attributed the British attitude to the tremendous pressure on Palmerston to keep peace in the Western hemisphere; a conflict with the United States, he wrote, "is the only thing he [Palmerston] could not stand for six months, or even half that time." British unwillingness to fight another war at this time was further demonstrated by the Parliamentary investigation of the troop reinforcements sent to Canada.[67]

Even as the recruiting question was reaching a *denouement,* the Central American question was further exacerbated by events on the isthmus. The Walker government in Nicaragua had maintained itself in power since the preceding October despite almost universal disapprobation. The American government had been hard-pressed to explain the large numbers of American citizens who joined the filibuster in that country; Crampton in particular had called attention to events in Central America to offset British embarrassment in the recruitment controversy. The danger to British lives and property in Nicaragua was in itself a potentially explosive source of conflict.[68]

The British had done more than register verbal protests to the Americanization of Nicaragua, for the country was of strategic importance as the logical canal route across Central America. When Costa Rica, fearing Walker's ambitions, declared war on its neighbor, Great Britain moved quietly in support of the effort to topple the Americans from power. The British sold 2000 muskets on credit to the Costa Ricans, advising them on the type of rifle best suited to combat the Americans.[69] In April, Walker intercepted some correspondence between Costa Rican authorities and Clarendon which referred to the arms purchase and included some favorable comments by the British Minister on Costa Rica's invasion of Nicaragua.[70] Copies of these documents were sent immediately to Washington, where the reaction was similar to that later expressed by Walker's biographer: "It is hard to repel the idea that British jealousy was a stumbling-block in the path of civilization at this time as much in the Caribbean as in the Crimea." [71]

Feeling flared up over this further instance of British "intermeddling" on the isthmus, as Congressional debates demonstrated; and Crampton was quick to report the surge of anti-British sentiment to his government.[72] News that a British naval vessel had stopped an American steamer in the Nicaraguan area to prevent recruits from reaching Walker was also received in Washington in early May.[73] A typical reaction to these events was registered by Dallas, in London, commenting on the intercepted correspondence:

> [This] shows Lord C.'s meddlesome and inimical spirit and policy to be rather worse than had been supposed in relation to Central America. . . . I am not sure that you have not been too scrupulous and cautious in your policy as to Walker. At all events, I hope that these meddling manifestations from this quarter may be made the avowed platform of a decisive movement on our part. We should displace this entering wedge by a quick and well-aimed stroke.[74]

Pierce had likewise determined that the time for action had arrived. The intercepted correspondence, the news of the naval incident, and Dallas' report that the British government was not going to recall Crampton all arrived in Washington in early May. In addition, Pierce's main hope for renomination in the rapidly approaching 1856 Democratic national convention rested upon strong support in the South, where demands for aiding Walker were strongest. The arrival of a representative of the Walker government on May 5, therefore, was considered a propitious event. Pierce decided to receive the envoy, Padre Vijil, thereby recognizing the Walker regime and laying down another challenge to Great Britain.[75] Not content with the act of recognition itself, Pierce sent a strong message of justification to Congress on the following day:

> The courageous and self-reliant spirit of our people prompts them to hardy enterprises, and they occasionally yield to the temptation of taking part in the troubles of countries near at hand. . . .
> It is the established policy of the United States to recognize all governments without question of their source or their organization, or of the means by which the governing persons attain their power, provided there be a government *de facto* accepted by the people of the country. . . .
> Another minister from the Republic of Nicaragua has now presented himself, and has been received as such, satisfactory evidence appearing that he represents the Government *de facto,* and, so far as such exists, the Government *de jure* of that Republic.[76]

The reaction to Pierce's move, in Latin America as well as in the Western European countries, was inevitably hostile.[77] Even so, the President continued his effort to force a conclusion to the crisis in Anglo-American relations. Immediately after receiving the official British reply to demands for Crampton's recall, the administration prepared two notes designed to put the British on the spot. The first, dated May 24, dealt with Central American affairs. While the conciliatory language of Clarendon's note on this affair had, said Marcy, prevented the President "from dismissing all hope of an amicable settlement," the British government was still too vague in its proposals; Dallas was instructed to press again for the desired concessions and bring the negotiations to a close in one way or another.[78] The second note, sent on May 27, informed the British government that Crampton and the British consuls had been dismissed because of their activities in the recruitment operations.[79]

The United States thus forced the choice of war or retreat upon Great Britain. Having challenged the British as far existing circumstances would allow, the Pierce administration could only wait and prepare for the worst. Dallas' advice from London was not out of place:

> Incidents affecting the relations between this country and the United States are crowding so rapidly upon us that too much vigilance and precaution cannot be exercised to ward off or to mitigate the consequences of an explosion which may possibly happen at any moment.[80]

The question was still whether Britain would fight a second war while recovering from the first. Another important consideration, of course, was the probable policy of her ally in the first conflict. The unpopularity of the Crimean War in France in its later stages and the end of the actual fighting that had allied the two countries, were taken as favorable indications that the French would not take part in any war between Britain and the United States. Mason was able to confirm this opinion in early June after an interview with Drouyn de Lhuys. Posing the actual possibility of war over the recruitment question and other complications, he was assured emphatically that France would not take part in the controversy. Mason concluded: "Instead of fleets and armies, France will send to the United States enormous orders for bread. This I confidently predict." [81] In his next despatch Mason added a note of caution; he conceded the possibility that Louis Napoleon might accede to British requests for support in spite of the French weariness of war, but again declared that "I cannot believe, that the Government can contemplate any measure, which may involve war with a country, whose friendly intercourse is so vastly beneficial to France." [82]

American statesmen assumed, therefore, that the Crimean alliance would not operate against them. Concern centered on the British alone. By June 6, Dallas, who was still convinced he would be dismissed in retaliation for Crampton's ignominious departure from the United States, was prematurely denouncing the expected action in melodramatic terms:

> I am disposed to think that the dignity of our country will make it necessary so to regard that measure, if it be resorted to, [as an original insult] and that, without the amplest apology, we ought never to permit an American minister, or diplomatic agent of any sort, even a consul, to show himself in her Majesty's dominions. My longing for historical fame would certainly be satiated if it were to turn out that I am to be the last of our ministers at this Court. [83]

Marcy, generally more moderate than many of his colleagues, was also infected by the war fever that pervaded the country in May and June, 1856. While waiting for news of the British reaction to his two notes of late May, he wrote Dallas a strongly worded letter denouncing the British as hypocrites for doing in India what they denied the United States the right to do in Central America: "Are not the United States the 'dominant power' of the North American Continent? Is not a safe transit across the Isthmus of vital importance to the integrity of our Union?" The United States, he remarked, "could not remain entirely inactive and see Great Britain obtain complete ascendancy in all the States of Central America." American recognition of the Walker regime, which Marcy now favored in spite of his initial reluctance, "was precipitated by the conduct of the British Government in furnishing aid to Costa Rica." [84] He felt, in short, that Britain should accept United States predominance in the Central American area.

People who thought as Marcy did assumed, at least implicitly, that the division between the Old World and the New World, embodied in American policy as the Monroe Doctrine, had a legitimate geographical basis, was essentially just, and as such, should be respected by the great European powers. Marcy, indeed, believed with some justification that his expressions were more moderate than most public opinion on the subject. Yet not all Americans were convinced that this doctrine of total separation corresponded to reality or should be pursued. The *North American Review*, for example, tried to inject a note of restraint by denying that the Monroe Doctrine had any relevance to the existing situation.[85] British statesmen, including those who opposed Palmerston's American policy, likewise denied that the United States could claim a division of spheres in defense of its Central American demands for British withdrawal. Benjamin Disraeli, who was considered a friend of the United States in British circles, gently reminded Americans during this crisis that, just as American foreign policy was inevitably connected to European events, European countries could not ignore the Western hemisphere:

> Now, sir, the Monroe Doctrine is one which, with great respect to the government of the United States, is not, in my opinion, suited to the age in which we live. The increase in the means of communication between Europe and America have made one great family of the countries of the world; and that system of government, which, instead of enlarging, would restrict the relations between those two quarters of the globe, is a system which is not adopted to this age. . . . Instead of vaunting that they build their greatness on the Monroe Doctrine, which is the doctrine of isolation, [the United States] should seek to attain it by deferring to the public law of Europe, and by allowing their

destiny to be regulated by the same high principles of policy which all the European communities that have a political system have invariably recognized.[86]

Had the Pierce administration examined its preconceptions objectively, and honestly reviewed the chain of events that led the United States to challenge Great Britain at this time, they might have been less hasty in making declarations for total separation of the two hemispheres.

# NOTES

1. Seymour to Marcy, May 3, 1855, Despatches from Russia, NA, RG 59.
2. Graham to Clarendon, November 17, 1854, cited by Van Alstyne, "John F. Crampton, Conspirator or Dupe?," *American Historical Review*, XLI (April, 1936), 493.
3. J. Bartlet Grebner, "Joseph Howe and the Crimean War Enlistment Controversy between Great Britain and the United States," *Canadian Historical Review*, XI (December, 1930), 303-04.
4. Crampton to Clarendon, February 12, 1855, quoted in Van Alstyne, *American Historical Review*, XLI, 494-95.
5. Clarendon to Crampton, April 12, 1855, quoted in Brebner, *Canadian Historical Review*, XI, 304-05.
6. Van Alstyne, *American Historical Review*, XLI, 496.
7. Brebner, *Canadian Historical Review*, XI, 307.
8. *Ibid.*, pp. 304-05, 310, 315-17; Crampton to Clarendon, March 26, 1855, quoted in Van Alstyne, *American Historical Review*, XLI, 497.
9. U.S. Congress, *Senate Executive Documents*, No. 35, 34th Cong., 1st Sess., 1856, p. 63.
10. Brebner, *Canadian Historical Review*, XI, 320.
11. U.S. Congress, *Senate Executive Documents*, No. 35, 34th Cong., 1st Sess., 1856, p. 17.
12. Marcy to Buchanan, June 9, 1855, Instructions to Great Britain, NA, RG 59. Most of the American diplomatic correspondence on this question is reprinted in U.S. Congress, *Senate Executive Documents*, No. 35, 34th Cong., 1st Sess., 1856.
13. Clarendon to Crampton, June 22, 1855, cited by Brebner, *Canadian Historical Review*, XI, 325. Clarendon to Buchanan, July 16, 1855, enclosure in Buchanan to Marcy, July 20, 1855, Despatches from Great Britain, NA, RG 59.
14. Marcy to Buchanan, July 15, 1855, Instructions to Great Britain, NA, RG 59.

15. Brebner, *Canadian Historical Review*, XI, 325.

16. *Ibid.;* Crampton to Clarendon, July 10, 16, 30, August 7, 1855, quoted in Van Alstyne, *American Historical Review*, XLI, 500-02. Italics Crampton's.

17. Marcy to Crampton, September 5, 1855, Notes to the British Legation, NA, RG 59.

18. Clarendon to Buchanan, September 27, 1855, enclosure in Buchanan to Marcy, September 28, 1855, Despatches from Great Britain, NA, RG 59.

19. Seymour reported that the Allies were guilty of crimes "which could well be done to revive the horrors of the wars of the middle ages," while the Russian troops had behaved in an exemplary fashion. Seymour to Marcy, August 2, 1855, Despatches from Russia, NA, RG 59.

20. Seymour to Marcy, August 1, 1855, *ibid.*

21. Seymour to Marcy, August 2, 1855, *ibid.*

22. M. Williams, *op. cit.*, p. 197.

23. *Ibid.*

24. Marcy to Buchanan, August 6, 1855, Instructions to Great Britain, NA, RG 59.

25. Buchanan to Clarendon, September 11, 1855, enclosure in Buchanan to Marcy, September 11, 1855, Despatches from Great Britain, NA, RG 59.

26. "The British Government share the conviction of the President of the United States that the two countries and their mutual desire to maintain existing friendly relations will alike inspire each party with a conciliatory spirit and enable them to overcome all obstacles to a satisfactory adjustment of Central American questions." Clarendon to Buchanan, September 28, 1855, enclosure in Buchanan to Marcy, October 4, 1855, *ibid.*

27. M. Williams, *op. cit.*, p. 200.

28. U.S. Congress, *Senate Executive Documents*, No. 35, 34th Cong., 1st Sess., 1856, pp. 100-218.

29. Marcy to Buchanan, October 1, 1855, Instructions to Great Britain, NA, RG 59.

30. Marcy to Buchanan, October 13, 1855, *ibid.*

31. Marcy to Buchanan, October 22, 1855, *ibid.*

32. Spencer, *op. cit.*, pp. 358-59.

33. Palmerston to Clarendon, October 24, 1855, cited by Rippy, *op. cit.*, pp. 117-18.

34. Buchanan to Marcy, October 26, 1855, Despatches from Great Britain, NA, RG 59. The three relevant articles, in the London *Times*, the *Chronicle*, and the *Morning Post*, were all reprinted in the *Washington Union* on November 14, 1855.

35. Buchanan to Marcy, October 30, 1855, Despatches from Great Britain, NA, RG 59.

36. Buchanan to Marcy, November 9, 1855, Despatches from Great Britain, NA, RG 59.

37. U.S. Congress, *Senate Executive Documents*, No. 35, 34th

Cong., 1st Sess., 1856, pp. 223-43. For a more complete account of the steamer built in New York (the "America"), see pages 234-35.

38. Marcy to Buchanan, November 12, 1855, Instructions to Great Britain, NA, RG 59.

39. *Washington Union*, November 15, 1855. This comment was reputedly written by Caleb Cushing. Scribner, *op. cit.*, p. 540.

40. Buchanan to Marcy, November 2, 16, 1855, Despatches from Great Britain, NA, RG 59.

41. Buchanan to Marcy, November 23, 1855, *ibid.*

42. Buchanan to Marcy, December 28, 1855, *ibid.*

43. Clarendon to Crampton, November 16, 1855, U.S. Congress, *Senate Executive Documents*, No. 35, 34th Cong., 1st Sess., 1856, pp. 38-43.

44. Marcy to Buchanan, December 28, 1855, Instructions to Great Britain, NA, RG 59.

45. Richardson, *op. cit.*, V, 331.

46. Seymour to Marcy, January 1, 1856, Despatches from Russia, NA, RG 59.

47. Buchanan to Marcy, January 11, 1856, Despatches from Great Britain, NA, RG 59.

48. Buchanan to Marcy, January 18, 1856, *ibid.* (Italics Buchanan's).

49. Buchanan to Marcy, January 22, 1856, *ibid.*

50. Van Alstyne, *American Historical Review*, XLI, 492.

51. Great Britain, *3 Hansard's Parliamentary Debates*, CXI (1856), 492.

52. Buchanan to Harriet Lane, January 25, 1856, in Moore, *The Works of James Buchanan*, X, 21.

53. Buchanan to Marcy, November 21, 1854, November 2, 9, 1855, Despatches from Great Britain, NA, RG 59.

54. Buchanan to Marcy, February 5, 1856, *ibid.*

55. Buchanan to Marcy, February 8, 1856, *ibid.* Clarendon to Crampton, November 10, 1855, U.S. Congress, *Senate Executive Documents*, No. 35, 34th Cong., 1st Sess., 1856, pp. 250-51; Crampton to Marcy, February 27, 1856, Notes from the British Legation, NA, RG 59.

56. See Buchanan to Marcy, November 9, 1855, Despatches from Great Britain, NA, RG 59.

57. Buchanan to Marcy, February 1, 1856, *ibid.*

58. Buchanan to Marcy, February 5, 12, 1856, *ibid.*

59. M. Williams, *op. cit.*, p. 209.

60. Richardson, *op. cit.*, V, 362.

61. U.S. Congressional Globe, 34th Cong. 1st Sess., 1856, XXXI, Pt. 1, 618-27, Appendix, pp. 175-77, 234-43, 300-06, 435-42.

62. *Ibid.*, pp. 620-21.

63. *Ibid.*, p. 624.

64. Dallas to Marcy, April 20, 7, 18, 25, 1856, Despatches from Great Britain, NA, RG 59.

65. Dallas to Marcy, April 20, 1856, *ibid.*

66. Clarendon to Dallas, May 3, 1856, enclosure in Dallas to Marcy, May 3, 1856, *ibid.;* Dallas to Marcy, May 6, 1856, *ibid.*

67. Dallas to Marcy, May 13, 1856, *ibid.*

68. Crampton to Clarendon, March 3, 4, April 29, 1856, cited by M. Williams, *op. cit.,* pp. 210-11.

69. Great Britain, *State Papers,* XLVI, 784-85, 794, 796, 803.

70. *Ibid.,* pp. 786, 789, 797.

71. William O. Scroggs, *Filibusters and Financiers* (New York: The Macmillan Company, 1916), p. 195.

72. Crampton to Clarendon, May 5, 1856, cited by M. Williams, p. 212; U.S., *Congressional Globe;* 34th Cong., 1st Sess., XXXI, Pt. 2, 1069-72.

73. Crampton to Clarendon, May 12, 1856, cited by M. Williams, *op. cit.,* p. 212.

74. Dallas to Marcy, May 16, 1856, Despatches from Great Britain, NA, RG 59.

75. Nichols, *op. cit.,* pp. 461-62; Spencer, *op. cit.,* pp. 371-72.

76. Richardson, *op. cit.,* V, 371-73.

77. See Scroggs, *op. cit.,* p. 250.

78. Marcy to Dallas, May 24, 1856, Instructions to Great Britain, NA, RG 59.

79. Marcy to Dallas, May 27, 1856, *ibid.;* also U.S. Congress, *Senate Executive Documents,* No. 80, 34th Cong., 1st Sess., 1856.

80. Dallas to Marcy, May 31, 1856, Despatches from Great Britain, NA, RG 59.

81. Mason to Marcy, June 8, 1856, Despatches from France, NA, RG 59.

82. Mason to Marcy, June 12, 1856, *ibid.*

83. Dallas to Marcy, June 6, 1856, Despatches from Great Britain, NA, RG 59.

84. Marcy to Dallas, June 16, Instructions to Great Britain, NA, RG 59.

85. "The Monroe Doctrine," *North American Review,* LXXXII (April, 1856), 478-512.

86. Great Britain, *3 Hansard's Parliamentary Debates,* CXLII (June 16, 1856), 1511, 1514.

# Success and Failure

## CHAPTER EIGHT

> I think, Sir, it would be wise if England would at last recognize that the United States, like all the great countries of Europe, have a policy, and that they have a right to have a policy.[1]

## BRITISH REVERSAL, 1856-1857

The decision that British statesmen faced in June, 1856 with respect to affairs in the western hemisphere, was much like the hard choices they had been forced to make in preceding years. Should opposition to further American expansion be maintained, whatever the risks, or should partial concessions be made in an attempt to preserve the desired balance of power? The issue was forced by the actions of the United States government, which had defiantly dismissed the British Minister in Washington for his part in an affair in which he had acted in good faith, and had simultaneously pressed for a final delimitation of the British presence in Central America. The Palmerston government, anti-American as it was, was forced by circumstances to choose the same

221

course that Great Britain had usually followed in past years
and was to follow in the future. In short,

> the British government had no resort but to retreat
> as gracefully as possible. The stubborn policy of the
> Pierce administration . . . undoubtedly emphasized
> the necessity for a prompt and definite concession.[2]

The Crimean War, symbol of the European involvement
that had restrained Britain in the Western hemisphere, influenced this decision. It has been claimed that "the reason
that the two nations averted war was British involvement in
another war, in the Crimea, a war which absorbed all the
strength of Great Britain, causing her to placate the United
States."[3] Such a judgment may seem exaggerated, since the
Crimean War had actually ended by this time and the large
British military organization was presumably free for use
elsewhere. But the underlying political tensions that had
brought on the war were not resolved, and Britain was still
occupied with preserving the European balance of power,
which was not a direct concern of American statesmen. The
Crimean War, moreover, dampened the enthusiasm of the
British public for foreign wars and thus undermined the
popular support of any British government seeking to use
force against the United States.
     British public sentiment in favor of a peaceful solution
to the difficulties with the United States grew. Pacifists, people with trading interests, and opposition political leaders led
the campaign against a threatening war which they saw as
potentially disastrous.[4] When many of Palmerston's own supporters joined the ranks of the critics, he found retreat the
only practical policy. Indications of this appeared before the
two notes of late May were received. News of United States
recognition of Walker's Nicaraguan regime, received in Britain on about the first of June, did not create the expected
uproar. The London *Times,* harshest critic of America, took
an unexpectedly light view of the matter:

It is no case of war, it is not even necessarily a ground of diplomatic complaint. The Clayton-Bulwer treaty has not been in terms, violated, and it may probably be expedient in the present critical state of the relations between the two countries, rather to pass this matter by in silence than to incur the risk of introducing fresh difficulties into a discussion already sufficiently perilous, or give an excuse to those who are even now only too ready to seek an occasion of quarrel.[5]

The following day the *Times* added that the recruiting question was likewise no cause for war, and declared that, even if Dallas should be dismissed in retaliation for Crampton's forced return, there was no need to regard the matter as a prelude to hostilities.[6] Other newspapers that had taken a strong anti-American stand also felt that the Walker affair should be handled tolerantly in order to preserve peace. The *News* hoped that Palmerston would not dismiss Dallas as a retaliatory act. The *Telegraph*, an anti-Palmerston paper, was openly alarmed at the government's dangerous policy of risking war with the United States: "Surely the war just terminated by a disgraceful peace, which we were obliged to accept, ought to be a lesson to curb the overweening pride of our countrymen." [7]

Dallas noted on June third that recognition of Walker's regime "has not produced the impression that was anticipated." Referring to the conciliatory tone of the *Times,* he remarked that the paper was "under the influence of more reason, or greater panic than usual. . . ." [8] One week later, as Dallas got a more complete impression of British sentiment, he reported to his government that criticism of Crampton "augments in force every day," and predicted that the British government would not, despite his earlier fears, send him back to the United States, much less hazard a war in defense of the unfortunate British Minister.[9]

With the stage thus set, it came as no surprise when Clarendon greeted Marcy's Central American note with a show of conciliation and a willingness to concede matters of substance. The British Foreign Minister predicted that the two countries could quickly clear up the whole dispute and indicated that he was prepared to offer unprecedented terms; as Clarendon phrased it, Great Britain "would not give three coppers to retain any post on the Central American territory or coast from which she could honorably retire." [10] The explosive recruitment question was similarly dampened in the House of Commons on June 16, after news of Crampton's dismissal had been received. By this time Palmerston had been under pressure to temper his response to the American act, not only from opposition leaders such as Benjamin Disraeli, but also from members of his own party—notably Lord John Russell. In his reply, Palmerston gave specific assurance that Dallas would *not* be handed his passport, and repeated Clarendon's statement of British willingness to settle Central American affairs. He agreed with his colleagues that it would be "lamentable in the extreme" for the two countries to be brought to war with each other.

As one historian of the subject has noted, "The attitude here displayed by Palmerston put an end to the recruiting dispute and really opened a new and more friendly era in the relations between the two countries." [11] Dallas wrote home in triumph:

> Everything since I communicated your two last despatches to Lord Clarendon has worked to a charm. The public excitement augmented every hour. The opposition in Parliament took an attitude not to be mistaken, and on Friday last, headed by Lord John Russell, opened their battery. Yesterday Lord John put his questions to the Premier in a handsome and impressive speech, and Lord Palmerston announced formally the determination of the cabinet, "not to terminate their present amicable relations with Mr. Dallas." The breakers are avoided; the legation is in deep water again; the Crampton squall has passed over, rather clearing the sky than otherwise; and there is bright promise of a goodly day to-morrow.[12]

The worst threat to the "goodly day" that still remained to mar British-American relations was the continued presence of the Walker regime in Nicaragua, which the United States had recognized. This threatened to affect the Central American negotiations adversely, since British withdrawal from the Mosquito Coast depended on a satisfactory arrangement with the government of that country. Furthermore, Honduras, Guatemala, El Salvador, and Costa Rica had vigorously protested Pierce's action and, supported by the British and Spanish, had drawn up a treaty of alliance in a war to drive out the invader. Walker's army of 1200 Americans was put to a severe test, and was finally destroyed in May, 1857. While the British, along with the French, encouraged the Central American states, they carefully avoided mentioning the Walker issue in negotiations with the United States over their withdrawal from the isthmus,[13] and concluded an agreement to retreat from the isthmus before the fall of the regime.

Soon after talks on Central America were reopened, Dallas reported that "I think I see land." [14] The British had demonstrated a willingness to yield on every major American demand, so long the withdrawal was accomplished in an honorable fashion. Progress in the talks between Dallas and Clarendon was held back because Dallas was not given full powers to conclude a treaty immediately, and because both sides wanted Britain to conclude an agreement with Honduras on the return of the Bay Islands before any Anglo-American agreement was made. By the end of July, Dallas had received detailed instructions with powers to draw up a treaty. At the same time he reported with regard to the Mosquito Coast, that "We shall ultimately adjust a plan by which the British obligation of honor may in no respect be violated in the abandonment of the protectorate." As British negotiations with the Honduran representative were drawing to a close, Dallas reported that there was "one only remaining snag to get over, or to get around, and that is the condition of Nicaragua...." [15]

The British change of heart continued to amaze and delight Dallas, who was not quite certain how to interpret it.

To a friend he confided his happiness with the state of affairs:

> All, aye all, that I came here to do will be suc-
> cessfully accomplished, if indeed it has not been already
> achieved, in the course of a week. The two countries,
> five months ago, were at that critical stand of mutual
> and morbid defiance when a prolonged war might have
> sprung from a few more hot words, or the hasty dis-
> charge of a gun at sea. People watched with suspended
> breath the news of every hour. Americans, all over the
> continent of Europe; and in particular, Commodore
> Breese, commanding our Mediterranean squadron,
> awaited a signal from this office to hurry home. Well!
> it all changed in the lapse of a month or six weeks;
> and the change has advanced, step by step, until now,
> before the entire expiration of five months, they who
> understand the condition and tone of international re-
> lations, are satisfied that a sounder basis for mutual
> harmony and respect has not existed since the Treaty
> of '83. I cannot tell you how this has been brought
> about. There is the fact.[16]

Dallas did recognize, however, that the continuing problems
of European international politics might have had some influence on the British decision to pacify the United States:

> I have had a little time to think on your question
> as to the cause of the present amicable tone toward
> us. It is impossible to answer it upon any but conjec-
> tural grounds. There may be serious anticipations as
> to the condition of Italy, and misgivings suggested by
> the extreme courtship between France and Russia. . . .[17]

A first draft of a treaty was completed in late August, to
which Marcy suggested a number of minor changes. After
Clarendon's acceptance of these alterations, the completed
agreement was signed on October 17.[18] The extent of the

British surrender, as summarized by Dallas himself was indeed considerable:

> The upshot is that Great Britain withdraws from
> her Colony in the Bay of Honduras, gives up her Pro-
> tectorate of the Mosquitoes, admits Greytown to be a
> Free City under the sovereignty of Nicaragua, pens
> up her Indian king and his subjects within a narrow
> and precise reservation, and promises never to over-
> leap the limits of the Belize as they were when the
> Clayton-Bulwer Treaty was made. That will do, won't
> it? [19]

Only in one respect did the Dallas-Clarendon agreement
depart significantly from the terms demanded by the United
States since the beginning of the Pierce administration. Instead of simply declaring the Bay Islands to be a part of the
Republic of Honduras, the treaty referred to the agreement
that almost had been concluded between Great Britain and
Honduras, which made the islands a free state under Honduran sovereignty—an arrangement intended to protect British citizens on the islands. Pierce approved the treaty despite
this one minor "defect," and recommended its ratification in
his fourth annual message in December.[20]

The Senate, however, struck out the offending article and
substituted one that affirmed Honduran sovereignty in the
Bay Islands. Clarendon offered another article designed to
meet American objections, but the Senate again insisted on all
or nothing. The dispute thus dragged on through the Buchanan administration until it was finally settled, again on
American terms, in 1860. By this time the British government
had, for all practical purposes, abandoned hope of maintaining a British presence of any real significance to oppose the
United States in this area.[21]

The failure of the Pierce administration to formalize, and
thus receive credit for, the British surrender in the isthmus

was due more to its tactical clumsiness than any other single factor. In general, the American government had made poor use of its advantages, despite the many external circumstances in its favor. One of the most important of these was the Crimean War, which, however poorly it may have been exploited on the whole, proved to be a powerful factor in the more successful episodes of American foreign policy during these years.

# CRIMEA: THE LOST CHANCE

The Crimean War left an important legacy in European international politics. It destroyed the diplomatic alliance that had united Austria, Prussia, and Russia at the center of European affairs since 1815. It temporarily brought together two traditional antagonists, Britain and France, in a coalition supported by Austria, but this combination proved unstable. The result was lack of stability in Europe which paved the way for the diplomacy of Cavour and Bismarck. The task of Great Britain, as the "balancer" of European politics, was made more difficult.[22]

American diplomats in late 1856 paid particular attention to the break-up of the Crimean alliance, as Napoleon III began to court Russia and to direct his attention to Rumanian and Italian politics. Because the alliance of Britain and France had been the chief debit of the conflict from the American point of view, the waning of this threat was quickly noted by such observers as Dallas:

> The great alliance is loosening. Something on this score is due to the insinuating diplomacy of Russia, which began immediately on the meeting of the Peace Congress in Paris,—something to the under-current of contemptuous remark in which the French indulge against the military capacity of their English Crimean heroes; something to the unavoidable diversity of sentiment and policy as to the Principalities. . . .

This question as to the union of the Danubian
Principalities has greater depth and importance in its
speculative futurity and in its immediate effects, than
may at first be supposed. It is vastly interesting as
bearing upon the relations hereafter to exist between
Russia and the rest of Europe. But its present operation in producing a disagreement on a great principle
between France and England, and tending to end the
alliance in angry quarrel, cannot be overrated. . . .
There would seem to spring out of it at once, a new
arrangement of European alliances: Great Britain,
Austria, and Turkey antagonistic to France, Russia and
Prussia.[23]

American statesmen had already shown their aversion to
any arrangement that seemed to give Britain strong and
constant support in the Western hemisphere. Britain was the
main obstacle to American policy in the New World, and
American statesmen welcomed any development in European
politics that tended to embarrass or encumber Her Majesty's
Ministers. American interest in the atrocity charges made
against Britain in the period following the war involved,
therefore, more than humanitarian sentiment. Dallas, for example, reported with glee that British military conduct at
Kerch and Odessa had created ill will which, according to a
German diplomat, "pervaded all Germany, if not all Europe." [24]

In another post-Crimean development—the reactivated
discussion of neutral rights in time of war—the United States
played an important role. Although the Pierce administration
had forced the British to follow a very broad definition of
neutral trading privileges during the Crimean War, efforts
to press Britain and her allies into permanent acceptance of
these principles had failed. There was therefore a good deal
of interest in the proposed statement of international law on
this subject signed by the belligerents at the peace conference
in early 1856.

The "Declaration of Paris" had the outward appearance
of a great victory for American principles. Under French

persuasion, the British had agreed to accept the twin rules of "free ships make free goods" and "neutral goods are safe under any flag," excepting in both cases contraband of war. To this was added the commonly accepted principle that all blockades must be effective in order to be binding. But the benefit of these rules, from the American point of view, was more than offset by the first of the four points in the declaration, which abolished all privateering. The United States regarded this as "a direct and intentional blow," which would "deprive it of what had been its greatest offensive weapon in case of war at sea." [25]

The affront was so great, in fact, that Dallas for one was led to suspect strong underlying malice:

> We have kept at peace, and I hope we may continue so. It is barely possible, however, that the late Congress at Paris intended their declaration abolishing Privateering as the groundwork of a coercive movement by a confederation of European sovereigns against America. If so, have at ye all, my lads! [26]

Behind this apprehension of European intentions was an appreciation of the hard military facts of international affairs. As mentioned above, privateering was the main American defense against the overwhelming strength of the British navy, and it was greatly feared by the British. Behind the extended technical arguments over international law lay the considerations of power expressed by Dallas:

> If the navies of England and France combined, or the fleet of England alone, are to be relieved from the necessity of dispersion, in order to convoy and protect their commerce, there is not a point of our immense coast on which they could not land any amount of force which they might deem necessary in order to countenance servile insurrection or separate the States. The danger of such a thing may be distant,

and on our own soil I should hope we could get the
better of any alliance: but I must confess that, until
by the vast increase of our national naval armament
we become more equal antagonists in the *national duel,*
I should prefer not to diminish the difficulties of our
invasion.[27]

The American campaign against the Declaration of Paris
was begun by approaching Russia, its tested friend in disputes
over the rights of neutral commerce. One month after the
peace had been signed, Dallas reported having reproached a
visiting Russian diplomat for entering into an agreement
"aimed exclusively at the great defensive weapon of the
United States against British disposition to go to war with
us." He remarked to the Tsar's representative with some as-
perity that American support of Russia was not being reciprocated: "See what the result is of having sympathized
with Russia for two years!—we have a fierce contest about
enlistments in violation of our neutrality laws, and at the
very first occasion Russia throws her weight into the scale of
our adversary. . . ." [28] The Russian government quickly
adopted the American point of view, announcing that it
viewed the document as inapplicable to any state not accepting it, and supported all subsequent American counterpro-
posals on the subjects of neutral rights and privateering. The
Tsar's approval of the Declaration of Paris thus became a
meaningless action.[29]

Marcy instructed Mason at about the same time to ask
the French government what its attitude to privateering by
American citizens would actually be "in case the United
States should unhappily be at war with any other power
which has acceded to the Declaration." [30] Since France, a
traditional "little navy" power, had usually supported American policies on international maritime law, the United States
hoped to complete the division of the Paris signatories by
obtaining an assurance that the French would not interfere
with American privateering.

No satisfactory reply was received from Paris, despite

continued urging.[31] But in the meantime Marcy had already
moved on another front to combat the effect of the declaration. The American Secretary of State revived a proposal,
first made in Pierce's second annual message of December 4,
1854, that private property at sea be made immune from
seizure by vessels-of-war as well as by private ships. In the
earlier message, also written by Marcy,[32] privateering had
been justified as a necessity for American policy on the
grounds that the United States navy was only a tenth the
size of Britain's while the merchant marines of the two
countries were of practically equal size. To renounce privateering, consequently, would leave all American commerce
and coastlines open to attack by foreign naval vessels with
no effective means of retaliation or defense. Only if the
safety of American commerce were assured could its right of
self-defense by raiding commerce be surrendered: "Should
the leading powers of Europe concur in proposing as a rule
of international law to exempt private property upon the
ocean from seizure by public armed cruisers as well as by
privateering, the United States will readily meet them upon
that broad ground." [33]

Marcy recast these thoughts into slightly different language and relayed the proposal to the French government on
July 28, 1856. If, he said, the Congress of Paris intended to
make war more civilized by limiting its effects to combatants,
there was no reason to allow naval vessels to do what private
ships were to be prohibited from doing. The United States,
since it did not keep large standing armies and navies, could
not assent to such an arrangement. To the contrary, it could
accept the whole declaration if the first point were amended
to include the provision that "the private property of the
subjects of citizens of a belligerent on the high seas shall be
exempt from seizure by public armed vessels of the other belligerent except it be contraband." [34] Marcy had made his coun-
terproposal appear to be an unprecedentedly liberal and
humane suggestion for changing the mode of warfare and
effectively countered the bad impression that might have been

created if the United States had simply refused to abolish privateering.

From the British pont of view, of course, the loss from the adoption of the amendment would more than offset the gain from the abolition of privateering. While the unequal American and British navies would be left to face each other, the vast superiority of the British force would be much less effective if private commerce were made inviolable. Although British commercial circles greeted the proposal with favor, Palmerston's organ, the *Post,* treated Marcy's move as an attempt to obscure the American refusal to abandon privateering by offering a dramatic but completely impractical program for the limitation of naval warfare.[35] The proposal was also regarded with some suspicion by those Americans who feared Britain most. Since privateering was the only American offensive naval weapon, it was argued, its abolition would leave the British navy free to invade the American coast, whatever the state of private commerce. Dallas expressed these misgivings privately to Marcy:

> Losing the right of privateering, in other words, of assailing the vital interests of our adversary, our means of aggression are nil. Our navy must be docked; and we must be content with whatever terms the adversary in this national duel may prescribe for a peace. . . . If our navy approached anywhere near to the power of the one displayed off Portsmouth last spring, I should be quite willing to let it take its chance in defending our coast:—but as it is now . . . it is impossible to say at how many points of landing along our coast, a war would rapidly become one of invasion.[36]

But the proposal, on the whole, was favorable to American interests, and Marcy continued to press for its adoption. Russia supported these efforts. When the British, in January 1857, indicated to the Russian Minister in London that they would consider Marcy's view, Alexander Gorchakov, the new Russian Foreign Minister, declared in elation to Seymour that it was the close ties between the United States and Russia that had brought Palmerston to this position.[37] But it was doubtful that Britain ever considered the scheme seriously, and in any event no positive move was ever made by that country. France rejected Russian overtures on the proposal, without even bothering to reply to Marcy.[38] Although the project collapsed, it did at least lessen the embarrassment caused by the Declaration of Paris. While the United States gained no lasting concessions on neutral rights from the Crimean War, quick action helped to neutralize a British move that would have crippled American naval power in any future engagement. The entire episode also furnished another illustration of the way in which the United States and Russia, the "villain" of the Crimean War, cooperated to their mutual advantage in world politics.

The Crimean War had, if anything, made these two countries more aware of the common interests that bound them. A strengthened friendship with Russia was a definite American gain in the Crimean War.

One indication of the high value placed on Russian friendship by the American statesmen is the fact that the United States knowingly allowed a Russian breach of neutrality laws at the same time they were forcing an international crisis over Crampton's unintentionally illegal activities in the enlistment controversy. This incident—one of the war's more unusual footnotes—involved the steamship "America," built in New York for the Russian government, which had used the names of American citizens as a cover. The fiction fooled no one but was never challenged by the American government. When the vessel was on its way to the Pacific, in late 1855, a British warship in Rio de Janeiro tried to seize it, but was stopped by an American naval officer. The boat proceeded on its journey, arriving at the mouth of the Amur River in early 1856. Marcy, who knew all the facts of the matter, commented, "If the English push us too hard we will tell them frankly that it ill becomes them who have received so much help from American citizens to complain because the Russians had a steamer built in this country." [39]

This was only one of a long series of events that had strengthened the ties between Russia and America during the conflict. The chief historian of the subject had made a striking summary of American "neutrality" during the conflict:

As the bloody war proceeded one European state after another left the neutral column and went over to the side of the Tsar's enemies. By the time it was over the United States was the only nation in the world that was neither ashamed nor afraid to acknowledge boldly her friendship for Russia. This friendship manifested itself in various ways and when the Russians counted up the numerous favors they had received they were both proud and pleased at the long list:

1. America had forced England to accept the principle that the flag covers the goods, and helped Russian commerce;

2. America permitted the sale of the Russian merchant marine interned in her ports after the declaration of war;

3. American naval vessels rescued the crew of the Russian ship "Diana" in the Far East;

4. America put a stop to recruiting for the English army;

5. America protected the "S.S. America" at Rio Janeiro;

6. American prestige and the fear of America prevented the allies from accepting the Spanish terms (guaranteeing Cuba) and consequently the Spanish help against Russia.[40]

The Russians extended numerous favors to the United States as well. For example, the Russian government offered to protect American citizens in Persia until the United States could gain diplomatic representation at the court of the Shah.[41] The two powers, as has been mentioned, cooperated in the discussions of neutral rights and privateering, especially those over the Declaration of Paris. The Russian government had extended the flat guarantee to the United States that, in spite of the declaration, "if in case of war between the United States and a third power, a legally armed American privateer presents itself before a Russian port, it will be admitted there." [42] Soon after the war American traders were welcomed into the Amur Valley and on Sakhalin Island, by special favor. Russia at the same time determined to coordinate its China policy with that of the United States: "The Emperor desires to march in accord with the American Government in this question as in all those related to the destiny of the United States." [43] The greatest advantage the Russians gave the United States, of course, was the deterrent effect of their war with the Western allies on British and French policy in the Western hemisphere.

That the United States, on the whole, gained little from the advantage it had been given by the Crimean War was due to the ineffective and inconsistent way in which American aims were pursued. Relations with Spain offer a prime example. In late 1856 the United States was still trying to resolve its controversies with the Spanish government. Marcy wrote Dodge that

> The President directs you to express his great disappointment that so little has been done by the Government of Spain to put the relations with the United States on a better footing. . . . If Spain is determined to make no arrangement with the United States upon the several subjects on which you were instructed to treat with her, that fact should be distinctly declared to this Government.[44]

But this effort proved as unavailing as those made before. The Spanish government had been antagonized by American behavior and particularly by Soulé's deportment in Madrid, and it was apparently determined not to make the slightest concessions unless forced to do so. The United States, with plausible if exaggerated pretexts for war, overwhelming superiority in war potential, and fairly definite assurances that Spain would receive no support from Britain or France, chose not to fight for Cuba or its other claims against Spain. Part of the explanation, of course, lay in the domestic situation, since the Pierce administration came to realize that a war over Cuba would not unify the country but would only arouse the violent hostility of antislavery groups. It was unable to gain even the minimal privilege of dealing directly with Cuban authorities (a right that had been granted to Great Britain).

With Mexico the story was similar. After he had purchased a small section of land in 1853, Gadsden could accomplish nothing more by his blustering attitude than to drive the Santa Anna government into the arms of the British, who, together with the French, effectively blocked American expansion in Mexico without arousing the Pierce administration to the point of hostilities. The United States, too ambitious and too truculent to pursue national aims by quiet pressure and negotiations during the enemy's hour of weakness, was however, too restrained to test British and French determination by the threat of physical force.

Where Britain was forced to retreat, it managed to do so with minimum loss. Neutral rights were conceded for the duration of the conflict on American terms, but efforts to give American principles a permanent status in international law were effectively blocked. Canadian waters were opened to American fishermen only after the British, in return, had won trade concessions that they hoped would cripple the annexationist movement north of the border. The Central American retreat, effected only after years of delay and evasion by the British, was help up once when the United States overplayed its hand, and once again by unreasoning American intransigence over a minor point of conflict.

In short, the United States gained very little from the Crimean War, when one considers the goals of the Pierce administration and its attempt to reap the greatest possible advantage from American neutrality. As far as positive results were concerned, the conflict was a lost chance. This should not, however, obscure the fact that the Crimean War was an important factor in the formulation of American policy, and influenced many American calculations—or miscalculations.

# NOTES

1. Benjamin Disraeli, June 16, 1856, *3 Hansard's Parliamentary Debates*, CXLII (1856), 1511.
2. M. Williams, *op. cit.*, p. 221.
3. Eugene Grigg, "The Political Career of William Learned Marcy" (unpublished Master's thesis, Department of History, University of Chicago, 1949), p. 71.
4. Rippy, *op. cit.*, pp. 117-18; M. Williams, *op. cit.*, pp. 221-22.
5. *Times* (June 2, 1856).
6. *Ibid.* (June 3, 1856).
7. *Examiner* (June 7, 1856). *Press* (June 2, 1856). *News* (June 4, 1856). *Telegraph* (June 2, 1856).
8. Dallas to Marcy, June 3, 1856, Despatches from Britain, NA, RG 59.
9. Dallas to Marcy, June 10, 1856, *ibid.*
10. Dallas to Marcy, June 13, 1856, *ibid.*
11. Great Britain, *3 Hansard's Parliamentary Debates*, CXLII (1856), 1502-1514; M. Williams, *op. cit.*, p. 218.
12. Dallas to Marcy, June 17, 1856, Despatches from Great Britain, NA, RG 59. See also despatch of June 20.
13. Scroggs, *op. cit.*, pp. 175, 250; John H. Wheeler, American Minister to Nicaragua, to Marcy, August 10, 1856, Despatches from Nicaragua, NA, RG 59.
14. Dallas to Marcy, July 8, 1856, Despatches from Great Britain, NA, RG 59.
15. Dallas to Marcy, July 15, 29, August 8, 1856, *ibid.;* Marcy to Dallas, July 26, 28, 1856, Instructions to Great Britain, NA, RG 59.
16. Dallas to Colonel Page, August 12, 1856, in George Mifflin Dallas, *A Series of Letters from London* (Philadelphia: J.B. Lippincott & Co., 1869), p. 74.
17. Dallas to Mr. Gilpin, August 22, 1856, *ibid.*, p. 78.
18. Marcy to Dallas, September 26, 1856, Instructions to Great Britain, NA, RG 59; Dallas to Marcy, October 10, 14, 17, 1856, Despatches from Great Britain, NA, RG 59.
19. Dallas to Gilpin, October 17, 1856, in Dallas, *op. cit.*, p. 93.
20. Richardson, *op cit.*, V, 410-11.
21. M. Williams, *op. cit.*, pp. 228-67.
22. See, for example, Gavin Henderson, "The Diplomatic Revolution of 1854," *American Historical Review*, XLIII (October, 1937), 22-23.
23. Dallas to Marcy, November 4, 7, 1856, Despatches from Great Britain, NA, RG 59.

24. Dallas to Marcy, December 1, 1856, *ibid.*

25. Francis Taylor Piggot, *The Declaration of Paris* (London: University of London Press Ltd., 1919), pp. 142-43; Spencer, *op. cit.,* p. 382. American records relating to the Declaration of Paris are collected in U.S. Congress, *Senate Executive Documents,* No. 104, 34th Cong., 1st Sess., 1856, and U.S. Congress, *House Executive Documents,* No. 1, 34th Cong., 3rd Sess., 1857.

26. Dallas to Senator G. W. Jones, August 20, 1856, in Dallas, *op. cit.,* p. 75.

27. Dallas to Marcy, December 8, 1856, Despatches from Great Britain, NA, RG 59. Italics Dallas'.

28. Dallas to Marcy, May 6, 1856, *ibid.*

29. Seymour to Marcy, September 16, 1856, Despatches from Russia, NA, RG 59.

30. Marcy to Mason, July 29, 1856, Instructions to France, NA, RG 59.

31. Marcy to Mason, October 4, December 8, 1856, *ibid.*

32. Spencer, *op. cit.,* p. 297, n. 40.

33. Richardson, *op cit.,* V, 276-77.

34. Marcy to Sartiges, July 28, 1856, Notes to the French Legation, NA, RG 59.

35. Spencer, *op. cit.,* p. 385.

36. Dallas to Marcy, December 12, 1856, Despatches from Great Britain, NA, RG 59. See also despatches of November 23 and December 8.

37. Seymour to Marcy, January 28, 1857, Despatches from Russia, NA, RG 59.

38. Spencer, *op. cit.,* p. 385.

39. Golder, *American Historical Review,* XXXI, 474; Stoeckl to Nesselrode, October 11/23, 1855, quoted *ibid.* Dvoichenko-Markov, *Russian Review,* XIII, 140.

40. Golder, *American Historical Review,* XXXI, 474.

41. Dvoichenko-Markov, *Russian Review,* XIII, 144.

42. Gorchakov, Russian Foreign Minister, to Stoeckl, June 10/22, 1856, quoted (in French) in Golder, *American Historical Review,* XXXI, 475.

43. Golder, *American Historical Review,* XXXI, 475; Gorchakov to Stoeckl, September 21/October 3, 1856, quoted (in French) *ibid.*

44. Marcy to Dodge, October 13, 1856, Instructions to Spain, NA, RG 59.

# Neutral But Not Isolated

## CHAPTER NINE

> But if it be contended that we must remain absolutely
> indifferent to the affairs of Europe—that the changes
> wrought in the institutions and mutual relations of
> European governments do not merit our consideration and
> challenge our watchfulness then, assuredly, our neutrality
> doctrine would amount to an injunction on ourselves, and
> condemn us, in our foreign relations, to absolute inaction.[1]

## THE CRIMEAN WAR IN
## UNITED STATES DIPLOMACY

When Townshend Harris arrived in Japan in 1856 as
the first United States diplomatic representative to the country, he based his appeal to the Shogun for concessions and privileges on the Crimean War, arguing that further conflict
between Great Britain and Russia would lead one or the other
of these two countries to seize Japanese territory as a base
of operations. Japan could best protect itself, therefore, by
accepting the tutelage of a neutral and "unambitious" coun-

241

try: the United States. The argument reportedly proved very useful in opening Japan to American trade and influence.[2]

Harris' action was but another small demonstration —however trivial—of the way in which American diplomats and political leaders accepted the Crimean War, almost instinctively, as advantageous to the aims of American foreign policy. No attempt was made to insulate that policy from the effects of war, nor was it suggested that such an effort would be desirable or possible. American statesmen, like all rational statesmen, followed a course determined largely by considerations of the objective national interest.

The expansionist aims of the Pierce administration made the underlying effects of the Crimean War on American policy more prominent than they might have been if American interests were being pursued less ambitiously. The extent of American ambition can be seen, for example, in the comments of Dallas on his convention with Clarendon regarding Central America:

> Those gentlemen who are unable to see the preponderating influence in Central America, and *all around* that region, secured, by the scheme of pacification, to the United States, her policy, and her citizens, had better give up the role of statesmanship. . . .
> Under the stimulus of a safe and uninterrupted trade, the cloud of British naval armament dispelled, and one or more free cities as *appuis,* we should in less than five years exercise controlling influence on the Isthmus, elbow out the Mosquitoes, render the Belise [*sic*] a comparatively neglected and dwindling settlement, and possibly entertain volunteered offers from their respective owners for the purchase of Cuba and Jamaica.[3]

As previously suggested, the greatest effect of the Crimean War on American foreign policy was the opposition it created to American ambitions in the Western hemisphere. The main obstacles to the expansion of American influence were the alarmed Latin American States and Great Britain, France, and Spain. The weak American states, by themselves, could maintain no effective balance against the Colossus of the North, nor could Spain, by itself, successfully resist the United States for an indefinite period of time. But France, and especially Britain, had both the motivation and the power to oppose American expansion in the Western hemisphere just as they opposed Russian expansion in Europe and the Near East. The British position was stated most unequivocally by the irreconcilable opponent of Yankee pretentions, Lord Palmerston:

> As to propitiating the Yankees by countenancing their schemes of annexation it would be like propitiating an animal of prey by giving him one of one's travelling Companions. It would increase his desire for similar Food and spur him on to obtain it. . . .
> There can be little doubt that in the Course of Time the Anglo Saxon Race will spread far South in America, but it is for our Interest that this Should not happen until the Swarms are prepared to separate from the Parent Hive.[4]

But when its two most important rivals in Western hemisphere politics found themselves engaged in hostilities in another quarter of the globe, they were less capable of countering American ambitions. Yet at the same time American leaders continued to declare their indifference: The United States had no interest in European power politics and European power politics had no effect on the interests or policy of the United States. This pronouncement has been taken by most modern historians as indicating one of the basic foundations of United States foreign policy in the nineteenth century. But the actions and private comments of the Pierce administration during the Crimean War provide evidence that the interpretation of neutrality proclaimed in Presidential messages was not the same one that was followed in practice.

In examining this evidence, the foreign policy of the United States must be viewed as a whole, united by considerations of national interest, and not as a series of episodes concerning unrelated legalistic arguments. The background of American relationships with the belligerents, as well as internal influences on American policy, must be considered in the analysis. If American diplomacy during these years is treated in this light, a pattern of underlying political relationships begins to emerge that is only superficially evident in specific incidents. This pattern is an impressive argument against the ideologically biased accounts of most literary sources.

American diplomats, in the first place, followed the conflict closely and made certain that the State Department was well informed on all phases and aspects of both the war and the diplomacy behind it. The attitude of most American diplomatic representatives abroad indicated that they felt the war was relevant at least to American commercial interests, if not to American political aims. In regard to the former, the United States acted along the same lines as, if not in association with, the neutral nations of Western Europe, seeking a broad definition of neutral rights and pressuring the maritime powers to allow the widest possible scope to its own trade. The attitude of the United States, in particular, was instrumental in winning from Great Britain unprecedented concessions. And respecting the political implications of the war, nearly all American observers of European politics were alarmed by inferences that an alliance formed to stop Russia might serve as well to contain American activities in the Western hemisphere.

In the eyes of American statesmen, this alliance was the greatest potential danger resulting from the war. If ties between Great Britain and France were strengthened by conflict with the Tsar, the two countries might indeed offer more effective opposition to other expansionist states. But, in the meantime, it was doubtful that either country would fight a second war while engaged in the East. This was an advantageous set of circumstances that the Pierce administration understood and upon which it based many calculations. While open admissions that such considerations underlay American policy were infrequent, there are enough indications in available sources to confirm the influence of the Crimean War on American policy. Needless to say, the effect of the war was also evident in the very tempo and extent of American activities during and immediately following it.

Faced with the threat of American privateering for Russia, the British had backed down on neutral trading rights. They were also forced to relent and in some cases, to retreat in their attempt to block United States expansion—particularly in Canada and Central America, where American pressure had reached a threatening stage. While the ways in which this pressure was exerted were not always effective or even consistent, the confident demands of the American government were backed by a persistent self-assurance that the British would eventually have to give way, as was indeed usually the case. The Crimean War was clearly related to the increase in American pressure upon Britain.

In Central America the Pierce administration enlarged its claims shortly after the onset of the Crimean crisis, demanding the almost total withdrawal of British occupation forces. These demands were based upon a contested view of a treaty designed to give the two powers equality in that area. While the British attempted to delay a showdown until their war with Russia was concluded, the United States tried several times (ineffectively) to force its demands, and had almost succeeded in mid-1854 when the Greytown bombardment stiffened British resistance. But American diplomats, still believing that ultimately the British would have to retreat, continued to apply pressure in the area, going so far in 1856 as to recognize the filibustering regime of William Walker.

British relations were finally resolved by the recruitment controversy, in which the United States made a grave issue of some inconsequential activities of British diplomats that were of questionable legality. (While this matter was being pressed, grounds for a similar complaint against Russia were overlooked.) When the Pierce administration took the extreme action of demanding the recall of the British diplomatic representatives involved and simultaneously asked for a final accounting in Central America, Palmerston was forced to accede. One reason the British gave in was that the Crimean War had exhausted the British public's willingness to fight a new and difficult war with their transatlantic cousins.

Relations with France were also characterized by a series of minor "incidents" blown out of proportion—such as the Raousset expedition, the Dillon affair, and the Soulé affair. In Mexico, Santo Domingo, and Hawaii, the anti-American activities of the British and French were challenged by the American government, which attempted to force their retreat in these areas by a forthright defense of "American rights." When the two powers, in framing the Declaration of Paris, tried to use their victory in Crimea to force the abolition of privateering upon the United States, the reaction was also swift and strong. In balance the advantage of the Crimean War remained with the United States as far as its relations with the Allies were concerned.

The United States also counted on the Crimean War to curtail Allied support of Spain in any war over Cuba. The administration, which believed that Spain would be left to fend for herself should her relations with the United States deteriorate to the point of hostilities, used two flimsy pretexts, the "Black Warrior" and "El Dorado" affairs, to create crises in its relations with Spain over Cuba; but in spite of the favorable opportunity presented by these incidents (strongly emphasized publicly and privately by such outspoken expansionists as Pierre Soulé) the United States government stopped short of belligerence. Nevertheless, in its extreme aggressiveness, typified by the Ostend "Manifesto" to Spain and her allies, the Pierce administration demonstrated its confidence that the British and French would not support Spanish rule on the island.

As we have shown above, the opposition of the British and French was a source of common concern to Russia and the United States, whose relations during these years were remarkable. Undisturbed by a single incident of the type that marred U.S. relations with the Western allies, they were marked by a series of small acts of friendship that did not pass unnoticed in London and Paris, and were certainly recognized by some members of the Pierce administration as a good means of gaining leverage against Britain and France. Mutual support on neutral rights and privateering was one example, and mediation offers by the United States in the Crimea was another. In both cases the legalistic, humanitarian arguments employed proved to have a foundation in political interest. The two states also cooperated diplomatically against British moves in Alaska, Persia, and elsewhere.

American diplomats openly attributed the sympathy of the American people for Russia to British and French opposition in the Western hemisphere. Public opinion thus revealed an instinctive appreciation of the way in which the conflict affected national interests. Only a set of ideological assumptions as deeply rooted as those in the American political tradition could maintain that the United States remained unaffected by European events; such is the isolationist view of the nineteenth century that has tended to dominate United States diplomatic historiography.

# UNITED STATES DIPLOMACY
# IN WORLD POLITICS

Throughout most of the nineteenth century American politicians generally supported the maintenance and spread of American influence especially in Latin America and in the Far East. Some diplomats at the end of the century could still subscribe literally to what John Quincy Adams had proclaimed in 1819:

Until Europe shall find it a settled geographical element that United States and North America are identical, any effort on our part to reason the world

out of a belief that we are ambitious will have no other
effect than to convince them that we add to our ambition hypocrisy.[5]


A corresponding, though less elegantly stated, sentiment was
expressed by the *Philadelphia Public Ledger* shortly after
Pierce's inauguration: "[America is bounded on] East by
sunrise, West by sunset, North by the Arctic Expedition, and
South as far as we darn please." [6]

In ideological terms, American aims were expressed
largely through the Monroe Doctrine: European states should
stay out of Western hemisphere affairs, leaving the United
States and the Latin American countries to evolve their own
destiny; in return the United States would let Europe alone.
These terms were highly favorable to the United States and
were evoked in almost every Presidential message, particularly during the Crimean War and other periods of European
turmoil.

The main international rival of the United States remained Great Britain. So long as the United States could
assume that Europe would be balanced without outside intervention, and Britain continued trying to keep the balance in
both the Old and New Worlds simultaneously, this did not
change. However, British diplomats differed on the degree
to which American moves should be opposed. Lord Napier,
who replaced Crampton in Washington, actually argued that
American expansion under certain circumstances was tolerable to British policy.[7] But he was perhaps forty years in
advance of his times; the British attitude at mid-century was
more clearly approximated by Palmerston's response to Napier's argument:


> This Despatch is not written with the good sense
> and judgment which naturally belong to Ld Napier;
> It is evidently the detailed Exposition of views argu-
> ments and opinions instilled into him by the Govt and
> others in the United States. It is a Tissue of Fallacies

and Sophistries. It tries to place on the narrow ground of Shop-keeping Considerations a Question which involves in its ultimate space the jeopardy of valuable possessions of the British Crown in the West Indies, and increased Danger to our floating Commerce. As to the argument that Concession as to Cuba would secure to England the permanent goodwill or future Forbearance of the United States, this is the worn out argument used by the Mouth Pieces of the Americans at each step of Encroachment on their Part. This was to be the Result of the Concession made to them by the Ashburton Treaty. This again was the motive urged by the Oregon arrangement. This is now put forward about Cuba and this would be repeated when successive Proofs of our weakness and Gullibility shall have encouraged them to demand our North American provinces.

I think Napier should have a Hint to cast one Eye at least to the Eastern Shores of the Atlantic and to remember that he has not become a Naturalized Citizen of the Union.[8]


Such opposed views of American and British interests were certain to be the cause of some dispute. In general, however, the British, with some support from France and Spain and the encouragement of the weak Latin American states, would naturally seek to keep a balance of power in the Western hemisphere and to prevent domination by the United States.

It is interesting to note that during the Crimean conflict Americans made no effort to hide their sympathy for, or interest in, European affairs, but unhesitatingly expressed their feelings about the war according to their ideals and to the way they understood those events to affect the United States. While some merely sought to encourage republicanism, some pacifism, some other ideals or moral standards, almost all recognized which power was the least threat to American interests and therefore best deserved American sympathy. Such conclusions were not based on passing fancies, which might suggest that the attitude of the American public toward the war was indeed an atypical episode in the country's emotional history, but upon considerations of greater permanence.

The Crimean War showed that the United States *was* involved with European powers in the pursuit of its goals, whether it chose to be or not. If Britain hindered American expansion at any point, the United States was forced to counter the opposition by pressure, subterfuge, open conflict, or otherwise. If Britain, or any other nation with which the United States had outstanding problems, was involved in events in another quarter of the globe, those events inevitably cast their shadow on American policy.

As a result, American neutrality in the war was shaped by political circumstances—there was nothing passive about it. The position was one of advantage, to be exploited. American statesman made use of European events in the pursuit of their own ends. The greatest challenges and threats to Britain and the "containing" powers were timed to coincide with their involvement elsewhere, and threats or concrete demonstrations of friendship with Britain's European opponents were also used to take advantage of the opponent's preoccupation.

It was a later generation of historians who tended to treat neutrality primarily as a doctrine of inaction. In 1860, Francis J. Grund gave an account of nineteenth-century United States neutrality in European politics that was closer to reality than the accounts of many historians who enjoyed the advantages of hindsight:

> If the map of Europe is to be changed—if Turkey is to be divided, and the nations of Europe are to extend their power and influence into Asia, we may consider how far this great historical movement of the people of the old world may affect the conditions of the new; and what steps it may be prudent for us to take, to balance the account. . . .
> If it be contended that we must remain indifferent

to the affairs of Europe—that the changes wrought in the institutions and mutual relations of European governments do not merit our consideration and challenge our watchfulness, then, assuredly, our neutrality doctrine would amount to an injunction on ourselves, and condemn us, in our foreign relations, to absolute political inaction. It would insure all other nations against harm from our growing energy and power; while it would not protect us from *their* intermeddling with *our* affairs.[9]

On every significant point, the events connected with the Crimean War support the view that the United States *was* involved in world politics, rather than the traditional theory of nineteenth-century isolationism usually accepted by twentieth-century historians. As opposed to a true policy of isolationism, the United States almost invariably opted for a course of action, determined by considerations of power and calculated to exploit existing circumstances to its advantage. The higher moral basis claimed for American neutrality in almost all policy pronouncements, was simply not evident in practice. American foreign policy, like all foreign policy, was conducted in a world of conflicting desires and aims, not in a state of quarantine maintained by assumptions of moral superiority.

Physical circumstances and considerations of concrete advantage made it possible during the Crimean War for the United States to follow and profit from a course of neutrality in European politics. Almost instinctively, the country was neutral in its international role, a position based on balance of power considerations and exploited to advantage. But it did play a role. The United States was actively neutral, not isolationist.

# NOTES

1. Francis J. Grund, *Thoughts and Reflections on the Present Position of Europe* (Philadelphia: Childs & Peterson, 1860), p. 225.

2. Bemis, *A Short History* . . . , pp. 188-89.

3. Dallas to Marcy, January 20, 30, 1857, Despatches from Great Britain, NA, RG 59.

4. Palmerston to Clarendon, July 4, 1857, quoted in Van Alstyne, *American Historical Review*, XLII, 499. Palmerston is advocating, in other words, a policy of "divide and rule"; no further areas in the Western hemisphere should be occupied by Americans until it is clear that the result would be independent states tending to oppose United States expansion rather than contribute to it.

5. Charles Francis Adams, ed., *Memoirs of John Quincy Adams*, IV (Philadelphia: J.B. Lippincott & Co., 1875), 439.

6. *Philadelphia Public Ledger*, July 8, 1853.

7. Napier to Clarendon, May 26, 1857, cited by Van Alstyne, *American Historical Review*, XLII, 492.

8. Palmerston to Clarendon, June 6, 1857, quoted *ibid.*, p. 499.

9. Grund, *op. cit.*, pp. 225, 233. Italics Grund's.

# Bibliography

*Unpublished Public Documents*

United States, Department of State, General Records. Record Group 59, National Archives, Washington, D.C.
 Despatches, 1853-1857
  Central America
  France
  Great Britain
  Hawaii
  Mexico
  Russia
  Turkey
 Instructions, 1835-1857
  Central America
  France
  Great Britain
  Hawaii
  Mexico
  Russia
  Spain
  Turkey
 Notes from Foreign Missions, 1853-1857
  France

Great Britain
Russia
Spain
Turkey
Notes to Foreign Missions, 1853-1857
France
Great Britain
Russia
Spain
Turkey

## Published Public Documents

Bartlett, Ruhl (ed.), *The Record of American Diplomacy.* Revised edition. New York: Alfred A. Knopf, 1954.

Delafield, Major Richard. *Report on the Art of War in Europe in 1854, 1855, and 1856.* Washington: George W. Bowman, 1860.

Great Britain, Parliament. *Hansard's Parliamentary Debates,* Third Series. Vols. CXXX-CXLII, 1854-1856.

Manning, William R. (ed.) *Diplomatic Correspondence of the United States. Inter-American Affairs, 1831-1860.* Vol. IV: *Central America, 1851-1860.* Vol. VI: *Dominican Republic, Ecuador, France.* Vol. VII: *Great Britain.* Vol. XI: *Spain.* Washington: Carnegie Endowment for International Peace, 1934, 1935, 1936, 1939.

Miller, David Hunter (ed.). *Treaties and other International Acts of the United States of America.* Vols. VI, VII. Washington: United States Government Printing Office, 1942.

Moore, John Bassett (ed.). *A Digest of International Law.* Vol. VI. Washington: United States Government Printing Office, 1906.

Mordecai, Major Alfred. *Military Commission to Europe in 1855 and 1956.* Washington: George W. Bowman, 1861.

Quitman, John A. *Speech on the Subject of the Neutrality Laws: Delivered in Committee of the Whole House on the State of the Union, April 29, 1856.* Washington: Union Office, 1856.

Richardson, James D. (ed.) *A Compilation of the Messages and Papers of the Presidents.* Vol. V. Washington: Bureau of National Literature and Art, 1908.

United States, Congress. *Congressional Globe.* Vols. XXVIII-
XXXI, 1854-1856.
————. *House Executive Documents* Nos. 1, 21, 76, 91, 103,
126. 33rd Congress, 1st session, 1853-1854.
————. *House Executive Documents* Nos. 1, 93. 33rd Con-
gress, 2nd session, 1854-1855.
————. *House Executive Documents* Nos. 1, 107. 34th Con-
gress, 1st session, 1855-1856.
————. *House Executive Documents* No. 1. 34th Congress,
3rd session, 1857.
————. *House Journal,* 33rd Congress, 2nd session, 1854-
1855.
————. *House Journal.* 34th Congress, 1st session, 1855-
1856.
————. *Senate Executive Documents* Nos. 1, 40, 53. 33rd
Congress, 1st session, 1853-1854.
————. *Senate Executive Documents* No. 1. 33rd Congress
2nd session, 1854-1855.
————. *Senate Executive Documents* Nos. 1, 35, 80, 85, 104.
34th Congress, 1st session, 1855-1856.
————. *Senate Journal,* 33rd Congress, 2nd session, 1854-
1855.
————. *Senate Journal,* 35th Congress, 1st session, 1857.
Van Alstyne, Richard W. (ed.) "Anglo-American Relations,
1853-1857," *American Historical Review,* XLII (April,
1937), 491-500.


### Published Private Documents


Burritt, Elihu, *Ten-Minute Talks on All Sorts of Topics.*
Boston: Lee and Shepard, 1874.
Claiborne, J. F. H. *Life and Correspondence of John A. Quit-
man.* New York: Harper & Brothers, 1860.
Curtis, George Tickner. *Life of James Buchanan.* Vol. II.
New York: Harper & Brothers, 1883.
Dallas, George Mifflin. *A Series of Letters from London.*
Philadelphia: J. B. Lippincott & Co., 1869.
Dallas, Susan (ed.). *Diary of George Mifflin Dallas.* Phila-
delphia: J. B. Lippincott Company, 1892.
Dix, Morgan (ed.). *Memoirs of John Adams Dix.* New York:
Harper & Brothers, 1883.

Forney, John. *Anecdotes of Public Men.* New York: Harper and Brothers, 1873.

Marsh, Caroline Crane. *Life and Letters of George Perkins Marsh.* Vol. I. New York: Charles Scribner's Sons, 1888.

Marshall, Thomas Maitland (ed.). "Diary and Memoranda of William L. Marcy," *American Historical Review,* XXIV (April, July, 1919), 444-462, 641-653.

Moore, John Bassett (ed.). *The Works of James Buchanan.* Vols. IX, X. Philadelphia and London: J. B. Lippincott Company, 1909, 1910.

Ogden, Robert Morris (ed.). *The Diaries of Andrew Dickson White.* Ithaca: Cornell University Library, 1959.

*The Political Correspondence of the Late Hon. George N. Sanders.* New York: The American Art Association, 1914.

Poore, Benjamin Perley. *Reminiscences of Sixty Years in the National Metropolis.* Vol. I. Philadelphia, Chicago, Kansas City: Hubbard Brothers, 1890.

Pryor, Mrs. Roger A. *Reminiscences of Peace and War.* New York: The Macmillan Company, 1924.

Ray, P. O. (ed.) "Some Papers of Franklin Pierce, 1852-62," *American Historical Review,* X (October, 1904, January, 1905), 110-127, 350-370.

Charles Sumner, *Works.* Vol. III. Boston: Lee and Shepard, 1875.

Wallace, Sarah, and Gillespie, Frances Elma (eds.). *The Journal of Benjamin Moran, 1857-1865.* Chicago: The University of Chicago Press, 1948.

White, Andrew Dickson. *Autobiography.* Vol. I. New York: The Century Co., 1905.

### Primary Articles

"Christianity-Islamism," *United States Review,* XXXVI (November, 1855), 375-380.

"The Czar of Russia," *United States Review,* XXXV (January, 1855), 1-13.

"A Few Facts in Regard to Nicholas of Russia," *United States Review,* XXXV (March, 1855), 225-233.

"The Isolation of our Country," *Nation,* LXVII (August 4, 1898), 86-87.

Mahan, Alfred Thayer. "The United States Looking Out-
ward," *Living Age,* CLXXIV (December, 1890), 816-824.
[Marsh, George Perkins]. "The Oriental Question," *The
Christian Examiner,* CCVII (May, 1858), 393-420.
Olney, Richard. "Growth of our Foreign Policy," *Atlantic
Monthly,* LXXXV (March, 1900), 289-301.
———. "International Isolation of the United States," *At-
lantic Monthly,* LXXXI (May, 1898), 577-588.
"Our Transatlantic Cousins," *United States Review,* XXXV
(April, 1855), 284-289.
Proctor, John W. "Isolation or Imperialism?" *Forum,* XXVI
(September, 1898), 14-26.
"Russia and the Anglo-French Alliance," *United States Re-
view,* XXXV (April, 1855), 237-247.
"Russia and the Mouths of the Danube," *De Bow's Review,*
XVII (August, 1854), 172-73.
"The Russo-Turkish Question," *De Bow's Review,* XVI
(March, April, 1854), 277-300, 329-350.
"Sultan Abdel Medjid," *United States Review,* XXXV (May,
1855), 394-398.
Trescot, William H. "An American View of the Eastern
Question," *De Bow's Review,* XVII (September, October,
1854), 285-294, 327-350.
"Turkey—Its Commerce and Its Destiny," *De Bow's Review,*
XVI (February, 1854), 109-128.

*Primary Books*

Adams, Charles Francis. *The Struggle for Neutrality in
America.* New York: Charles Scribner and Co., 1871.
Alger, William R. *An American Voice on the Late War in the
East.* Boston: John P. Jewett and Company, 1856.
Bownton, Charles Brandon. *English and French Neutrality
and the Anglo-French Alliance in their relations to the
United States and Russia.* Cincinnati: C. F. Vent & Co.,
1864.
———. *The Russian Empire: its Resources, Government,
and Policy.* Cincinnati: C. F. Vent & Co., 1856.
Grund, Francis J. *Thoughts and Reflections on the Present
Position of Europe.* Philadelphia: Childs & Peterson,
1860.

Loring, Charles. *Neutral Relations of England and the United States.* Boston: W. V. Spencer, 1863.

Lyman, Theodore. *The Diplomacy of the United States.* Boston: Wells and Lilly, 1826.

Martineau, Harriet. *History of the Peace.* Boston: Walker, Fuller, and Company, 1866.

Oliphant, Laurence. *The Russian Shores of the Black Sea.* Third edition. New York: Redfield, 1854.

Squier, Ephraim G. *Notes on Central America.* New York: Harper & Brothers, 1855.

### Primary Periodicals, 1853-1857

*American Review: A Whig Journal*
*Brownson's Quarterly Review*
*De Bow's Review*
*Democratic Review*
*Harper's New Monthly Magazine*
*Living Age*
*The Nation*
*National Intelligencer*
*New Orleans Picayune*
*New York Atlas*
*New York Herald*
*New York Times*
*New York Tribune*
*North American Review*
*Portland Transcript*
*Putnam's Monthly Magazine*
*Richmond Enquirer*
*United States Review*
*Washington Union*

### Secondary Articles

Bourne, Kenneth. "The Clayton-Bulwer Treaty and the Decline of British Opposition to the Territorial Expansion of the United States, 1857-60," *Journal of Modern History*, XXXIII (September, 1961), 287-291.

Brebner, J. Bartlett, "Joseph Howe and the Crimean War Enlistment Controversy between Great Britain and the

United States," *Canadian Historical Review*, XI (December, 1930), 300-327.

Curti, Merle E. "George N. Sanders—American Patriot of the Fifties," *South Atlantic Quarterly*, XXVII (January, 1928), 79-87.

————. "Young America," *American Historical Review*, XXXII (October, 1926), 34-55.

Dvoichenko-Markov, Eufrosina. "Americans in the Crimean War," *Russian Review*, XIII (April, 1954), 137-145.

Earle, Edward Meade. "Early American Policy Concerning Ottoman Minorities," *Political Science Quarterly*, XLII (September, 1927), 337-367.

Golder, Frank A. "Purchase of Alaska," *American Historical Review*, XXV (April, 1920), 411-425.

————. "Russian-American Relations during the Crimean War," *American Historical Review*, XXXI (April, 1926), 462-476.

Henderson, Gavin. "The Diplomatic Revolution of 1854," *American Historical Review*, XLII (October, 1937), 22-50.

Janes, Henry L. "The Black Warrior Affair," *American Historical Review*, XII (January, 1907), 280-298.

McPherson, Hallie M. "The Interest of William McKendree Gwin in the Purchase of Alaska, 1854-1861," *Pacific Historical Review*, III (March, 1934), 28-38.

Nuermberger, Gustave A. "The Continental Treaties of 1856: An American Union 'Exclusive of the United States,'" *Hispanic American Historical Review*, XX (February, 1940), 32-55.

Oliva, L. Jay. "America Meets Russia: 1854," *Journalism Quarterly*, XL (Winter, 1963), 65-69.

Schmitt, Bernadotte E. "Diplomatic Preliminaries of the Crimean War," *American Historical Review*, XXV (October, 1919), 36-67.

Urban, C. Stanley. "The Ideology of Southern Imperialism: New Orleans and the Caribbean, 1845-1860," *Louisiana Historical Quarterly*, XXXIX (January, 1956), 48-73.

Van Alstyne, Richard W. "British Diplomacy and the Clayton-Bulwer Treaty, 1850-60," *Journal of Modern History*, XI (June, 1939), 149-183.

————. "John F. Crampton, Conspirator or Dupe?" *American Historical Review*, XLI (April, 1936), 492-502.

Weinberg, Albert K. "The Historical Meaning of the American Doctrine of Isolation," *American Political Science Review*, XXXIV (June, 1940), 539-547.

————. "Washington's 'Great Rule' in Its Historical Evolution. *Historiography and Urbanization*, ed. Eric F. Goldman. Baltimore: The Johns Hopkins Press, 1941.

*Secondary Books*

Adams, Randolph Greenfield. *A History of the Foreign Policy of the United States*. New York: The Macmillan Company, 1924.

Bailey, Thomas A. *America Faces Russia*. Ithaca: Cornell University Press, 1950.

————. *A Diplomatic History of the American People*. New York: F. S. Crofts & Co., 1940.

Bemis, Samuel Flagg. *A Diplomatic History of the United States*. First, second, and fourth editions. New York: Holt, Rinehart and Winston, Inc., 1936, 1942, 1955.

————. *A Short History of American Foreign Policy and Diplomacy*. New York: Henry Holt and Company, Inc., 1959.

Bigelow, John. *American Policy: The Western Hemisphere in its Relation to the Eastern*. New York: Charles Scribner's Sons, 1914.

————. *Breaches of Anglo-American Treaties*. New York: Sturgis & Walton Company, 1917.

Blumenthal, Henry. *A Reappraisal of Franco-American Relations, 1830-1871*. Chapel Hill: The University of North Carolina Press, 1959.

Borchard, Edwin, and Lage, William Potter. *Neutrality for the United States*. New Haven: Yale University Press, 1937.

Brebner, J. Bartlett. *North Atlantic Triangle*. New Haven: Yale University Press, 1945.

Callahan, James Morton. *The Alaska Purchase and Americo-Canadian Relations*. ("West Virginia University Studies in American History," Series 1, Nos. 2 and 3.) West Virginia University, 1908.

————. *Russo-American Relations During the American*

*Civil War*. ("West Virginia University Studies in American History," Series 1, No. 1.) West Virginia University, 1908.

Carnegie Endowment for International Peace. *American Foreign Policy*. Washington: Carnegie Endowment for International Peace, 1920.

Casper, Henry W. *American Attitudes Toward the Rise of Napoleon III*. Washington: The Catholic University of America Press, 1947.

Chadwick, French Ensor. *The Relations of the United States and Spain*. New York: Charles Scribner's Sons, 1909.

Clark, J. Reuben. *Memorandum on the Monroe Doctrine*. Washington: United States Government Printing Office, 1930.

Curti, Merle E. *The American Peace Crusade, 1815-1860*. Durham, N.C.: Duke University Press, 1929.

————. *Austria and the United States, 1848-1852*. ("Smith College Studies in History," Vol. XI, No. 3.) Northampton, Mass.: Smith College, 1926.

Davis, Forrest. *The Atlantic System*. New York: Reynal & Hitchcock, 1941.

De Conde, Alexander. *A History of American Foreign Policy*. New York: Charles Scribner's Sons, 1963.

————. "On Twentieth Century Isolationism." *Isolation and Security*, ed. Alexander De Conde. Durham, N.C.: Duke University Press, 1957.

Dealey, James Quayle. *Foreign Policies of the United States*. Boston: Ginn and Company, 1926.

Dulles, Foster Rhea. *America's Rise to World Power*. New York: Harper & Row, 1954.

————. *The Road to Teheran*. Princeton: Princeton University Press, 1944.

Dunning, William A. *The British Empire and the United States*. New York: Charles Scribner's Sons, 1914.

Earle, Edward Meade. *Against This Torrent*. Princeton: Princeton University Press, 1941.

Ettinger, Amos Aschbach. *The Mission to Spain of Pierre Soulé, 1853-1855*. New York: Yale University Press, 1932.

Fish, Carl Russell. *American Diplomacy*. New York: H. Holt and Company, 1919.

———. *The United States and Great Britain, 1776-1930*. Chicago: University of Chicago Press, 1932.

Foster, John W. *A Century of American Diplomacy*. Boston: Houghton, Mifflin and Company, 1900.

Fuess, Claude M. *The Life of Caleb Cushing*. New York: Harcourt, Brace and Company, 1923.

Garber, Paul N. *The Gadsden Treaty*. Philadelphia: Press of the University of Pennsylvania, 1923.

Garner, James Witford. *American Foreign Policies*. New York: New York University Press, 1928.

Gazley, John G. *American Opinion of German Unification, 1848-1871*. ("Studies in History, Economics and Public Law," Vol. CXXI, No. 267.) New York: Columbia University, 1926.

Gibbons, Herbert Adams. *America's Place in the World*. New York & London: The Century Co., 1924.

Gibbs, Peter. *Crimean Blunder*. London: Frederick Muller Limited, 1960.

Gilbert, Felix. *To the Farewell Address: Ideas of Early American Foreign Policy*. Princeton: Princeton University Press, 1961.

Gordon, Leland James. *American Relations with Turkey, 1830-1930*. Philadelphia: University of Pennsylvania Press, 1932.

Graber, Doris Appel. *Crisis Diplomacy: A History of U.S. Intervention Policies and Practices*. Washington: Public Affairs Press, 1959.

Graham, Malbone W. *American Diplomacy in the International Community*. Baltimore: The Johns Hopkins Press, 1948.

Greene, Lawrence. *The Filibuster*. Indianapolis: The Bobbs-Merrill Company, 1937.

Hart, Albert Bushnell. *The Foundations of American Foreign Policy*. New York: The Macmillan Company, 1901.

Hodges, Henry G. *The Doctrine of Intervention*. Princeton: The Banner Press, 1915.

Hodgson, Michael Catherine, Sister. *Caleb Cushing, Attorney General of the United States, 1853-1857*. Washington: The Catholic University Press, 1955.

Howe, Quincy. *England Expects Every American to do His Duty*. New York: Simon and Schuster, 1937.

Johnsen, Julia (ed.). *United States Foreign Policy*. New York: The H. W. Wilson Company, 1938.

Johnson, Willis Fletcher. *America's Foreign Relations*. New York: The Century Co., 1916.

Jones, Robert L. *History of the Foreign Policy of the United States*. New York: G. P. Putnam's Sons, 1933.

Klein, Philip Shriver. *President James Buchanan*. University Park, Pa.: The Pennsylvania State University Press, 1962.

Laserson, Max M. *The American Impact on Russia*. New York: The Macmillan Company, 1950.

Latané, John Holloday. *A History of American Foreign Policy*. Garden City, N.Y.: Doubleday, Page & Company, 1927.

Lawson, Leonard. *The Relation of British Policy to the Declaration of the Monroe Doctrine*. New York: Columbia University, 1922.

Learned, Henry Barrett. "William Learned Marcy." *The American Secretaries of State and Their Diplomacy*, ed. Samuel Flagg Bemis. Vol. VI. New York: Alfred A. Knopf, 1928.

Leopold, Richard W. *The Growth of American Foreign Policy*. New York: Alfred A. Knopf, 1962.

Lowenthal, David. *George Perkins Marsh*. New York: Columbia University Press, 1958.

McElroy, Robert. *The Pathway of Peace: An Interpretation of some British-American Crises*. New York: The Macmillan Company, 1927.

McLaughlin, Andrew C. *Lewis Cass*. Boston and New York: Houghton, Mifflin and Company, 1891.

Manning, Clarence A. *Russian Influence on Early America*. New York: Library Publishers, 1953.

Marraro, Howard R. *U.S. Opinions on the Unification of Italy: 1846-1861*. New York: Columbia University, 1932.

Marriott, J. A. R. *The Eastern Question*. Oxford: The Clarendon Press, 1940.

Martin, Charles D. *The Policy of the United States as regards Intervention*. New York: Columbia University, 1921.

Mathews, John Mabry. *American Foreign Relations*. New York: The Century Co., 1928.

May, Arthur James. *Contemporary American Opinion of the*

*Mid-Century Revolutions in Central Europe.* Philadelphia: University of Pennsylvania, 1927.

Moore, John Bassett. *Four Phases of American Development.* Baltimore: The Johns Hopkins Press, 1912.

———. *The Principles of American Diplomacy.* New York and London: Harper & Brothers, 1918.

Morgenthau, Hans J. *In Defense of the National Interest.* New York: Alfred A. Knopf, 1952.

Mowat, R. B. *The Diplomatic Relations of Great Britain and the United States.* London: Edward Arnold & Co., 1925.

Mowrer, Paul Scott, *Our Foreign Affairs.* New York: E. P. Dutton & Company, 1924.

Nichols, Roy Franklin. *Advance Agents of American Destiny.* Philadelphia: University of Pennsylvania Press, 1956.

———. *Franklin Pierce.* Philadelphia: University of Pennsylvania Press, 1931.

Northend, Charles (ed.). *Elihu Burritt; a Memorial Volume containing A Sketch of His Life and Labors.* New York: D. Appleton & Company, 1880.

Perkins, Dexter. *America and Two Wars.* Boston, Little, Brown & Company, 1944.

———. *The Evolution of American Foreign Policy.* New York: Oxford University Press, 1948.

———. *Hands Off: A History of the Monroe Doctrine.* Boston: Little, Brown and Company, 1946.

Piggott, Francis Taylor. *The Declaration of Paris.* London: University of London Press Ltd., 1919.

Pinchon, Edgcumb. *Dan Sickles.* Garden City, N.Y.: Doubleday, Doran and Company, Inc., 1945.

Potter, Pitman B. *The Myth of American Isolation.* ("A League of Nations," Vol. IV, No. 6.) Boston: World Peace Foundation, 1921.

Pratt, Julius W. *A History of United States Foreign Policy.* New York: Prentice-Hall, Inc., 1955.

Puryear, Vernon John. *England, Russia and the Straits Question, 1844-1856.* ("University of California Publications in History," Vol. XX.) Berkeley: University of California Press, 1931.

Rauch, Basil. *American Interest in Cuba: 1848-1855.* New York: Columbia University Press, 1948.

Rippy, J. Fred. *America and the Strife of Europe.* Chicago: The University of Chicago Press, 1938.

————, and Debo, Angie. *The Historical Background of the American Policy of Isolation.* ("Smith College Studies in History" Vol. IX, No. 3.) Northampton, Mass.: Smith College, 1924.

Roche, James Jeffrey. *By-Ways of War: The Story of the Filibusters.* Boston: Small, Maynard & Company, 1901.

Scroggs, William O. *Filibusters and Financiers.* New York: The Macmillan Company, 1916.

Sears, Louis Martin. *A History of American Foreign Relations.* First and third editions. New York: Thomas Y. Crowell Company, 1927, 1936.

Smith, Theodore Clarke. *The United States as a Factor in World History.* New York: Henry Holt and Company, 1941.

Smith, W. L. G. *The Life and Times of Lewis Cass.* New York: Derby & Jackson, 1856.

Spencer, Ivor Debenham. *The Victor and the Spoils.* Providence: Brown University Press, 1959.

Spykman, Nicholas John. *America's Strategy in World Politics.* New York: Harcourt, Brace and Company, 1942.

Steiner, Bernard C. *Life of Henry Winter Davis.* Baltimore: John Murphy Company, 1916.

Tansill, Charles C. *The Canadian Reciprocity Treaty of 1854.* Baltimore: The Johns Hopkins University, 1922.

Tarsaidze, Alexander. *Czars and Presidents: The Story of a Forgotten Friendship.* New York: McDowell, Obolensky, Inc., 1958.

Thomas, Benjamin Platt. *Russo-American Relations, 1815-1867.* Baltimore: The Johns Hopkins Press, 1930.

Thompson, Kenneth W. "Isolationism and Collective Security." *Isolation and Security,* ed. Alexander De Conde. Durham, N.C.: Duke University Press, 1957.

Travis, Ira Dudley. *The History of the Clayton-Bulwer Treaty.* ("Publications of the Michigan Political Science Association," Vol. III, No. 8.) Ann Arbor: Michigan Political Science Association, 1899.

Trescott, William Henry. *The Diplomatic History of the Administration of Washington and Adams.* Boston: Little, Brown and Company, 1857.

Van Alstyne, Richard W. *American Diplomacy in Action.* Second edition. Stanford University, Calif.: Stanford University Press, 1947.

Ward, A. W., Prothero, G. W., and Leathes, Stanley (eds.).
    *The Cambridge Modern History.* Vol. XI. New York:
    The Macmillan Company, 1909.
White, Elizabeth Brett. *American Opinion of France from
    Lafayette to Poincaré.* New York: Alfred A. Knopf,
    1927.
Williams, Benjamin H. *American Diplomacy.* New York and
    London: McGraw-Hill Book Company, Inc., 1936.
Williams, Mary W. *Anglo-American Isthmian Diplomacy,
    1815-1915.* Baltimore: The Lord Baltimore Press, 1916.
Williams, William Appleman. *American-Russian Relations,
    1781-1947.* New York: Rinehart & Co., 1952.
Willson, Beckles. *America's Ambassador's to England, 1785-
    1929.* New York: Frederick A. Stokes Company, 1929.
————. *America's Ambassadors to France, 1777-1927.* New
    York: Frederick A. Stokes Company, 1928.
Woodford, Frank B. *Lewis Cass.* New Brunswick, N.J.:
    Rutgers University Press, 1950.

*Unpublished Dissertations and Theses*

Grigg, Eugene, "The Political Career of William Learned
    Marcy." Unpublished M.A. thesis, University of Chicago,
    1949.
Schodt, Eddie William. "American Policy and Practice with
    Respect to European Liberal Movements, 1848-1853."
    Unpublished Ph.D. dissertation, University of Colorado,
    1951.
Scribner, Robert L. "The Diplomacy of William L. Marcy."
    Unpublished Ph.D. dissertation, University of Virginia,
    1949.
Silverstein, Mary Poindexter. "Diplomacy and Politics: A
    British View of the Reciprocity-Fisheries Negotiation,
    1853-1854." Unpublished Master's thesis, University of
    Chicago, 1961.

# Index